To Pop-Pop,

Stay Safe!

OUR PATH
TO
SAFETY

A U.S. Secret Service Agent's Guide
to Creating Safe Communities

Jason Wells

DTAC
Publishing

Baltimore, MD

For permission requests, write to the publisher at the address below.

DTAC Publishing
6604 Greenoch Dr.
Catonsville, MD 21228
info@dtacpublishing.com

Ordering Information:
Quantity sales. Special discounts are available on quantity purchases by corporations, associations, and others. For details, contact the publisher at the address above.

Orders by U.S. trade bookstores and wholesalers. Please contact:
info@dtacpublishing.com.

Author Photo by Lia Joell Photography.

Printed in the United States of America.

Publisher's Cataloging-in-Publication data
Wells, Jason.
Our Path to Safety: A U.S. Secret Service Agent's Guide to Creating Safe Communities / Jason Wells.

ISBN-10: 0-9982488-0-0
ISBN-13: 978-0-9982488-0-6

1. Social Sciences. 2. Education. 3. Safety — Security — Terrorism. I. Wells, Jason. II. Our Path to Safety: A U.S. Secret Service Agent's Guide to Creating Safe Communities.

First Edition

Dedication:

For my wife, Blythe, and our wonderful children, Abigail and Samuel.

I will always keep you safe.

CONTENTS

ACKNOWLEDGMENTS

There have been so many people in my life over the last several years who have helped make this book possible. Although I cannot mention all of them here, they know who they are and they have my sincere thanks for their support.

Thank you Leigh Thompson for your positivity, your innovative thinking and your belief in me. Through this venture you have become a trusting business partner and a good friend. Many additional thanks to your lovely wife, Whitney, and Bhodi, for loaning you to me over many hours.

Thank you Rus VanWestervelt for all that you have taught me about the world of book development, editing and publishing. You have become both a trusted advisor and a literary mentor to me, and I look forward to your continued guidance.

To Bill and Sandra. You never believed that I would fail. It was as simple as that. Thank you for your support and your encouragement.

To my mother, Cathy. It's so good to have a mother's thoughts and insight once more in my life.

Thank you Richard, Larissa, Matt, Audra, Galen, Jenn, Sibley and Colin for your support. I don't say it enough, so I hope that immortalizing it in these pages makes up for it: I love you all.

Thank you, Susan. We miss you so very much.

Thank you, Jim and Traci, for all of your support and thoughtful words of encouragement.

Many thanks to Dr. Harvey Goldstein for his encouragement and enthusiasm for this project. Your professional tutelage has always been inspiring.

To Heather, thank you for sharing your story, and your friendship, through all of these years.

Thank you to the VMI Family, and particularly to Elaine Wood with the VMI Alumni Association, for reaching out to me, supporting me, and promoting my work. It is greatly appreciated, and Rah Virginia Mil!

Thank you to the entire Resurrection-St. Paul School and Church of the Resurrection Community. The staff, students and families have been enthusiastic and wonderfully supportive with this, and to them I owe my sincere gratitude.

Of course, sincere thanks to my lovely wife, Blythe. You have been my best friend, the best partner in life I could have ever wished for. I hope I have made you proud.

Thank you, my darling Abigail. I love you so very much.

Thank you, Samuel. We'll always be best buddies.

And I proudly proclaim that I give all the glory, all the greatness that may come from this writing to my Lord and Savior Jesus Christ. He has carried me through the challenges in my life, and has always been there for me even when I have failed. I will praise You forever; I am so grateful for all that You have done for me.

And thank you, the reader, for your interest and support. You were the reason I wrote this book, and you will be the ones who make our community a safer place.

OUR PATH
TO
SAFETY

A U.S. Secret Service Agent's Guide
to Creating Safe Communities

INTRODUCTION

1. Heather and the Navy Yard Shooting

For Heather, the morning began like any other with a 3:15 a.m. wake-up. For a commute on the single stretch of Interstate 95 northbound to the nation's capital, that was a fairly standard morning rise for most people. The tradeoff of making a home in a lovely Virginia community was living far enough away from Washington, D.C. to afford the lifestyle. When more than one hundred thousand people have the same idea in mind, the earlier start of the day means less time in traffic. For those like Heather, 3:15 a.m. was the time to start the day.

By 4:40 a.m., she was out the door and on her way to meet with her carpool. If misery ever loved company, then the right group of people to share a ride to the office made all the difference. Heather had that: a close sorority of modern-day working women who bonded and laughed through the commuting push together. Up every morning, back every afternoon. It was a good group, one that had actually been through a lot together. For most people, the drive to work was the worst part of the day; for Heather, it was almost… enjoyable. After all, it gave her and the other girls time to chat.

By 5:45 a.m., she was at her office at the Washington Navy Yard. Her office building, Building 197, was starting to come alive. The employees were easing into their offices, getting their coffee and socializing with their co-workers, their friends. It was a Monday, and people were sharing their stories with each other about the weekend. The Green Bay

Packers' fans were giving the Washington Redskins' faithful a healthy ribbing for the defeat they handed them the day before. The weather was still pushing the last remnants of summer's warm front, and the forecast was calling for a bright and sunny day.

"I still remember what I was wearing that day," she told me. "I still have the outfit. I haven't worn it since, but I still have it…." Her thoughts drifted for a second and she stared down at her iced tea before she spoke again.

"I don't know why I kept it."

I had known Heather since I was a young man. During middle school, our families moved into a newly developed neighborhood outside of the small rural community of Stafford, Virginia. As both my parents had been some of the early pioneers of the Interstate 95 commute, I was left to my own devices to get ready for school and find things to occupy my time. It was Heather's family, and in particular her father, who helped me to forge a personal path of responsibility rather than one of trouble. As a career military Non-Commissioned Officer, Heather's father was gone for long periods of time all over the world. If he couldn't be there to watch over his two young daughters, the next best thing was train the teenage boy down the street to do it in his absence. That was exactly what he did, and I took my responsibilities very seriously. Those years growing up, I looked on Heather and her little sister, Heidi, as my sisters; they helped to fill a void in me that too often is there for those who are burdened with being an only child.

Now, over 20 years later, Heather sat across from me at the local coffee shop in Stafford. I had not seen her since just before I had left for college. Even in her mid-thirties and as a single mother, she had not changed. Sadly, the reason for my visit was not merely a social call, but to hear about one of the most harrowing and emotional days of her life.

In September of 2013, she had been with her contracting firm for nearly ten years. The work was good, and the mission was important. The United States Navy was (and still is) one of the most innovative and forward-thinking organizations in the world. There has never been a shortage of bright people who support the mission of the Navy, and for the intellectual, the work they do is more than enough to stimulate their brilliant minds. For Heather, it was an ideal position.

"Did you know any of the victims personally?" I asked.

"I knew two." She said. "One was the man who was the security guard.

I knew him casually, in passing. I saw him every morning when I came in. The other was a man who was a maintenance worker in the building. I knew him well. The security guard went by Mike and the maintenance worker was Arthur."

Heather then remembered a particularly bad morning she was having when she had come across Arthur in passing. He inquired as to what was bothering her, and Heather opened up to him. He listened and offered nice words of encouragement to keep her chin up. Later in the day, he left her a poem on her work cubicle. Heather still has the poem, thankful for the positive influence he had on her that day.

THE ESSENCE OF NEW DAY

THIS IS THE BEGINNING OF A NEW DAY
YOU HAVE BEEN GIVEN THIS DAY TO USE AS YOU WILL
YOU CAN WASTE IT OR USE IT FOR GOOD
WHAT YOU DO TODAY IS IMPORTANT BECAUSE...
YOU ARE EXCHANGING A DAY OF YOUR LIFE FOR IT
WHEN TOMORROW COMES
THIS DAY WILL BE GONE FOREVER
IN ITS PLACE IS SOMETHING THAT YOU HAVE LEFT BEHIND
LET IT BE SOMETHING "GOOD"

Arthur

Heather continued her story about that fateful day.

As she entered her building on the morning of the incident, she saw Mike. His real name was Richard, but for some reason, everyone seemed to address him by his middle name. Mike was her familiar security guard buddy, and he was always good for a bit of morning banter to add a smile to her face to start the day. Heather and Mike spoke for a few moments and shared pleasantries before Heather moved through the checkpoint and on to her office. Unbeknownst to both of them, it was the last time they would ever see each other again. Within 3 hours of their conversation, Officer Richard Michael Ridgell would be shot and killed.

"What was the first indicator that something was wrong?" I asked.

"The fire alarm."

At sometime around 8:30 a.m., the office fire alarm went off. Fire alarms were a common practice in office buildings across the country, and the Navy Yard was no different. But for so early in the morning, that was unusual. Fire alarm drills typically occurred later in the day to ensure that everyone who was working had arrived. For Heather, her secured section had over 100 personnel, with her seat near the back of the massive cell. As she began to exit, she felt the urge to go back to her desk and grab her purse. By the time she had done this, all but 12 people had left the room. As she moved to the massive security door, the faint but audible sounds of popping resonated through the halls.

"I still don't know what it was," she said, reliving that scene. "We were right by a hallway. It could have been people moving through the halls or something else. I had heard it before, I'm familiar with the sound of gunfire. But the sound was muffled from the room we were in."

As Heather came to her office door, she heard someone pounding on it from the other side. She instinctively opened it, which swung inward, and was met by one of her co-workers from the office across the hall. The co-worker was a retired Marine female, and a contractor like Heather.

"She was yelling, 'gunfire, gunfire, gunfire' over and over. She pushed me back into the office and closed the door behind her. Then we locked the door." Heather and her co-workers stood there in numb silence for a moment, almost waiting for this person who had just entered the room to spring the "surprise, just kidding" joke on them. But it was no joke; it was a very real and suddenly very deadly situation.

On the morning of September 16, 2013, 34-year-old Aaron Alexis entered the Washington Navy Yard and made his way directly to Building 197. In the duffel bag that he was carrying were the broken-down parts of a Remington 870 Express Tactical 12-gauge shotgun and a complement of ammunition. His security badge for entry was legitimate, as Alexis was a vetted contractor with a security clearance allowing access to the facility. He had worked there for some time, and he knew the security measures of the building. The officers on post randomly conducted bag checks on the employees, but it was not frequent. Whether Alexis had some inside information on the schedule of the bag checks or he just chose to play the odds is unknown. On that day, he passed through the security checkpoints without incident. From there, he proceeded to the men's bathroom and reassembled his shotgun. It was approximately 8:10 a.m. Within 5 minutes, Alexis had loaded the shotgun and proceeded to an upper level of the office that overlooked an interior atrium of the building. At approximately 8:15 a.m., he took position on the high vantage point and began raining shotgun blasts on the innocent employees below.

When Heather heard the fire alarm, she made her way to her supervisor's corner office. His work area offered an ideal spot for seeing the main entrance of the facility from his window. Only three stories up, the emotions of people leaving the building were clear. Their faces told a story that this was no ordinary fire alarm. Typically, people would leave the building in a meandering, slow pace, sometimes enjoying the reprieve of the office to bask in the lovely morning like this one. Today however, there was a frantic pace to leave the building, to get away as quickly as possible without starting a stampede. And just as the employees were rushing to get out, others were sprinting to come in.

"They must have been 19-20 years old, in their civilian clothes, " she said. "Some of them were in shorts; it was warm out. I just remember thinking, 'How do these kids even know that this is going on right now?'"

Her hands began to shake, and she had to take a sip from her iced tea to calm her nerves.

For Heather, that was the moment that reality had set in. Marines from the base across the street had been the first to get the call about the attack at the Navy Yard, and they were responding in the way that they were trained to respond. Without reservation, they grabbed their rifles and what gear they could – be it a flak vest, ammunition, or a helmet – and they made way into danger. The security guards at the main gate quickly followed; they grabbed their own gear and moved in with their military counterparts.

"Did you feel relief when you saw that?" I asked.

She shook her head, "No. I felt anxious. I felt nervous. I saw a security guard who I had seen every day when I drove in suddenly come running in wearing a helmet and carrying a machine gun. He's never done that, I knew something was very, very wrong." Heather later told me that she was worried for her acquaintance-friend, as part of her didn't want him coming into the building where there was danger.

"I was really worried for him," she said.

"What happened then?" I asked.

"I called my father."

Heather's father is nothing short of a legend in the United States Army Special Operations Command. A retired Command Sergeant Major with a distinguished career of serving his country for over 40 years, he is a true patriot. Only 5 months prior to the morning of the Navy Yard attack, Heather's father survived the bombing of the Boston Marathon while there to cheer on his fellow soldiers. He would later be awarded the Superior Civilian Service Award for his exceptional and decisive actions on that day, helping the injured and helping to secure the crime scene. But on the morning of the Navy Yard attacks, he would receive one of the most distressing calls of his life, one that no parent wants to ever have. His daughter was trapped in a building with a deranged killer on a shooting rampage.

"How did that conversation go?" I asked, a bit comically. Anyone who knew her father knew he wasn't one for talk, but of action.

Heather caught my humor and laughed before responding, "Well, it didn't last long," she admitted, "but I'm glad I made the call. He really got me focused. He just sort of said, 'You know what to do. I've trained you. I'll let Mom know that you're okay.' He then said that he would stay focused on the news, and then he sort of hung up. And he was right, I did know what to do.… so I did it."

Heather understood her father, and she knew that it wasn't like him to lose his cool or show any emotion on the phone. Heather was later told by several of his co-workers that he was watching the news for updates all day, but showing her his concern would have only made it worse for her. There was time enough to talk when she was safe. For now, Heather had to look at everything around her, and it was then that she realized she needed to change her clothes quickly. The bright orange cardigan she had on was a shout-out to any shooter who came in the room. As she made her way to join her co-workers, Heather ditched the cardigan and started looking for the best cubicle to hide under.

After several minutes of firing at the people in the atrium below,

Alexis moved to one of the stairwells and proceeded to make his way down. It was there that he confronted Security Officer Richard "Mike" Ridgell, who was en route to stop the attacker. Alexis shot Officer Ridgell in the stairwell, killing him. Alexis took Ridgell's service weapon, a Beretta 92SF semiautomatic pistol. He then returned to his original vantage point and began shooting once again into the atrium.

Heather contacted one of her closest friends who was an officer with the Metropolitan Police Department. He told her that he had just been called into work on some emergency. The two surmised that it was the same incident, and they were right.

"At that point, I just started giving him as much information as I had: [the] times things started happening, who was in the office with us, where we were… anything." While Heather and her co-workers were providing what they could, the officer was relaying the information to his operation supervisor. Simultaneously, the group was able to see several people that they knew who had been able to get out safely from their window during the initial fire alarm. Heather and her co-workers began to look for people they knew in the crowds and used social media to let their families know that they were okay. For accountability of concerned family and friends, it was something.

"I remember asking him what else he wanted us to do," she told me.

"And what did he say?" I asked.

She sipped her tea again and then responded, "He told me to lock down, don't leave the office, and wait. Help was on its way."

Sometime during the first fire alarm and the evacuation, Alexis had finished his second volley of attacks from the upper floor. For reasons unknown he left his shooting spot once again and began meandering his way through the building. During this time, he came across 51-year-old Arthur Daniels who was returning from a cigarette-smoking break with his supervisor. The supervisor would later report that Daniels was the first of the two of them to hear gunshots. He pushed his supervisor back into the hallway that they came from, and then told him to run. Daniels' actions would become one of sacrifice, as moments later he was shot and killed by Alexis. The supervisor survived the attacks that day, and he credited his survival to the selfless bravery of Arthur Daniels.

Alexis then continued moving through Building 197, killing people at random.

Heather and her co-workers did what they were told. They made sure that any entrance into their office was secured tight, and they waited and wondered what was going to happen next. They were able to call out and talk with some friends and family, and the news gave them snippets of information to what was happening. The eerie irony of watching a life-and-death situation unfold on the news, showing it to the very people who were living it at that moment, was not lost on anyone.

Co-workers started to wonder what they were hearing throughout the building. In much the same way that a first-time mother thinks she hears the "phantom crying" of her newborn in the crib only to find her child asleep, the sounds of possible "phantom gunshots" seemed to take hold. "Did you hear that?" was a common question for a time among the co-workers, as their nerves and senses were heightened in a way that they had seldom felt before.

But they likely did hear something. Shortly after Alexis left his position, he was met by the Marines and law enforcement who rushed in to stop his rampage of indiscriminant killing. What ensued was a gun battle lasting for nearly 30 minutes. Although the specifics of the fight were never made public, the results were what was expected: Aaron Alexis was killed in the firefight. The psychopath who single-handedly attacked the Washington Navy Yard on the morning of September 16, 2013 had finally been stopped. The harm was done, though. In his attack, Alexis had killed 12 people and injured 8 more. The Washington Navy Yard shooting would be the second deadliest mass-murder incident on a U.S. military base, with only the attack at Fort Hood 4 years prior having more incidents of fatalities.

Heather's small party remained in their office for just over 4 hours. Other people throughout Building 197 were there much later, some hiding in spaces until very late in the night. At the time of the attack, there were reports that multiple shooters had been identified during the shootings. As such, every room, office, and hallway needed to be thoroughly cleared so no one else would be exposed to any more senseless violence. For 4 long hours, people waited to leave their office to go home and let their families see them, hold them, and hear their voices. Telling them over a phone that they were fine was one thing, but no one is truly reassured until they are there in the flesh. Four hours after the first fire alarm sounded, Heather and her co-workers were escorted to safety and away from Building 197.

"I didn't feel safe, though; I was still on edge," she told me. "I didn't feel like myself until I got home that evening."

There were several hours of interviews with law enforcement, accountability issues with personnel, and informal reunions with fellow employees, providing comfort and tearful relief that each was alive. During one such exchange, Heather found a friend who had actually been shot at by the attacker and was fortunate to escape with his life. For her, the aftermath of the attacks melded into crowds of confused civilian employees and Navy personnel meandering about with dazed, haunted gazes. The occasional tears and breakdowns could be heard amidst the questions being asked by law enforcement.

It would be several more hours before Heather returned home. One of Heather's carpool friends had arranged for both of them to be dropped off at their cars in Stafford. When she arrived at her house, Heather was met by her closest friend, who had been waiting desperately for Heather to come home.

Now, two and a half years later, Heather believes security wasn't an issue at the Navy Yard.

"I think that security at the building was sufficient. I have never questioned the security of the building; I always felt very confident. They did an amazing job."

She went on to tell me that the security personnel were the last people she blamed for the tragic events at the Navy Yard. I have certainly seen enough situations myself where the security are the ones who are the recipients of blame when an attack occurs. No one thinks to blame those who allowed the attackers access in the first place, though.

"He had a security clearance," she went on. "What were the security guards supposed to do? That's where the system failed. I don't blame the security guards at that building."

For those who knew Aaron Alexis on a personal level, they paint a picture of him as anyone but the homicidal maniac for which he will always be remembered. People who were interviewed about him described Alexis as "very intellectual" and "sound of mind." He was also described as a "very polite" and "friendly" man. According to record, Alexis had been enrolled at the time at Embry-Riddle Aeronautical University where he was pursuing a bachelor of science in Aeronautics. Alexis had somewhat close ties to his family, and they stated they were in a state of shock that he had committed such a brutal, horrific tragedy.

When interviewed shortly after the Navy Yard massacre, Alexis' own mother apologized for what her son had done and added in a statement: "[Alexis] is now in a place where he can no longer do harm to anyone.... I don't know why he did what he did, and I'll never be able to ask him why.... I'm so, so very sorry this has happened. My heart is broken."

But there was dark side to Alexis that those closest to him did not know, a part of the person that ultimately led to him attacking the Washington Navy Yard. This dark alter ego was one that would be the instigator in a series of violent and unstable behaviors throughout Alexis' professional and personal life. Even more disturbing was that these instances had been documented at length from accounts including those in the medical, law enforcement, and military communities. Nevertheless, Alexis was still able to hold prestigious, highly secured clearance positions working for the federal government. It would be this security clearance that would grant him unfettered access to the Navy Yard on September 16, 2013.

Nearly 10 years earlier, there had been multiple reports of Alexis' behavior and entanglements with law enforcement. In 2004, while living in Seattle, Alexis brandished a Glock pistol and fired two shots into the tires of a co-worker's parked vehicle. The police report cited that Alexis had suffered an "anger-fueled blackout" after Alexis believed that the co-worker had disrespected him. This incident led to Alexis being arrested and charged with malicious mischief.

Later in 2008, Alexis had another run-in with law enforcement. While at a nightclub in downtown Atlanta, Georgia, he was removed from the premises for damaging business property. The police were called to the scene when Alexis became belligerent and defied police and business authorities. After refusing to comply with the officers' orders to calm down, he was arrested for disorderly conduct.

In 2010, Alexis yet again had an encounter with law enforcement, this time in Fort Worth, Texas. Police were called to Alexis' apartment residence when it was reported that he had discharged a firearm through his neighbor's ceiling. When police arrived, Alexis explained that he had been cleaning his loaded gun, and the gun had fired accidentally. Alexis was not charged for the incident, but it was documented.

Despite this last occurrence possibly being a genuine accident, Alexis clearly showed patterns in his life of misconduct and (at the very least) poor decision making. During the Atlanta incident in 2008, Alexis was in the U.S. Navy and had only 5 months before being granted a "secret" clearance with the U.S. government. Additionally, the Navy used this incident as reason to begin the process of having Alexis issued a "general discharge." His personal decisions reflected in his professional tenure with the Navy, as he was constantly reprimanded for insubordination, disorderly conduct, unauthorized absences from work, and drunkenness. The events in Atlanta seemed to be the "last straw," and the Navy began a 3-year process to have Alexis removed from the service.

Despite these damning charges, for reasons only cited as a "lack of evidence," Alexis was granted an "honorable discharge" upon release from the military. Had Alexis received the general discharge that the U.S. Navy sought, it is entirely likely that he would have not maintained his security clearance and therefore not been given access to the Navy Yard. Obviously, this is speculation, and who is to say that Alexis would not have committed his atrocious actions elsewhere? Nevertheless, it is unsettling that he was given such access with so many previous issues in the first place.

As if these issues were not enough, Alexis displayed symptoms of an individual who was not mentally healthy. Records indicate that prior to the attacks, Alexis contacted a local police department while he was temporarily assigned to a job in Rhode Island as a government contractor. He gave a statement to law enforcement that he was being harassed by people who were following him, and he had already moved from two previous hotels for this reason. Additionally, Alexis stated that he had been hearing voices, and he was convinced that these people were using a "microwave machine" to send vibrations into his body to keep him awake. The report showed validity in his personal belief, as he made two separate attempts to have prescriptions filled with the VA Hospital for sleep deprivation. The police department notified the Navy base where Alexis was employed of the unusual report, but it doesn't appear that further action was taken on the part of any party. Lastly, the report was filed 4 weeks before Alexis reported to his new contract assignment at the Washington Navy Yard. Eleven days after arriving, Alexis would commit his violent massacre. (See "Charging Documents" in *Appendix A*).

In the post-attack investigation, law enforcement discovered evidence suggesting the true depths of just how disturbed Alexis was. The FBI concluded that he was "delusional" and felt like he was being controlled or influenced by "extremely low-frequency magnetic waves." The authorities were able to further access thumb drives, computers, and phones that he owned. On these devices, they found the following statement:

Ultra low frequency attack is what I've been subject to for the last 3 months… to be perfectly honest, that is what has driven me to this…

At the crime scene, Alexis' Remington shotgun was etched with multiple statements including:

"Better off this way!"

"End to the torment!"

"Not what y'all say!"

"My ELF Weapon"

This last statement to ELF is believed to be a reference to low-electromagnetic waves; this is a technology that is commonly used for communication in submarine operations. It is also a popular target for conspiracy theorists that believe such technology is employed by the government to monitor and manipulate people without their knowledge.

According to all parties affiliated, none of this information came up during the numerous background investigations into Aaron Alexis. This suggests that the background investigation system is either flawed or dishonest. Whatever the case, there was ample information to suggest that Alexis needed help, and multiple parties were aware of it.

I looked at Heather who sat across the table from me. "Do you think anything could have been done to stop him at any time?" I asked softly.

Heather thought about my question for a long moment, then replied, "I don't think it matters how secure you make a building, an office, a shop…. If someone wants to do something, they're going to do it. They're going to find a way around it to do it. Security did the best they could do."

She paused and collected herself. She took another deep breath and finished her thought. "He shouldn't have been on the base in the first place. Nobody was safe while he was there. As bad as it was, it could have been much worse."

I was inclined to agree with Heather's assessment. The great failure of the Navy Yard shooting was not the response to the attack, but rather the authorizing body choosing to ignore the indicators of threat-related behavior that Alexis was showing in his life. These indicators should have been identified; they should have inhibited such a person to be granted access to a secured facility. With Aaron Alexis and others like him, the hint of violence is there for those who are willing to recognize it.

2. Identifying the Fire

L et me pose a question: If you were asked to identify a fire, from either a photograph, a video or in person, would you be able to do it? Let me apologize if I have insulted your intelligence. I assume that if you are reading this, then you should be perfectly capable of identifying the properties that make up a fire.

Let me now ask you a follow-up question: Are you able to identify a fire that is dangerous? Again, you most likely are. If you happened upon a flaming car in the middle of the street, you would be much more concerned than if you came across a group of campers encircling a roaring fire while singing songs and playing a guitar. I also assume that you would likely try and do something about the fire that consumes the car. You might call the fire department or possibly even try to put the fire out. Whatever the case, you understand what a fire is, when it is bad, and when it is harmless.

How did you get this way? If you were like the vast majority of the members in our society, you were educated at a very young age in the usefulness of fire, as well as its dangerous properties. As you grew older, you were given more responsibility for dealing with fire if it became a hazard. You were taught how to use 9-1-1, you were given permission to pull the fire alarm if it was necessary, and you may have even been taught how to use a fire extinguisher. In today's society, you are still expected to know these social mores, and it is widely considered your civic duty to render any assistance you can if you come across such a dangerous situation. You do so freely, with no demand for further training, no expectation of future liability, and no reservations at the possibility that you could endanger yourself.

Yet, are you trained in dealing with a fire? Unless you are a certified firefighter (as most of us are not) then it is highly likely that the answer to this question is "no." The emphasis that is placed on you by your community, however, cannot be ignored. In matters of dangerous, uncontrollable conditions of fire, you are expected to be able to identify the seriousness of the situation, assess the level of danger that it presents, and then act accordingly to see that it doesn't harm anyone else. What an awesome responsibility! It's almost deserving of thanks.

The same could be said of providing help to someone who is injured or incapacitated. Just like a fire, it is usually easy to identify a person who is in some kind of distress, be it a physical injury or an ailment of some kind. And also like a fire, you are expected as a member of society to do your best to provide some kind of care to another person in need of immediate attention. Even though medical training of some kind is more common than firefighting skills, it is still rare to find people who are trained enough to handle a medical condition at any moment. Nevertheless, the onus of caring for an injured person in some capacity falls on you until emergency medical personnel arrive to take over.

When I was 19 years old, I knew everything (like most at that age). Either I have become more ignorant as I have gotten older, or I didn't know as much as I thought I did (either way, it's not very good for me how it turned out). One particular Sunday, I had gone out with a friend to our local diner for breakfast. It was still fairly early in the morning, long before the rush of churchgoers and weekend shoppers had taken over the streets, so it was an ideal time to have eggs and coffee. I was always an early riser anyway, and my friend who was with me (whom I will call "Bill") was recently out of the Marine Corps. Anyone who knows the U.S. Marine culture knows that marines don't tend to sleep in.

As we finished our morning meal, we left the restaurant and proceeded to return to our car. The morning was brisk but not uncomfortable, and the slight chill in the air was both refreshing and energizing. The town we were in had deep roots in antebellum Virginia culture, with a particular emphasis on Civil War history. As such, the streets were a bit narrow and still cobbled from mismatched bricks and settled foundations. Nonetheless, it gave the small town a personality that many enjoyed.

As we moved down the walkway, our conversation was slowly drowned out by the increasing sounds of construction. Across the narrow road a man was doing some kind of handiwork on a scaffold. The worker was approximately two stories high and alone. The building that he was working on was interconnected with a series of other buildings, and the one under construction looked as though it were in the midst of a refurbishment. The windows and door were still in place but covered with thick commercial-grade plastic tarps. In the building, music from a radio was broadcasting, and there were familiar sounds of construction and other workers shouting to each other over the shrieks of construction tools at work.

As Bill and I continued down the sidewalk, there was a faint but audible "pop" from the construction site. I still don't know what exactly happened, but from the left corner of my eye I caught something like the flash of a camera going off. A moment later, I saw something very large hurling my way. Instinctively, I ducked down to avoid the massive projectile.

The "object" was none other than the man on the scaffolding whom I had just seen a moment before, only now he was in a crumpled heap directly in front of me. He had landed more in the street, but his momentum caused him to roll and rest on the sidewalk. The most vivid things I remember about the situation were the smells and the sounds. There was the clear aroma of burned hair and some kind of coppery, metallic smell. The sounds of the man indicated that he was still semi-conscious and in considerable pain. His writhing was an indicator that he was in great distress and suffering. His face was contorted in a show of confusion, disorientation, and fear. It was a horrible scene; as an observer, it was something that gave an impression of revulsion, hopelessness, and terror. I will remember it all my life.

I'll take this moment and pause to pay my deepest respects to our armed servicemen and women. Throughout history, our country has sent these brave individuals into life-or-death combat, oftentimes when they were no more than 18 years old and barely adults.

They were then expected to brave situations that would cripple others with fear. As a testament to them, American courage is the standard by which the rest of the world endeavors to hold to its own citizens.

I am embarrassed to say that I am likely one of those who would experience such fear, as I did on the day that a man was thrown into my path, a victim of an unfortunate accident. Fortunate for both the victim and me, my friend, the marine, was also nearby to see the events unfold. I stood there, unable to move, unable to avert my eyes from this man as he twisted and turned under the burden of his suffering; I, on the other hand, remained motionless, still trying to comprehend what I was witnessing. Please keep in mind, this was the mid 1990's; there were no cell phones or wi-fi or YouTube. I had just advanced into carrying a "phone card" in my wallet, complete with money charged on an account and usable at any nearby pay phone.

My friend stood next to me; it was still early in the morning, but there were enough people out to start making a small crowd. Everyone was just in shock. I remember that Bill first moved to the man and, removing his coat, placed it under the man's head and said something to him too soft for me to hear. After a moment, Bill stood up, came to me and told me to keep my back turned to the scene and to start telling people to not get too close. In a daze, that's what I did. I just remember my body moving into a "cruise control" and doing what it was directed to do, all while my conscious was still trying to process the events as they were unfolding.

I don't really remember the rest; it was such a blur and over 20 years ago. I know that my friend told someone to find a phone and call 9-1-1. I know that he also asked people if anyone was trained in first aid, and I know someone came out of the crowd and helped him. I also know that the man was terribly injured, both with broken bones, severe burns and a head injury. I know that the emergency medical personnel showed up and stabilized the victim. Lastly, I know the victim's life was saved because my friend acted when no one else did, including me.

Bill was not trained in medicine. The extent of his medical training of any kind consisted of a one-day CPR and first-aid course he received while in the Marine Corps. Ironically, I was better suited to assist, having had three summers of American Red Cross training as a lifeguard. Yet, it was Bill who was credited with saving the man's life. How did Bill know what to do? The answer is that he basically used common sense and kept his head. Furthermore, Bill was empowered to act because he recognized the seriousness of the situation, and knew that time was critical. Bill observed the situation unfold; he then assessed the condition of the individual based on the reaction that the victim was giving moments after he hit the ground. Bill then acted decisively when he determined that no one else was going to do anything.

That is the point of this book. Like fires, injuries, and accidents that occur every day in our country, our culture has an ability to learn how to observe, assess, and act on life-threatening situations before they manifest into their dangerous conditions and often tragic outcomes. We have all kinds of fires in our communities today, and they are in the form of threat-related violence from others. This may be an active shooter, an individual who wishes to take his or her own life, or even an individual driven by a zealous religious fervor, to name a few.

Whatever the case, all of the assailants are driven by behavioral motivations. These behavioral motivations have been studied and identified as indicators of future possible violence. Our mental health professionals are familiar with these indicators, as are our law enforcement personnel. In fact, the United States Secret Service trains every single special agent in these indicators so that they can identify and proactively address threats against some of the people that they protect, including the President of the United States. Although federal agents are some of the best and brightest in our law enforcement community, they are by no means trained in mental health diagnosis or treatment. Rather, they are provided effective training to identify behavioral conditions in others who might show a propensity to threat-related violence. Once that condition has been identified, professionals can treat it in a proactive, positive manner. But like the firefighter who is called to stop the fire, mental health professionals and law enforcement officers are largely reactionary. These positions are in fact dependent on being called to a crisis that they are uniquely qualified to handle. Right now though, we haven't trained the community in identifying the "fire"; we've only set up the "fire department" to come if they are called. Our health providers and law enforcement personnel do great work, but they cannot be in all places monitoring all members of society for threat-related indicators. It is the responsibility of the community to be the eyes and ears for identifying danger, and then contacting the professionals to deal with it in a proactive manner.

It sounds fairly straightforward, something that we should be educating the public to do on a regular basis. I bet that if you are reading this book, however, it is likely because you are not familiar with the concept of behavioral indicators that can identify threat-related conditions.

The truth is that you may already know the indicators; you have just lacked the confirmation of what you see in others to justify taking action. By teaching you what to look for in other people's behavior and by assessing the seriousness of the indicators you are identifying, you will then be empowered to take decisive action.

That is the key: making the call and bringing it to the attention of someone of authority who can do something.

As a former U.S. Secret Service agent, my training has not diminished even though I am no longer a part of their cadre. I still watch the news with the eyes of one who has been trained in this identification of threatening conditions. For me, reading the news reports about rampage violence is frustrating. After a day or two, the media begins to piece together the profile of the assailant: his lifestyle, professional background, and conditions leading up to the attack, all corroborated by interviews with those who knew him. It never fails. Every one reads like a case study from my days as an agent. The most disturbing things are the interviews with other people; their responses are always the same:

"I knew something was wrong; I just didn't know what to do or who to call…."

"He said things every now and then that seemed a little weird…. "

"He posted some stuff online that I thought was a little disturbing…."

I don't blame those people who felt like they knew something was up. It's not their fault. We're not trained to see these indicators, and we don't have the clear path laid out to take action. Some places, like school districts, have started to take on a proactive approach to setting up "Threat Assessment Teams," but they are more like call centers for dealing with reports as they come in. Are they training their school staff? Yes, somewhat. But are they training their student body? I have yet to find a school in America that teaches the students what conditions to look for in other students pertaining to threat-related behavior. I don't blame the schools for this shortcoming, as they are teaching in a system that is mandated by government oversight. In addition, there are many parents who would refuse to allow their child to participate in a training session on threat-related behaviors and what to watch for in potential killers. It's a disturbing mental picture, imagining our children being briefed on how to identify and report behavioral issues and threats in others.

But it is a necessity. The truth is that no one wants to expose their families to the gruesome realities of the world, so we choose to refrain from learning what we can about threats to our community. But this has created a cultural understanding that we should turn our eyes away from the dangers of today when we should be facing them head on. We don't want to scare our children, so we justify that it is better to not educate them on threat-related behavior as a way to protect those most dear to us.

As a father, I understand this thinking. I police what my children watch on television; I constantly ask them what they discussed with their friends at school; I monitor what they are doing online very, very closely. And I am also realistically aware that I cannot keep them censored from the atrocities and dangers of the world. As such, I give them the best defense to an uncaring and predatory planet, that of education.

We have to train our entire community in identifying the indicators of danger to the community if we want to stop threat-related violence from occurring. It's that simple. All of the laws and regulations in history have not curbed violence in our community; reactive measures such as law enforcement interventions have not deterred others from committing violence. The solutions we have in place are missing a crucial, critical piece, that of proactive interventions and identifications of behavioral observations and assessments.

In early 2016, a charter school in Alaska suspended three females in first grade for plotting to kill one of their own classmates. The children believed that the silica gel packets that are often found in sealed food products were poisonous, and they planned to use the packets to poison the student. The reason the plan was discovered was because fellow first graders had the presence of mind to recognize the threat and report it to the teachers.

These were first grade students. They were not adults who lived independently in the world. They were children. If not for the student who had the fortitude to report the incident, who knows what would have happened? Granted, the silica gel packets are not fatal, but the effort on the part of the students is what is important, and that it happened with those so young. This should be a cautionary tale to those who don't believe violence-identification should be taught in our schools.

This book will hopefully be a guide that anyone can use at the pace with which they want to teach themselves, their companies, schools, or families. It provides a thorough outline of the indicators of threat-related behavior, as outlined by the foremost authorities in law enforcement and mental health. In addition, it provides templates that can be used in a corporate or academic environment to assist with compiling a valid assessment of a case. Lastly, it outlines a "garden-variety" plan of action in the event that an assessment has been deemed a serious matter.

This book is not meant to fan the flames of paranoia. You may, however, become a bit concerned when you read through some of the symptoms that are known to manifest with threatening conditions. In fact, you may have experienced a few in your lifetime (as I have). First and foremost, the vast majority of our population HAS experienced some of these conditions in their lives, and the majority of us have NOT acted on them aggressively. Second, it is important to remember that the goal of this program is PROACTIVE intervention. It is NOT to have an individual arrested, prosecuted, and sent away for the rest of his or her life. It IS to get individuals to the professionals who can help that person before the condition manifests into one of a threat – to you, your family, your co-workers, your classmates, or himself/herself.

Remember: You are being trained to identify a fire, assess its level of danger, and if necessary, call the fire department.

In other words, you are being trained to Observe, Assess, and Act® (OA²®). I am a firm believer that there is no safer community than the one that we forge together. I thank you reading and for taking steps to ensure a safer place for us all to live.

3. Eric and Dylan and the Columbine Massacre: Where It All Began

On the morning of April 20, 1999, 18-year-old Eric Harris and 17-year-old Dylan Klebold entered Columbine High School in Littleton, Colorado, and changed our country forever. At approximately 11:19 a.m., Harris and Klebold began executing a carefully planned massacre of as many students and faculty as they could attack at the school. The attackers carried four semi-automatic firearms, one shotgun, and four knives between them. In addition, they planted an additional 99 explosive devices, propane tanks rigged to explode, and vehicle bombs throughout the area to delay the arrival of emergency services.

For the defenseless school, the attack was an absolute massacre. Klebold and Harris began a spree of random killing, shooting both faculty and students alike. Based on post-attack investigations, the attack lasted for approximately 49 minutes. In that time, 12 students and 1 teacher were executed, and an additional 21 students were injured by gunfire; 3 additional students would be injured while attempting to escape the attacks. Ultimately, the massacre ended when Harris and Klebold both took their own lives.

We will discuss Eric Harris and Dylan Klebold in greater detail later, but for now, we need to understand what the Columbine High School massacre did to our country and how we began addressing such violence. For our national community, the attacks were a watershed moment. Although rampage violence had occurred before in the United States, Columbine was violence brought upon innocent children by (seemingly) innocent children. In truth, we had seen incidents of violence at schools before, and in grand scale; in just 2 years before Columbine, there were 11 incidents of rampage violence in schools throughout the United States where all the assailants were between the ages of 11 and 15. In total, 20 people were killed and 54 people were injured.

So what made the Columbine attack so "special"? The idea that a child could conceptualize such a horrific act, and subsequently act on it, was so outlandish and disturbing that it was difficult to believe. That two children were able to act out such macabre ideation proved that evil did in fact exist in the world and was right next door. It was unnerving, but it was not unusual. It had happened 11 times before, with the 2 years prior being a small snapshot of attacks of child-upon-child violence in schools. The difference was the evolution of modern media and technology.

In 1999, the media was beginning to experiment with live-streaming video; video that would find its way onto the fairly new "internet." Footage that was once edited and cleared for public viewing was now a real-time matter and came across to viewers in raw scenes that were as real as amateur video at the moment of recording. As Columbine unfolded in the small town of Littleton, it also unfolded in the corporate offices, school campuses, and homes when mothers had just dropped their own children off at schools throughout the country.

Just as America watched Columbine, so did the American government. Within a month after the attacks, the Department of Education (DOE) took decisive action. Committing itself to ensuring that there was a plan to prevent future violent attacks like the one in Columbine from ever occurring again, the DOE met with the United States Secret Service (USSS) to find a solution to the problem. It made sense to contact the USSS, as they were the premier federal agency in matters of protective capabilities. Already mandated by the United States Congress to protect the lives of the President of the United States, The Vice President, and other political figures and their families as necessary, the USSS were the ideal candidate to tackle the project of outlining better methods of protection for our nation's schools.

The project was completed with a final report published in July 2004. It was formally known as the "Final Report and Findings of the Safe School Initiative: Implications for the Prevention of School Attacks in the United States" or the "SSI" and was released jointly through the DOE and the USSS. Although the publication was not highly anticipated when it was released (society had since forgotten the shock of Columbine and was reeling from a new threat, that of terrorist attacks after 9/11), the SSI did provide great insight into school rampage violence. Equally surprising, however, were its recommendations for effective protective measures in schools. Where readers were expecting a thorough outline of security programs and precautionary measures, the SSI offered none of that. Instead, the recommendations focused on proactive interventions into a student's behavior.

Specifically, the SSI focused on studying incidents of targeted school violence that occurred between 1974 and May 2000. The total number of incidents that occurred numbered 37, with 41 assailants. I encourage anyone reading this book to find the SSI online and peruse it, as it both validates the information that you will read here as well as provides additional data for those needing quantitative support. Briefly, the SSI states these following points:

1. Preparation

Targeted violence is rarely impulsive; it is meticulously planned. We have all felt a flash of anger during some point in our lives. Even today, I personally experience it when I am driving. The person I am supposed to share the road with doesn't want to share with me, and inevitably I find myself on the receiving end of being cut off or nearly hit. It is at that moment that I want to make sure my fellow road-sharer knows my displeasure. Most of the time I don't get my point across, though. The person who nearly ended my life with his car has moved on down the road, leaving a path of disgruntled drivers who feel as I do. For me, I stew for a bit and then I am drawn back to the melody playing in my speakers.

Those who target a location or group don't let things go, though. In fact, they go home after they have gotten the license plate of the other driver and start planning. They try and find out where they live, where they work and what a typical day is like. They collect intelligence through observation, they analyze when their target is weakest, and they sometimes test security measures to see what is effective and what needs improvement. Their violence is the opening night performance, and their planning is the rehearsal. Simply put: rampage violence attacks are carefully planned, meticulously scripted, and oftentimes rehearsed operations that go into production months, sometimes years, before the attack. So why is this important? Even the most confidential, carefully laid plan will have moments that will interact with the public. It is likely that indicators that point to a plan of attack can be identified sometime prior to the attack itself.

While planning attacks of this nature likely display indicators, it is important to note that threatening the target is not one of them. Oftentimes, an individual will not threaten his or her target before attacking. Attackers understand that, by drawing attention to themselves, they risk losing a "soft target" or one that has minimal defenses. In addition, the target is often a group of people, and the target becomes the place where that group gathers. In the summer of 2015, 21-year-old Dylann Roof entered the Emmanuel African Methodist Church in Charleston, South Carolina and executed nine innocent people, all of whom were of African American descent. We know that Roof harbored ill-intent to multiple minorities and religious affiliations, with sympathetic leanings toward white supremacist groups.

There was no evidence to suggest that Roof ever threatened the Emmanuel Church prior to his attack. Obviously, he felt some deep-seeded malevolence toward the people there and what he perceived they represented. That is a certainly proven by his actions. But, can his hatred be enough to proactively identify him as a threat? Can a person with this kind of vile toward a specific group of people also be considered a person with threatening behavior? Is it fair to identify the Dylann Roof's of the world as threatening solely based on their feelings (albeit disgusting) toward others?

What is fairly certain is that, although Roof did not communicate his hostile intent to his victims prior to his attack, it is very likely that he voiced his opinions and intentions in some manner, to someone, before he killed. Even voicing such angst may not be enough to alert law enforcement, but it should at least raise a red flag of concern in your community.

Are such actions enough to pay closer attention to that person? To see if they are doing or saying other things that should give concern? Absolutely.

2. Communicating Intentions

Attackers usually communicate their plans to friends, family, or associates through social means. Have you ever bought something that you were really excited about getting? Maybe it was a house, or a car. Perhaps it was something that you could wear, like a pair of shoes or jewelry. You saved up for it for a long time and you waited until you felt financially secure enough to buy it, or you had earned it from all of your hard work or patience. When you finally got it, how did you feel? When I bought my first new car, I wanted to shout it from the rafters. I stood outside my house, admired it at every possible angle, and took pictures from those viewpoints. I forwarded the pictures to all my friends and family, and I volunteered to drive anyone anywhere for a month. I was brimming with pride. It was so important to me, and I wanted to share my excitement over my new toy with the world.

We are all, by nature, ego-driven creatures. If something is important to us, then more times than not we will express our enthusiasm in a search for accolades from others. "Facebook" and "Twitter" that have made a fortune off of this concept. "Selfies" are such a trend because people want to share their beautiful appearances, the places they are visiting or the celebrities that they just met. People truly enjoy expressing things that are important to them, and they want to tell everyone else.

This may seem a bit disturbing, but someone who is planning an attack is just as excited about what they are planning as you and I are about our new car. It's a morbid thought to us, but for an assailant, it is a labor of love; it has been planned and re-planned, studied and rehearsed, and soon the assailant is preparing to set his nightmare into motion. He is metaphorically bursting at the seams to tell people, and he often will. It may be a cryptic utterance, or possibly an online communication, or a personal journal but make no mistake; the assailant has communicated his intentions to others prior to the attack. He may say it on the internet and through chat lines. Jeffery Weise, the Red Lake attacker who we will discuss later, told multiple people about his plans the night before in an online chat service. He had reached the point where he could not contain his dark secret any longer.

Others would argue that it may be a "cry for help" as well, and that is very possible. Whether it is an attempt to reach out to others for assistance, or a sick excitement about what is going to happen, communicating an intention is likely to occur. If you find that you're the one who is being told about something like this, you should act promptly. Don't assume that a person is joking or that someone else will handle it. Do something about it.

In many cases, other people learned about the plans and then helped to carry them out. Like Harris and Klebold, the thought that multiple people could devise and execute such blatant violence against innocent civilians is unnerving and frightening. It's also a very realistic scenario. More likely than not, attackers have some sort of supporting cast to see their plan come to fruition. In the case of Columbine, for example, Harris and Klebold were able to obtain all of their weapons through what is popularly known as the "gun show loophole." The post-Columbine investigation determined that the attackers researched the state laws and determined that, through a third party, they could have a person purchase weapons at gun shows for them. That person was (at the time) 18-year-old Robyn Anderson, who was a legal adult and, as such, legally able to procure firearms at the Tanner Gun Show in December of 1998. Anderson successfully bought the Hi-Point 9mm Carbine, Savage 67H pump-action shotgun, and a Savage 311-D 12-gauge shotgun used in the Columbine massacre. Additionally, another person named Mark Manes sold the attackers the TEC-DC9 for $500, even though Manes was well aware that the boys were under the legal age of gun ownership at the time.

3. Profile

There is no one profile of attackers who engage in targeted violence. If we could judge a book by its cover, then you wouldn't have had to read this far to know that you had a great book in your hands. Unfortunately for me (and those profiting from this writing), you needed to read on before you decided to recommend it to your friends and family. In other words, the content matters.

People are the same. We have to look deeper into a person's actions and behavior to determine if they have the potential to be a true threat to our community. Is this profiling? Yes, but it's behavioral profiling. It's not judging a person by his physical characteristics, or a religious belief or mental state. It is however an assessment based on his own personal actions, and there is nothing wrong with that at all. If you were walking through a dark parking garage and you saw someone breaking into cars, you wouldn't judge the person based on their skin color or what they were wearing. You would assess them by the actions that they are committing, and you would likely be concerned since they are doing something illegal. From that alone, I hope you would take appropriate action and notify the proper authorities. This is the same concept.

The studies show that there is no one discriminating religion, age, or class status of an attacker. Ages vary from as young as 11 to as old as 89. Attackers have come from wealthy, established families and from broken homes. They have been diagnosed with mental disorders and they have been certified geniuses. The only glaring similarity in assailants of rampage violence in the United States is that they were virtually all male. It's important to note that females also display these conditions, except studies suggest that their aggression is internalized. In other words, females are more prone to suicidal tendencies and other kinds of self-harm. If you have a mother, sister, daughter who shows some of these indicators, you should not ignore them because of her gender. You should be concerned that she might hurt herself rather than others.

4. Coping Issues

Most attackers are known to have recently suffered significant losses or personal failures. We have all experienced incredible failures, tragedies and hardship in our lives. How we have dealt with these issues often define us later in life. The most telling factor in identifying who may be a threat to themselves or others are those who have these drastic, sudden changes in their lives and cannot cope the way most of us do. It's a terrible situation when someone loses the sense of hope for a better tomorrow. That is usually the first sign of a person who will continue into a downward spiral. In some cases, those individuals blame others and want to enact some kind of vengeance for the pain that they feel.

This is the most obvious indicator for future threatening behavior in an individual, and it's one that we'll discuss later. For now, it is important to understand that significant changes for the worse in an individual's life can have drastic and sudden emotional, mental, and behavioral consequences. As I mentioned before, you have likely experienced something like this yourself in your life, as we all have. I am not suggesting that you were capable of committing rampage violence, but that stress coupled with a sense of any number of emotions (anger, humiliation, regret, etc.) can send someone to the point where he or she feels that the only reprieve is violence.

Many times, the attackers are experiencing significant losses and failures after coping, sometimes for years, with feeling bullied, persecuted, or injured by others prior to the attack. I still remember the first "bully" I ever had to deal with. I was only seven years old, and this boy, Robbie, was about ten. Although only a few years apart, to me Robbie might as well have been an adult. He was much taller, had a deeper voice and was already on his way to middle school. He terrified me in every conceivable way. When I would walk to school, I would try to find ways through the woods to avoid him. My shoes would get wet from the creek-bed that I had to cross, and my clothes would be covered in those thatches that would stick to cotton. I would be late for school; I was humiliated by how I looked. And I didn't care. I was just so thankful to have survived another trip to my school without be hunted, demeaned and beaten like a scared animal. This went on for years.

Even into my adulthood, the thought of my bully was still fresh in my mind. As I grew into manhood, I became aware that I was becoming larger than most boys my age, and sports helped. I saw others getting bullied and I took it upon myself to intervene when I could. It was one summer that I had returned from my military college that I had stopped for gas a station that was nowhere near my home. As I paid the attendant I noticed that it was my bully, my Robbie. I stood there looking at him from across the counter, a full foot taller than him. He was sickly now, covered in an unkempt beard and stunk of cigarette smoke. He politely handed me my change, told me to have a nice day, and moved on to the next person in line behind me. I walked away, stunned at what had happened. He never even recognized me. This person who had single-handedly been responsible for some of the worst moments in my childhood, this bastard who had me crying myself to sleep at night didn't even have the decency to acknowledge a memory of me. As I returned to my car, I had a sudden urge to walk back into the shop and destroy him. It would have been easy; his ill frame would have been a dry twig in my hands. But the moment passed, and at that time I found comfort in finally facing my great opponent. I knew I could ruin him, but the cost would be ruining myself. My future would be tainted and my life broken. No, it was not worth it. I collected myself and continued down the road.

Sadly, there are those in our community who never get the opportunity to have any kind of closure. It festers and the fear stays. It even translates into the workforce. The ugly truth is that bullying doesn't go away into adulthood. With a society of bullies, there is an equal volume of victims. I am going to bet most of you have experienced bullying in some way in your life, and if you think about it, those painful memories are still clear and haunting.

Thankfully, our communities are starting to recognize the real damage that bullying causes, and we're starting to do something about it. Anti-bullying programs are starting to really take hold in our schools. Where kids were once expected to settle their differences on the playground, dealing with a gut full of fear and humiliation at the same time, positive interventions are now the norm. School programs like Positive Behavioral Interventions and Supports (PBIS) and the Olweus Bullying Prevention Program (OBPP) can be credited for attempting change. So, what about bullying outside of school? Public humiliation and degradation has never been easier to do since the creation of the internet. We are seeing adults in our society who are still living with the bullying of their youth, and they continue to be attacked in online forums and in their adult lives. Also, bullies can find refuge in the anonymity of the online attacks, and their words are more hurtful than any sticks or stones.

5. Indicators

Most of the time, attackers displayed concerning behavior to others suggesting they were a danger or needed help. In previous incidents of rampage violence, people who were somehow affiliated with the attacker prior to the attack knew something was wrong. Most of the time, however, self-doubt of their feelings or observations usually kicked in, and they ignored how they felt. They justified to themselves that they were being paranoid, and they let the matter go. Also, the all too familiar "someone else will do something" argument became the foundation for not acting on his or her personal concerns.

This is the most glaring, obvious reason for this book. This is the very reason why it is critical that you, as a member of the community, recognize the behavioral conditions that I will define in this book. Most likely, an attacker will display concerning behavior before attacking a target. Law enforcement, counseling services and other support professions cannot be there all the time to identify these conditions — but you can and you must make every effort to do so.

That is what this book is all about: identifying these conditions and telling those community services so they can intervene.

The SSI is not the only study that supports these arguments, but it is a good starting point to build the foundation of discussing threat-related behavior. It outlines a thorough analysis of similarities that span over decades to include age groups, locations, and social dynamics. All of this makes for a quality report. The data are supported by clinical and behavioral studies that are far too voluminous to detail here. For now, it is important to keep in mind that our efforts here are an attempt to recognize what behavioral conditions we, as a society, should be watchful for. One additional study that we will reference is the Exceptional Case Study Project (ECSP) published in 1997 by the U.S. Secret Service. Although nearly 20 years old at the time of this writing, the ECSP is still considered the federal law enforcement standard for recognizing threat-related behavior. It is also the first exposure for all agents in the U.S. Secret Service when learning the fundamental traits and behaviors of an assassin and their motivations for committing such violence. The project itself was a study into individuals known to have engaged in assassination-type behaviors directed at prominent public officials in the United States since 1949, totaling 83 attackers in all. The ECSP makes it clear that there have been other attacks that go further back in history, but the limited amount of information outlining an attacker's behavioral condition in his life made for inaccurate data analysis. As such, these individuals were not considered in the study.

The conclusion of the study indicates that assassinations and attacks on public officials resulted from an understandable and discernible process of thinking and behavior. What is most intriguing though is that those who were studied in the ECSP had very similar characteristics of those individuals who are referenced and studied in the SSI. With both reports, the findings conclude that there is no accurate profile of an attacker; persons who have attacked or come close to attacking public officials often exhibit attack-related behaviors (like those we will discuss later); a high percent of attackers had an interest in assassinations or were motivated by some kind of historical attack before they attacked or approached their targets. Attackers communicated their intentions to others in some way, strategized a planned method for the attack, did not display erratic, non-rational behavior in society, showed an interest in radicalized or militant groups, and (most importantly) had suffered a severe negative impact in their lives prior to the attack.

Why is this so important? During my training as a special agent with the U.S. Secret Service, and my subsequent tenure with the agency in the agent ranks for over 8 years, the ECSP was the professional standard on which we as agents based the vast majority of our protective investigations. As special agents, my counterparts and I were mandated by federal law to investigate every single threat that was made to those under our umbrella of protection. Every single one. No exceptions. In this day and age of heightened political angst, coupled with the ease of accessibility of social media, you can imagine how many people would send an emotionally filled rant into a public forum online. If any of those rants even implied a threat to a political figure under our shield of protection, then the person who sent that post was probably going to get a call from a few federal agents. In extreme circumstances, those individuals would be prosecuted for a federal crime.

But I will ask again: Why is this so important? So what? What's the point? Well, here it is. The United States Secret Service, the agency that is responsible for the safety and well-being of the person who occupies one of the most powerful political offices in the world and is the Commander-In-Chief of the greatest military force in history, uses behavioral identification, assessment, and (when necessary) action to keep that person who is under their veil of protection, the President of the United States, safe. If there is so much as a sniff of a possible concern of a threat to the President, then it is addressed. That should be a more than obvious testament to the credibility of the methodology of using identification of threat-related behavior to protect people. Observations and assessments of threat-related behavior are the backbone for Presidential protection; it is certainly a valid means at ensuring safety in our community as well. As if that is not justification enough, then let it sink in that Secret Service agents are not certified psychologists, clinical practitioners, behavioral psychiatrists, or any other specialist in the mental health field. They have been trained to identify concerning behavior of an individual, assess the seriousness of the concern, and then act in a proactive manner to thwart any potential danger later on.

Remember the example of what to do if you came upon a fire. You would instinctively identify it and then you would assess its level of danger. If you found that it was a serious issue then you would contact the fire department. We're doing the exact same thing with behavioral indicators: You are identifying the behavioral issue that is being presented; you are assessing its level of danger and you are contacting a support group or professional assistance to take care of the situation. Like the fire, the goal is to act proactively to prevent something terrible from possibly occurring.

If this makes you feel confident about being able to identify threatening behaviors in others, then that's a good thing! We as a community should feel empowered to proactively address behaviors that give us concern. Ultimately, we want to be able to stop future incidents of violence; those that prompted research studies like the SSI and the ECSP in the first place.

Some things to note before we continue: it is very important to stress that the behavioral indicators that we will be discussing are by no means a guarantee that the person who displays them will commit rampage violence. In fact, the odds suggest that they will very likely not harm anyone at all. But it is equally important to note that if an individual does commit rampage violence, that several of these indicators will be identifiable in the person's life and behavior.

So what should we do? Do we continue to look the other way and play the odds? Or should we be cognizant to the possibility that there may be some concerning behavior manifesting in someone? Our society has opted to play the odds and live with the occasional incidents of rampage violence. I say we now err on the side of caution.

Additionally, I have every confidence that this book will also have its share of critics, likely those whose studies I cite throughout the writing. In response to their criticism, I can only state that the research studies that have been cited were released in 1997 and 2004, each concluding with recommendations that there be a furtherance of sponsored training for members of the community into identifying threatening behavior in others. After nearly 20 years since the first publication was released, little effort has been made to reach out to the private sector, the national schools, college campuses, local law enforcement, and neighborhood watch programs to jumpstart such programs. Yet our country has watched threat-related behavior bear the fruit of rampage violence time and time again, be it Columbine High School, Sandy Hook Elementary, Virginia Tech, Aurora Cinemark, or any number of victim targets.

The limited motivation to promote the findings of the SSI and the ECSP to the public is a failure on behalf of our federal government and a tragedy to our mourning country. The research is deeply appreciated, but the follow-through on behalf of its originators is both disappointing and unacceptable. Let the theorists criticize while we the national community take action to make our country safe.

Let's begin, shall we?

I. OBSERVE

4. Timothy

It begins with an observation. Most likely it will be something that you were not prepared for such as overhearing a conversation or seeing something posted on a social network. It could be something like a person making a veiled threat ("I wouldn't cry if a piano dropped on that guy's head") or something much more direct ("You better watch your back next time you're around here…."). Whatever the case, if you have lived in the United States, then you've been around enough of these kinds of statements. You have also probably heard the tired, antiquated defense of such statements with "it's a free country; I can say what I want." And yes, that is true… but not without consequences. The law does not protect individuals from threatening people. They cannot imply a threat to a person, and they further cannot make such threats and then expect that the rights of the U.S. Constitution will grant immunity from punishment. Just as a person making the threat believes he has a right to free speech, the person he has threatened has a right to living a life devoid of such threats. And in the eyes of the court, the victim will win every time.

Maybe you have overheard something or seen something that is much more subtle. I have a friend who was concerned when, during a ride home from school, she overheard her kids and a neighbor's child tell a story about a classmate who had implied he was going to hurt a teacher (which my friend immediately reported to the school, thankfully). In one of my first jobs out of college, I had an employee who had overheard a fellow co-worker talking to himself in his office as she walked by. She heard him say, "I just can't go on." On an impulse, she asked him to meet after work for some dinner. In the conversation, he confessed that he was trying find a reason to not take his own life and that he was fairly certain he was going to soon (again, the intercession likely saved him as he was convinced to get help). There are a nearly infinite number of scenarios that you could be exposed to that get your senses tingling like these two instances.

As I write this, (even though I don't know you), I am fairly certain that you know what I am talking about because you probably have experienced some kind of situation like this many, many times in your life. Most of the time, you (like me) usually brushed it off and moved on with your day. Let me offer a suggestion: from now on, let's pay closer attention to the things we are hearing other people say, reading what they write, and viewing how they act. Let me put your mind at ease a bit and stress that what we are observing is probably nothing, but we may be the key element in stopping something tragic from happening.

Even as you are reading these first few words, your mind has accessed memories that you have, associating those personal memories with what you are reading. Memory retrieval is one of the great resources of your mind. As you go through your day reading an article (or a book) or listening to a presentation or talking with other people, your subconscious will immediately start accessing your memories, finding similarities to what you are seeing and hearing at that moment and bringing similar memories to the attention of you consciousness. It is like a servant eagerly awaiting an order and following through on it before you can decide whether you want him to or not. I know that this is happening because it is exactly what happens whenever I start discussing OA²® (Observe, Assess, Act®) with people. OA²® is the phrase I use to describe the three-step approach to engaging the community in proactive safety. I have found that my audience tends to first grasp the concept fairly quickly, then they agree that it is a major need in our society today, and finally they reflect on something that happened in their personal lives where the concepts of OA²® could have been a difference maker if they had been trained in it.

A few months ago, I had the opportunity to attend a sporting event with my sister-in-law. I was coming home from Greensboro after a business road trip, and I stopped for the night in my wife's hometown of Richmond, Virginia. My sister-in-law, Audra, had tickets she had won from the local radio station to see the Washington Redskins at their new practice facility. It was a great opportunity, as they were sharing a few sessions with the Houston Texans, and I was eager to see some terrific players take the field. After some schedule adjustments, I was on board with the plans. Audra and I met at the radio station and enjoyed a complimentary breakfast while waiting for the bus to take us and the other winners over to the practice facility.

I began an idle conversation with Joe, one of the winners (just to pass the time more than anything). We talked a bit about football, and that moved into talking about the business of the sport, which eventually got to us talking about what we did for a living. Joe was the manager of a prestigious car dealership in the city, and he had been given the tickets for being such a great client. I explained what I did (I was presenting OA²® almost exclusively at the time) and what the program entailed.

Joe listened intently, almost to the point that I couldn't tell if he was really paying attention or just politely keeping his eyes on me while his imagination ran amok. I soon found that Joe was not only listening to what I was saying, but internalizing it into aspects of his own life.

After a polite pause, he began to tell me about how he volunteered as the assistant head coach for his son's high school junior varsity football team, comprising mostly freshman and sophomore students. Joe's own son, a sophomore, was a linebacker. As such, Joe's responsibilities were overseeing the defensive unit of the team. One of the other members of the defense was a young man named Timothy, who played defensive end and was also a sophomore.

"He just didn't fit in." Joe told me. "It's not that he wasn't welcome; he was just different. Like the way he acted with the boys, and how they treated him. Not bullying. Just kind of like 'Okay, he's here on the team, so it is what it is.' I don't really know how to explain it; it was kind of sad." Joe went on to tell me about how Timothy was pretty terrible as an all-around football player. He had the physical ability and athleticism to play the game, but his performance at practice was sluggish at best. There was no doubt that he understood the plays that needed to be executed, but he seemed to be comfortable with going through the motions rather than showing a crisp, effective response to an offensive play. After practice ended, Timothy would find himself on the bleachers alone, waiting for his mother to pick him up.

One of these afternoons, Joe approached Timothy, sat down with him after practice, and started talking to him.

"I just knew something wasn't right, ya know? He just wasn't acting like a kid." Joe told me.

Joe started talking with Timothy and asking him how things were going, and if there was anything he wanted to get off his mind. As the father of a son Timothy's age, Joe explained that he wasn't expecting much, but thought it best to make the effort. However, Joe's simple gesture toward Timothy might very well have saved lives.

"He just started breaking down, telling me about all of these things at home and how he's just so angry all the time," Joe explained. Timothy started speaking softly about his home life, how it was an uncomfortable place for him and his family. I was never told if Timothy referenced a sibling, but he said that his mother had married a man a few years before and he turned out to be very belittling and mean spirited. From the perspective of Timothy, a virtual stranger had come into his home, taken over, and subjected the boy to ridicule and verbal abuse. After telling Joe about this for several minutes, he finally explained that he was filled with so much rage that he knew if he didn't do something about it, then he was going to try and kill his stepfather.

"And that was why he joined the football team, to release some of that rage. " Joe finished.

"So what did you do?" I asked.

"Well, I moved him from Tight End to Linebacker so he could really hit some people." Joe replied.

Even with the seriousness of the story he had just told, I couldn't help but laugh. I always thought it was a great response. Nevertheless, I pressed the issue and Joe told me that Timothy was starting to give up on football. He didn't find the fulfillment he thought he would and still felt the boiling rage in him even after a long, exhaustive practice. Joe interceded at just the right time, apparently, as Timothy later told the coach that he was planning on quitting that week.

Much to my surprise, Joe had not done anything about the Timothy issue since. I recommended to him that he contact either the school guidance counselor or the mother to take some kind of action. Joe admitted that he thought about doing that, but didn't want to seem like he was overreacting. One thing Joe did do, however, was stress to his football team the importance of including Timothy as part of the "family," and he put the responsibility on his own son to keep a watchful eye on Timothy in school, where the coach's eyes could not be.

I don't blame Joe for not doing more; he did what he could with the information that he had (which sadly, is not enough). We just don't train our community in identifying these indicators in others like we should. But you still have the ability to pick up on those things that are "off" in other people, like Coach Joe did in Timothy. And also like Joe, you can probably do more than you realize. Just reaching out to someone could make a difference before he or she resolves to do something unthinkable to him or herself or others. Yours may be the light that returns to their gray horizon and makes them rethink what they are contemplating.

After my conversation with Joe, it occurred to me that what happened with him happens a lot. I don't mean running into a teenager professing his desires to kill his stepfather. I mean someone starting to tell me a story that had happened in his or her life that could be linked to the work I was doing. The other thing that I realized was that, not only did people relate these stories to me a lot, but the things they said were (for the most part) fairly recent. Every now and then, someone would reflect on a situation that may have happened in their childhood, but mostly the things that they told me were happening now. It might have been a friend or family member, a co-worker or someone that attended school with their kids, but it was most assuredly happening recently enough that it was fresh in their memories.

As you are thinking about incidents you've heard about or possibly things that have occurred in your life, start to think about what you could be looking for—what could you observe that would help? There are three categories in the "Observe" phase of OA²®. They are:

- Early Indicators
- Danger Indicators
- Mental Health Indicators, or those mental illnesses commonly associated with threatening behavior.

Each of these categories is divided into sub-categories, and each comes with a unique outline to include what to watch for and how each might manifest.

I have stressed before (and will continue to stress throughout the book) that the indicators that are listed in the "observe" phase are by no means a guarantee that an individual will commit any kind of violence against themselves or other people. In fact, it is highly probable that they will not. However, these behavioral identifiers are those that are most common in people who have committed such atrocities despite age, their individual backgrounds, or the lifestyles in which they grew up. There have been attackers who were raised in deeply religious, loving families and there were those who were physically, mentally, and emotionally abused the first 20 years of their lives. Just like most people in society, we have all types of individuals who have come from various backgrounds (sometimes negative, traumatic ones) and they have gone on to lead productive, positive lives in our community. Theirs are inspirational testaments, and this book should not discredit them.

Additionally, the ultimate goal is positive, proactive interventions. If these indicators have been identified, it is important not to take steps to isolate the individual in question. Rather, it should be to get that person help as to avoid a possible incident later.

There are many, many individuals out there who are dealing with something in their lives that cause others to be concerned. Everybody, most likely, has an opportunity to proactively intervene. Everybody has a story about people they know like Joe and Timothy. Everybody—even me.

I grew up in the rural community of Stafford, Virginia. Stafford has since grown into a kind of "rural metropolis" offering the best of acreage, privacy and close proximity to Washington, D.C. or Richmond, depending on your work. But during my day, Stafford still had the small-town feel of a close-knit community. You could walk down the old-cobbled streets of Fredericksburg and probably run in to someone you knew. It was a wonderful place to grow up.

I attended Stafford Senior High School, one of only two high schools in the town at the time. While there, I became an avid long-distance runner and was actively involved with track and field and cross country. For those years, long-distance running became my life.

Like anyone so committed to a sport, the bonds that come with those who are going through it with you become stronger as time goes on. Track was no different. The friends I made with the boys' and girls' teams were some of the closest I had developed in my life, and I am pleased to say that I still keep in touch with many of them. Sadly, one of our own did not have a future that once seemed so promising.

Michael was in many ways the "baby" of the group. He was a sophomore when the corps of our best runners were Juniors. I was the juxtaposition of Michael, being the lone Senior on the distance team in my final year. Just as Michael was the baby, I was the "grandpa." For adults, a few years' age difference is inconsequential, but for high school, a year or two apart in school was a lifetime. I found myself in a mentor role for Michael as the oldest runner, keeping an eye out for him, and assuring the rest of the team that we were a "family" as we watched out for one another. The message was effective, and minus the occasional jabs and ribbing, Michael was welcome into our inner circle.

Michael was there with the varsity team for one simple reason: he was good. He wasn't the best runner, but he was certainly good enough to keep up with the pack. I remember thinking – envying – how fast I might have been as a Senior if I had been able to run the speeds Michael was running when I was a Sophomore. I often thought about how much potential Michael had in long-distance running, and I was genuinely happy for my younger friend.

As good as he was on the track, Michael truly excelled in the classroom. As a sophomore, he was taking classes at the advanced placement level with those a full 2 years ahead of him academically. We even shared a chemistry class together. As I struggled through the rudimentary basics of hydrocarbon bonds and the periodic table, Michael eased through the studies without ever cracking a book. He was one the best students in the school, and he hadn't even tested for his driver's license. Again, I marveled at his potential.

After I graduated from high school, I like most people, moved on to other parts of the world. The life of college and adulthood took me away from the life I had experienced in my youth. I kept in touch with some of my friends from my earlier years, but Michael was not one of them. I had every confidence that he himself had moved on to greatness and was conquering the world with God-given talents. I could not have been more wrong.

Shortly before I started writing this book, I saw a news article one morning that shook me to the core. I was having my coffee on a Sunday morning, enjoying the time with my family as we lounged around our home and planned out our day. While I was reading the news on my computer, a quick blurb came across my ticker about a murder that had occurred in my hometown of Stafford. The sad truth is that we live in a society where, if a person tried to read every news article that was online concerning a murder, it would be a full-time job with no rest. What drew me to it was that it was my childhood home, and the unlikely possibility that someone I may have known was involved.

There, staring at me from my computer screen, was the photo of an assailant accused of a brutal, unthinkable murder. It was also my friend from high school. Michael's police photo left no doubt that it was the person I once knew. Obviously he was 20 years older, but the facial features matched the name without a doubt. He looked at me with dead eyes, a thousand-yard stare of a person devoid of consciousness, so very different from the person I once knew.

The news article told of how a neighbor called the police at around 5 a.m. the morning before after hearing ramblings and shouting coming from the next-door yard. When the neighbor went to investigate, he found Michael walking around in the moonlight with his hands and clothes covered in blood, talking out loud in gibberish. When police arrived at the home, they found a scene of horror: Michael's mother had been killed, having been bludgeoned to death by a hammer. Michael admitted his guilt to police and, after a bit of brief resistance, was arrested without incident.

My friend, a person that I had spent many hours with and who I admired for all of his natural abilities as a human being, had just committed one the most horrific crimes I had ever known. In a moment of anger and insanity, he had killed the woman who thought him more important than any other on Earth. He had done so with repeated blows to her skull with a hammer. Even now, it is still difficult to process.

The media never really provided much in the way of useful information as to the "why" this occurred. There were some follow-up reports that Michael began to deteriorate mentally and emotionally shortly after high school. Individuals who have committed such violence after living normally have shown similar breakdowns in their early adulthood. It was not reported that Michael had been diagnosed with a mental or emotional condition, but people who knew him had said that Michael showed symptoms of an individual who was "troubled." I don't presume to know what drove Michael to his madness, but multiple studies over decades support that individuals who commit murder, particularly those who begin to digress after adolescence, seem to be more likely to commit their crimes based on psychotic symptoms rather than those that have issues with social conduct. There is evidence to support that youth who are committing crimes, behaving with deviance, or are exposed to criminal circles, will have tendencies for violence. But those individuals who are in a seemingly stable lifestyle are totally susceptible to murderous actions with little warning. This seemed to be the case with Michael. Believe it or not, I even had pangs of personal guilt for a time about Michael. Although my association with Michael was as a good friend in our youth, I wonder if there might have been a different outcome to this tragic story if I had been more involved in his life as we grew older. I often thought to myself how I could have made a difference in the outcome of Michael's story if I had only kept in touch with him through the years.

I can't do anything for Michael anymore. But I can help to show you these indicators that are present and relevant when someone is on a downward spiral toward violence.

Some of these indicators may already be familiar to you. You may have been (or are one of) these people who have experienced an episode or felt emotionally or mentally unstable at some time in your life. Does that mean that you are going to go out and commit a murder? No, of course not. But it certainly shows that this is an issue that is more common than our society gives due attention. You have probably already been a part of something involving a behavioral concern in another person; maybe you've seen it, or even acted on it. In fact, I am going to bet that you have observed something, and that you have been thinking about it while you were reading this section. As I stated earlier, everyone has a story, and perhaps my story has helped you relate to your own. From personal experience, I can tell you that when you start watching for the conditions in others, it becomes very difficult to ignore them. I want you to be cognizant of concerning behavior so that you will do something about it. The information is meant to provide empowerment, and the ultimate goal is a safer community.

I hope that as you review the list of those things to watch for, you see similarities with conditions that may have happened in your life. I don't wish this out of any kind of spite, but association is one of the better kinds of understanding. Since you are reading this, I can assume that you are stable mentally and eager to learn more about what to do to protect our community. Therefore, if you have been through some of these tough spots in life and turned out okay, is it not safe to say that someone else can turn out okay as well? Maybe they need a bit of help getting over the road bump. That's where you will come in.

5. Early Indicators: Introduction

Specials Agents in the employ of the United States Secret Service are given an overwhelming amount of training and are painstakingly vetted before they are officially recognized as a federal agent in the organization. Upon completing a rigorous and extensive application process consisting of background investigations, panel interviews, polygraph examinations, and a battery of written and physical tests, only the top qualified recruits are selected for training. The training itself is nearly a year in scope, with the first half conducted at the Federal Law Enforcement Training Center (or FLETC) in Glynco, Georgia. From there, recruits are sent to the United States Secret Service James J. Rowley Training Center (affectionately known as "RTC") to complete the process. The two academies are intensive, highly stressful programs that are meant to test the limits of cadets while simultaneously determining if the candidate is a realistic fit for a career in federal law enforcement. Although the graduation rate is high, the programs do a fine job of filtering those who are not meant to carry a firearm and enforce law.

Needless to say, the classroom training is conducted by some of the brightest and best minds in the world. The United States Government spares no expense in ensuring that only the top individuals in their respective fields are contracted to teach the cadets the fundamentals of their trade. I felt privileged to receive such training, having been trained by some impressive individuals in all manners of defensive driving, control tactics, constitutional law, firearms proficiency, and other similar programs.

One of these training programs was unique to the mission of the U.S. Secret Service, that of "protective intelligence." As I have mentioned before, the agency has made its name in the study and practice of identifying threats to those under their protection based on certain displayed behaviors. It is these behaviors that we will discuss. In order to under-stand what to look for, we need to start with the earliest indicators that are common with threat-related behavior. Enter Dr. Harvey Goldstein.

For the past 30+ years, Dr. Goldstein has provided human behav-ioral assessment and analysis consulting and training to local, state and federal law enforcement agencies. Dr. Goldstein is widely considered one of the foremost experts on the psychology of dangerous individuals. He has trained special agents with the Federal Bureau of Investigation, the Drug Enforcement Administration, the U.S. State Department, and others. Dr. Goldstein has instructed courses at the University of Vir-ginia, Johns Hopkins University, Columbia University, and New York University as well. He has been recognized as a subject matter expert from media outlets such as 60 Minutes, CNN, and ABC's Nightline, to name a few. Dr. Goldstein was the ideal instructor to introduce rising agents in the U.S. Secret Service to the art of identifying indicators of threat-related behavior.

I had the opportunity to work with Dr. Goldstein on two differ-ent occasions while with the Secret Service. The first time was during the overview training on psychological dangers in threatening people, which all agents receive while at RTC. The second was a much more advanced course, specifically designated for those agents who were in-dividually selected to conduct protective intelligence investigations and interviews. It was during this second course that I was able to study the work that Dr. Goldstein provided us, and then apply it in a real-world setting against those who sought to do harm to U.S. Secret Service pro-tectees. What I determined was this: after conducting my own investi-gations, Dr. Goldstein was right. The behavioral indicators that we were trained in became a "check box" of sorts when analyzing individuals who we were investigating. It was extremely valuable information that let us know our investigation had legitimate merit to stopping threats against the people we protected.

Granted, the material that you are reading is a very high-end, "snap shot" for what I was trained in, but that's how it is supposed to be. My training was meant to assess an individual who had come across the pro-verbial radar of the federal government, and it was likely because they had made some kind of threat to some of the most powerful political figures in the world. I was responsible for determining the seriousness of a danger, and then possibly building a federal case against them. At the very least, I was mandated to get them some kind of professional help.

I'm not implying you build your own federal case, but you should feel empowered to use the following "tools in your tool belt" that will help alert you to possible issues. I call these "Early Indicators of Threat-Related Behavior." They are:

- Maladaptive Behavior
- Disregard of Social Norms
- Irrational Behavior
- Observer Discomfort
- Unconventional Beliefs
- Behavioral Suffering

Early Indicators are deemed so because they do not require immediate attention. These are indicators that present first and allow you the greatest amount of time to make further observations. They are also the likeliest you will observe in a person and they do not necessarily require an immediate action. Therefore you have time to draw your own conclusions on whether you see a pattern that is cause for concern. They will draw your attention to a possible situation, and give you time to determine your next course of action.

6. Maladaptive Behavior

After high school (and a two-year stint of traveling the country and doing odd jobs while saving up for college), I applied and was accepted into the Virginia Military Institute. I knew that I lacked the discipline that came with being a regular freshman at a standard four-year college, and a semester at college would only result in failing grades after my first semester. At VMI, I knew that if I failed I wouldn't have the temptations of a typical college lifestyle to blame. Ultimately, the decision turned out to be the right one. VMI provided me with the education of character, discipline, and academia that I would not have found anywhere else, and it is that education that has made me the man that I am today.

But that education was, at times, a painful one. And it started shortly after I arrived. Within a week of matriculation, I and 400 other recruits were whisked into a military college life, complete with shaved heads, uniform clothes, reveille, marching, taps, reveille, marching and taps (again). Week 1 was called "Hell Week," where we were quickly trained to exhibit all the characteristics of the VMI cadet. From there, it was an entire school year of walking "The Rat Line." This was a miserable year of heavy class work coupled with upperclassmen harassment and age-old initiations.

In many ways, it was a traumatic experience. I'm not criticizing the system, as the results speak for themselves. It was modeled after the "boot camp" methodology of the modern military, the foundation for which the United States Armed Forces continue to develop and strengthen the mightiest military force on Earth. But the training that I went through at VMI had its effects. If a teenager is not properly prepared to handle the duress and is still subjected to it, those effects can be severe.

During Hell Week, each of us in our company (approximately 30 cadets) was paired up with a "buddy." Our buddy was the person we marched next to in formation, ran alongside during morning workouts, made sure we made it to breakfast on time and more. The point of the buddy system was to keep an eye on each other. My buddy was a young man who I will call Sullivan. We had been at school for a week, and during Hell Week, you didn't get too much time to socialize. Any attempt at talking or even turning your head was met with a healthy order of pushups and running. I knew my buddy's name was "Sullivan" because it was the name freshly stenciled on his new uniform gym shirt, and it was what all the other cadre instructors were yelling when they came toward him. They said his name a lot.

Sullivan was a mess. I don't know how else to describe it. He was constantly being berated for his disheveled appearance, his failure to understand simple instructions, and his forgetfulness. Granted, we were all in an environment where our instructors were looking for mistakes, and we all made them. But Sullivan took the art of being a soup-sandwich to the next level. As such, he suffered tremendously. In fact, we all suffered. What happened to one freshman happened to the whole company. In addition to his issues with the learning curve of VMI, Sullivan wasn't making friends with any of us who were suffering with him.

The week of marching, running, and breaking in new combat boots and dress shoes had taken its toll on everyone's feet. No one was without their share of blisters, scabs, and cuts. To the credit of VMI, EMT-trained cadets were readily available to help and were proactive in their care. As we were completing a march, a team of EMT's met up with us, had us remove our boots and socks, and had us show them our feet to make sure that we could continue.

After we finished the inspection, our cadre started barking out commands to get our boots back on. Maybe it was that my feet had swollen up, but I was having the worst time getting my boots back on. Sullivan, much to my surprise, had finished putting on his socks and boots, and had already laced both pairs up. For once, Sullivan was ready to go.

"Wells, you've got to get yourself some of these speed laces," Sullivan whispered to me as I started tightening my boots. I looked over, and I noticed that his laces were a little different. He was referring to "speed laces," which were bootlaces that were made of a specialized material for a quicker lace-up. I don't know where he got them (since we weren't allowed to exactly go out shopping or anything) but Sullivan had them on his boots, and they seemed to have worked out well for him.

"Yeah, speed laces, man. You get these and they'll make..." Sullivan went on for a moment, and then stopped in mid-sentence. Our eyes met, and his became bulging and frantic.

"Are you okay?" I whispered quietly

Sullivan only continued to look at me. After a very long second, he reached his arms out to me, grabbed my shirt forcefully and started making gurgling, animal-like sounds. Shocked, I instinctively pulled away and shouted for help.

The next few moments were a blur. The cadre pulled him off of me, one of the EMT's raced to put something in his mouth to bite down, and another EMT was calling on a handheld radio for help. I remember one of the upperclassman peppering me with questions. "What happened? What did you do to him, Wells?" I only stood there with the rest of my classmates, perplexed and scared at what was happening. Sullivan had begun shaking and his body was racked with spasms. After another minute, we could hear the ambulance sirens coming from the distance.

Later that evening, one of the upperclassman in our company brought us all together and informed us that Sullivan had been medically discontinued at the school. The student did not have any more information. He only added that Sullivan had suffered some kind of seizure, and that it was likely that it had been the result of an intense week of stress, sleep deprivation, and severe anxiety. I was never told how our upperclassman knew this, as it was privileged medical information that I assumed would not be given to cadets. It might have been the cadet was just surmising based on what he had observed from Sullivan in the previous week, but I did not think it out of the realm of possibility. As for Cadet Sullivan, I never saw him again, and judging by what had happened, it was for the best that he moved on to another school.

I am not diagnosing the condition of Cadet Sullivan, but based on his symptoms, what I was told by the upperclassmen and what I witnessed, his condition appeared to have been caused from his inability to cope with the stressful environment. By definition, this is maladaptive behavior, when an individual is unable to provide an appropriate adjustment to an environment or a situation. Another popular example of maladaptive behavior is from the film *Full Metal Jacket* by Stanley Kubrick. The first 45 minutes of the film take place at the U.S. Marine Corps Boot

Camp, Parris Island in the 1960's during the Vietnam War. One member of the company, who is coined "Private Gomer Pyle," is incapable of dealing with the emotional and mental stress of the training program, and the results are the character kills himself and his drill instructor.

Many students who experience a sudden decline after changing schools associate their issues to being unable to fit in, make friends, and adapt to the new environment. This goes for people who are forced to change jobs or need to move, as well. You or a family member may be in a situation like this, and it is important to recognize when there is trouble with adapting to the new world. Maladaptive behavior is a condition where the individual is isolated from others, unsure of their actions in an environment, and continues to regress the longer they stay there. The more that they regress, the more unstable they can become. It is not common, but it does happen. Naturally, everyone feels apprehensive when being thrown into a new environment of some kind, but most of us adapt as time goes on.

It is important that a community recognizes these symptoms in an individual and works to make that person feel socially accepted, especially before they begin to manifest dangerous conditions. Such was the case in 2005, with 16-year-old Jeff Weise. On March 21 of that year, Weise killed nine people at the Red Lake Indian Reservation in Red Lake, Minnesota, including himself.

Weise' upbringing was a tragic, sad story. He was born to a 17-year-old mother and a 21-year-old father, who were already separated before Weise was born. Even at a young age, he was transferred between both parents and his grandparents on multiple occasions. After living the first three years of his life like this, Weise was sent to live with his mother and her new husband. Weise would later go on to claim that they physically, emotionally, and mentally abused him regularly. While this persisted for years, Weise was given the sad news at 9 years old that his father had committed suicide. Within two years after his father's death, his mother was in a car accident that left her brain damaged. Weise' stepfather filed for divorce from his now permanently handicapped wife. In the divorce settlement, his stepfather had no legal claim to Weise, despite providing him residence for most of his childhood. Weise was forced to live with his paternal grandmother, while sharing time at his paternal grandfather's home on the Red Lake Native American reservation. His grandparents were divorced.

Weise became a child without any stable support. He was forced to move from the only environment he had known for much of his childhood. This likely created feelings of abandonment by the family he had known in his youth; that being his mother, his stepfather and their two children (Weise's half-siblings). You see, Jeff Weise was not recognized as part of the custody agreement when his stepfather left, and was effectively left behind.

Weise' issues on the home front translated themselves to his schooling. Lacking any kind of upbringing that cultivated a healthy social childhood, Weise found himself the target of bullying, ridicule, and isolation. He quickly became withdrawn in the halls of Red Lake High School. There were reports that the school administration recommended that Weise should be home-schooled, rather than work to help Weise adjust to his environment. According to these reports, Weise' introverted behavior was seen as a hindrance to officials; it was considered for the greater good that Jeff Weise should quietly go away.

Jeff Weise had been banned from Red Lake High School and was in his fifth week of homeschooling on the day of his attacks. Sometime in the morning, Weise shot his grandfather ten times in the head while he slept. He then shot his grandfather's girlfriend twice in the head while she carried a basket of laundry upstairs. Weise proceeded to Red Lake High School in his grandfather's police car. Jeff Weise entered the school and killed a security guard, a teacher and five students before turning a shotgun on himself.

I am not going to try and justify Jeff Weise' reasons for committing the atrocities that he did. There is no question that the rampage violence that happened in Red Lake, Minnesota was tragic and undeserving to all who were affected and there is no question that Weise is to blame. It seems that Jeff Weise was dealt a pretty terrible hand in life, and there were multiple factors that played into his eventual breakdown into violence. But that is no excuse. There are plenty of people in life who have it as bad or worse than Weise ever did, and they still go about their lives without killing innocent people. I lastly cannot blame any school administrators for recommending that Weise be home-schooled, as that was the best course of action of the day. No one could have assumed that Weise was going to do what he did.

However, one has to wonder what course Jeff Weise might have taken if the community had been more cognizant of what maladaptive behavior is and the violence for which it could be an early indicator. Perhaps the bullying would have stopped; school clubs and sports programs would have invited Jeff to become more involved and they could provide some solace from his shattered life. It is people like Jeff Weise that make maladaptive behavior so important to identify, and it is so important that your community makes the effort to welcome those isolated individuals.

7. Disregard of Social Norms

Walking around inside with an open umbrella.... Saying "goodbye" when answering a phone.... Talking to yourself in public.... These are actions that disregard social norms; they are easy to spot but difficult to use as a foundation for threat-related behavior because, frankly, we're all guilty of them in some form or another.

A disregard of social norms is an action or a behavior that goes against something that is otherwise socially acceptable. They are actions that stand out as unusual or even disturbing to the general populous that shares space with us. Sometimes these things are illegal, or a violation of some kind of code or law that is regulated in society. For example, it is a health code violation for a person to urinate in public. But if you have been to any major city in America, it won't be long before you see this regulation violated. You may have also been in a public place and seen someone enter without wearing shoes. Sometimes it is in direct violation of laws or regulations, sometimes it is outright unacceptable behavior, and sometimes it is just a minor "glitch" in our actions when we forget where we are. I am notorious for talking to myself, the habit developed from a life of living without brothers or sisters. But that doesn't mean I am a threat to society.

From time to time, these deviations in behavior are understandable too. A grocery store near a beach probably shows leniency toward its customers who enter barefoot in their swimsuits to make a few quick purchases. I won't bother asking you to confess if you had to relieve yourself somewhere because there wasn't a facility nearby, and how dare I judge... but you know what you've done. Like I mentioned, we're all guilty of something at one time or another. Most of us are conscientious of when we are closing in on disregarding social norms. We begin to feel self-conscious, embarrassed, maybe even ashamed. As such, we quickly get through whatever it is that we are doing or we correct ourselves before someone corrects the situation for us. This social filter is what keeps us operating as a decent society.

How do we detect when someone who displays this condition could be considered a threat? People who have displayed threatening behavior have had some history of going against the grain of socially acceptable normalcy. As such, it warrants paying extra attention to those who show the condition with regularity. Therefore, it starts with the frequency of the action. Where you and I may have only done something that society frowns upon just a few times, someone else who acts in such a way with regularity may be a person of concern. Additionally, our concern of embarrassment keeps us in line; we don't want others to judge us. A person with concerning behavior will likely not care what anyone else thinks.

But even then, does it count as a threatening condition? No, we can't assume that. There's no question it's easy to identify, but we just can't single out a person because they enjoy talking to themselves in public or decide to eat soup with a fork.

The additional challenge is the time that we live in. Today, it seems people almost seek out this kind of behavior for attention or "shock theater." The most risqué music videos of the 1980's pale in comparison to today's social norms that are shared through the internet. If a disregard of social norms is the only thing you recognize in someone, good on you for seeing it. But if you think that it is enough to be concerned that it is threatening behavior, I must admit that you will need more to go on. Like the other early indicators, a disregard of social norms should only act as an initial red flag that there may be something wrong. The first step is identification for further observation.

So how do we determine if this person could be a problem? If it has been observed, it is worth watching for further issues. That is the point of early indicators; to recognize behaviors in others and be mindful of them.

8. Irrational Behavior

Irrational behavior is exactly that: It is behavior that defies reason, defies logic. From the legitimately mentally ill person who thinks that wearing aluminum foil around his head will stop voices that he hears, to the thrill-seeking free climber (in the United States known as free solo climbing) who scales a mountainous rock face with limited safety equipment, we know that we live in a world where irrational behavior is not in short supply. When does this behavior manifest into a concerning condition?

Many early indicators are identified by one's own "feel" rather than just a definition that can be provided in a book. Let's take a look at my example of a "free climber." Although this is extremely unusual behavior, and defies most individual's concepts of safety and rationality, it is still considered a socially acceptable (and even admired) practice. Why? For one, it is putting only the person performing the climb at risk. No one else needs to worry about his or her well-being, and there is no danger to the public environment, be it a school campus or an office setting. Additionally, the climber is most likely not delving into this as a sudden pursuit. Free climbers are those individuals who have been active mountain climbers for many years. They choose to take their level of danger up a notch by losing the equipment that keeps them safe. Lastly, free climbers typically train constantly and are in peak physical shape; many focus themselves through meditation, breathing control, and even religious prayer. Although a radical endeavor, the act of free climbing is irrational but by no means is it a threat to the community. In fact, free climbers are displaying more mental, physical, and emotional discipline than the average person. If they do not have the right stability, their lives will come to an abrupt and painful end at the base of a mountain.

Now let's take another scenario from the sports world: the riotous crowds of a European soccer match. From a global perspective, soccer matches are the most popular sporting event in the world. Although they have not caught on in the United States with the same fervor as the rest of the world, they are the premier athletic scenes. But anyone who has seen one of these at a European venue, either in person or from the safety of a room with a television, knows that professional soccer matches overseas typically degenerate into something resembling riotous anarchy. In 2015, the Wall Street Journal reported that Germany had an estimated 7,863 soccer-related offenses, Italy had 1,515 incidents, and Spain had an increase in their violence by 22%. The practice of soccer riots has led to the creation of the term "hooliganism," and it has even taken on a cultural place in what is considered an international pastime.

There is little doubt in anyone's mind that the behavior of hooliganism is irrational. Additionally, it would give anyone cause for concern for ones own safety. Why? What makes this irrationality so different from our free climber? From my personal perspective, if my family and I parked our car at a campsite next to one of these climbers and we got into a discussion about the climber's pursuits, I would certainly think it unusual, terribly dangerous and a bit insane. But I doubt I would be concerned for my own safety because of what the climber was getting ready to do. On the reverse, if I was in a European restaurant and a hooligan came into the establishment, was gregarious, loud-spoken and emotional about the upcoming football match, I would probably try and find my waiter, pay the check and get the hell out before more of them showed up. Why? He wasn't doing anything violent. He's just excited about the match.

It comes back to the aspect of the behavior itself, when the irrationality of the person has aligned him/her with a venture that is dangerous to the community. If the free climber who I had met at the campsite in the morning turns out to be the same hooligan I see at the restaurant in the afternoon, I would see him in a different light, one that is not so positive. Some would argue that such behavior is brought on with a groupthink mentality. With a larger group of likeminded people, it becomes easier to justify harmful actions. I mean, if he is doing it, it must be okay. Groupthink can be a very powerful mechanism for spreading violence. Look no further than your run of the mill riots. Most recently I witnessed this first hand on the streets of Baltimore in 2015. Any and all respect for law enforcement authority was non-existent, and rioters gave very little regard to the consequences of their actions. Their behavior was irrational, and was fueled by the sense that it had great strength in its number of participants. When irrational behavior has created someone who has lost touch with long-term consequences of his actions, does not reflect on (or care) what effect his actions might have on other people, and continues to act out even if it is socially unacceptable... it is then that irrational behavior becomes dangerous.

One final point on the topic: in addition to the points that have been made, an individual with irrational behavior cannot be reasoned with in that moment. When I was a Secret Service agent, it was not unusual to see adults lose their composure in the presence of the person that I was protecting (whom we called the "protectee"). In my time escorting protectees at fundraisers, along the rope line as they were shaking hands, and at public functions throughout the country, people regularly lost control of their rational behavior. I understand it, as these people are meeting someone who in many ways, is their great hope for a better tomorrow. I have seen grown men break down into tears and women faint, and I even saw one young lady wet her dress when meeting one of our former presidents. It is at this escalated moment of passion when rationality disintegrates. They would instinctively reach out and try to grab or hug our protectee. People would often try to grab our person's tie or their hair, all of which would result in a very forceful and stern response from agents. At that moment, the person would immediately "snap back" into reality and realize the seriousness of the situation. A person who is truly irrational does not return to reality if the situation calls for it. They continue to remain irrational. Just like the hooligans at the soccer stadiums, they fit the bill on a grand scale. Despite law enforcement intervention, even under the threat of lethal force, the rioting continues. It is easy to understand how irrational behavior can quickly escalate into a much more serious situation, and it should be given close attention if recognized.

Our free climber? He can be reasoned with. If his family begged him to stop doing what he was doing, that they feared for his safety, he could probably be convinced to take precautions or give it up all together for the good of those he loves. A hooligan or a rioter? Unlikely. They are perfectly content in their destruction and cannot be reasoned into a state of rational behavior.

9. Observer Discomfort

Have you ever been around an individual who made you incredibly uncomfortable? We all have, of course. Maybe you felt exposed around the person, or disgusted in his/her presence, or even frightened for your safety. Here's another question: Did you do anything about it? You probably didn't since you felt like you were overreacting, and you didn't want to offend the person. The thought of looking a person in the eye and telling them, "I'm sorry, I just don't want to be in your presence because you make me uncomfortable" is a very difficult thing to say to another. It is demeaning, belittling and it will probably hurt the person's feelings very much. Even as evil as the human race can seem at times, we still are a very benevolent global society, and caring and nurturing is our human nature. For anyone who disagrees, I encourage you to spend the day in a kindergarten class and watch the children play and share. Children will show you that it is our natural instinct to be good; we learn to be bad as we grow. So, it is a difficult thing to confront a person who makes us uncomfortable and then tell them to go away, even if it means our safety might be at stake.

Despite all of this, it doesn't mean that the discomfort you felt was wrong. In fact, studies suggest that you felt a physiological instinct that manifested based on self-preservation. Mr. Gavin de Becker has written a series of books on this subject, with his first being *The Gift of Fear*, published in 1997. I encourage anyone to read Mr. de Becker's books, as they are both fantastic and insightful into this topic. With that, it is equally important to understand that your observer discomfort is not something that should be ignored, but rather you need to pay close attention as you feel the discomfort when that certain kind of person comes into your safe zone.

On April 16, 2007, Seung Hui Cho walked the campus of Virginia

Polytechnic Institute (Virginia Tech) and, with several firearms in his possession, killed 32 students and teachers, wounded an additional 17 people, and then took his own life. The Virginia Tech massacre was the deadliest shooting attack by a single gunman in United States history until June 2016 when Omar Mateen killed 49 people at the "Pulse" Nightclub in Orlando, Florida.

For several months prior to the tragic shooting, there were multiple, blatant signs of threat-related behavior by the attacker. It is easy for me to say that now, as I sit writing these words on an event that occurred nearly a decade ago. But the post-attack investigation showed that there were multiple reports of concern from different people on campus; even members of Cho's family had attempted to report their concern for Cho's safety even before he left for college. One of the most dominant issues that people expressed repeatedly about Cho was their fear of being in his presence. Cho spiked people's observer discomfort levels at all times. The report reveals that many students at Virginia Tech were frightened of Cho, sometimes because of his behavior and oftentimes just from his presence. One of Cho's professors, Nikki Giovanni, had so much concern for her and her students' well-being that she demanded Cho be transferred from her class and sent elsewhere. When the request was denied, Giovanni threatened to resign from her position.

The final report to the Governor of Virginia about the Virginia Tech Massacre was nothing short of damning (and justifiably so) about the failure of the school to take proactive measures against Cho. It was determined that the system at Virginia Tech failed on multiple levels to include safety and security procedures as well as to administratively address a troubled student and his apparent issues. One of the key supporting points made in the report included the many notifications from individuals experiencing observer discomfort about the student. There were even reports that some of the professors had established a "duress code" among each other. This was an obscure statement such as "please remember the red chair" or "don't forget the cannonball tonight." It was something that they could say to one another with a phone call if Cho happened to appear. The call would alert the other instructors that Cho was present and the teacher did not want to be alone with him. To the credit of the students and staff, they did what they were supposed to do; they listened to their instincts and they responded by protecting themselves and each other as best they could. It appears that Virginia Tech did not appropriately respond to their concerns.

If there was any silver lining to be found from the Virginia Tech tragedy, it is that schools are (or should be) paying closer attention now. This feeling should have permeated itself into other factions of the community to include law enforcement, corporations, religious entities, and philanthropic groups. Of course, even after nearly 10 years, the transition to proactive safety is pathetically slow. To the credit of the Commonwealth of Virginia, upon review of the final report of the Virginia Tech Massacre, lawmakers passed a resolution that mandated all public universities to comply with establishing a threat-assessment program. We'll discuss threat-assessment programs in detail in Section II. For now, know that for these programs to be effective, they need to receive the report on a situation that you may observe. You should still feel empowered to say something if someone continuously makes you uncomfortable. Like Seung Hui Cho, it is entirely probable that if you feel that way about a person, then other people do as well. Cho had multiple reports of concerns from various individuals throughout the school campus spanning different periods of time, but no one successfully connected the dots until after the shooting.

10. Unconventional Beliefs

Individuals in our society who believe that the events of 9/11 were a U.S. government conspiracy are a perfect example of those who are practicing unconventional beliefs.

I have met a few people like this in my day, and most were very intelligent individuals who did not show any kind of indicators associated with threat-related behavior or mental illness (any that I was aware of, at least).

"Unconventional beliefs" are a belief in something that someone has that does not conform to what is generally done or believed in the rest of society. In the case of the 9/11 Truthers, they fit the example for this definition. They are a small group of individuals who believe that the horrific events of 9/11 were actually an elaborate multi-agency government plan concocted by the Bush Administration. The theory is that the ultimate goal of 9/11 was to force the United States into a Middle East conflict. The results of such action would include the overthrow of Saddam Hussein and a power shift in control of the world's oil. The group has differing sub-theories, but many revolve around the belief that the planes used in the attack were either shot down by military fighters, or they never existed in the first place. There are further beliefs that the towers and the Pentagon were destroyed by a series of charges that were strategically placed at spots in the buildings, allowing them to implode. This belief is not meant to suggest that the person who believes them is a violent person. It just shows that it could be an early indicator of other, more serious conditions. Sometimes, conspiracy theorists tend to move into more paranoid ideations. A person who might have unconventional behavior, believing that their government is conspiring to kill thousands of its citizens for oil and power might start to feel like their government is against them too.

Let's turn the tables a little bit and talk about something that was once considered unconventional but is now widely accepted as fact.

Prior to the late 1400's, the popular belief in society was that the world was flat. It was such a strong certainty that it affected international commerce, war-fighting strategies among countries, and global exploration. It was more than a belief in the learned world; it was accepted as a guarantee. Anyone who even attempted to suggest otherwise was deemed insane or possibly even blasphemous. This was in a culture that would burn such heretics at the stake without a second thought.

There was, however, a small group of people who slowly and methodically pushed against the grain of this belief. They were scientists, explorers, and even theologians. They presented evidence to support their claims; they pointed to the round moon and sun in the sky, and they compared maps and charts from other lands with their own and pieced together a different concept. Even royalty took a risk and looked at the evidence and supported the alternative thinking. What was once seen as something radical eventually became progressive. Obviously, we now know how this cultural shift turned out, and we know that those pioneers of the theory were right all along.

But in their day, these scientific progressives promoted unconventional beliefs. Despite the fact that they were right, their thinking and beliefs were so against the social structure of the day that they were considered radical to the point of seeming unstable.

600 years from now there may be evidence that the 9/11 Truther Movement was right all along, too. There may be an overwhelming amount of information that vindicates their arguments through evidence and facts. One day, we may look back as a society and concede that this group, these 9/11 Truthers, was justified in their beliefs. Like the scientific progressives of yesteryear, we may be thankful for the 9/11 Truthers and their efforts to bring a dark government conspiracy to light so that we can prepare it to not happen again.

But right now, in this day in age, this is not the case. All of us must acknowledge (whatever you believe) that most of society believes that the terrible, tragic events of 9/11 occurred at the hands of a band of terrorist cowards who lack any consciousness for humanity and understand only zealous lunacy. For now, the 9/11 Truther Movement practices unconventional beliefs; their beliefs lack credible evidence, they promote an argument that the vast majority of the world refuses to acknowledge, and their only defense is based on thinking that mirrors conspiracy theory.

This last point is very important. As I mentioned earlier, oftentimes, unconventional beliefs go hand-in-hand with individuals who promote paranoid propaganda. Things like conspiracy theory and government cover-ups tend to have in their possession "proof" for some of these seemingly outlandish accusations. As such, it is natural that individuals who genuinely suffer from paranoia and other ideations would be attracted to these groups and follow them or even join. These people often fit into different behavioral criteria for threat-related behavior models. I continue to stress that not everyone affiliated with unconventional beliefs are a lock for determining violence. In fact, they are most likely not going to cause themselves or others harm. But if they are displaying an unconventional belief in some manner, it is worth paying close attention to further actions. Although they are likely stable, they could also be suffering from other threat-related conditions that drove them to these groups in the first place.

11. Suffering

The sad truth is we have become a society that is so littered with the symptoms of suffering that we are desensitized to it. What is more concerning is that we've learned to market it and make it a very profitable business venture.

When it comes to behavioral indicators, one thing that I take great comfort in is how proactive our society is with training, studying, and identifying one very specific type of condition: suicidal ideations. If you remember the "fire" analogy that was at the beginning of the book, you will realize that this is exactly what we do in terms of identification of suicidal tendencies. When we feel it is the appropriate age, we begin to expose out young adults to the "danger terms" that they need to be mindful of in others. In addition, we instruct them in the possible symptoms and thoughts that they may be experiencing that could bring them to self-harm. Lastly, we train them to reach out for help, and we let them know that there is no shame in talking about what they have seen, heard, or felt. As we grow older, this training is further reinforced in the workforce, as we are usually required to complete a training course that outlines the steps for getting help. If that's not enough, fliers for anonymous hotline numbers are readily available on the break-room tack board. From a business perspective, we have anti-depressant medications in bulk, alternative healing options, meditation clinics, music tones to create positivity, oils and herbal supplements, and the list goes on. I am not criticizing these potential remedies; I am merely stating that emotional suffering is big business. The reason it is so profitable is because many people are dealing with these kinds of conditions.

We still fall short of identifying behavioral indicators; one of those conditions that we need to identify is that of suffering. Suffering can be defined as when a person is undergoing depression, pain, and/or hardship. It's also easy to see how it can be a precursor to suicidal thoughts and action. And yet, with all of the care and concern we take to prevent suicides in our society, we rarely train our community to look for these conditions in others. Only until we hear or read the words from someone implying that they want to die, or that they plan to kill themselves, are we expected to take action. Why? The cold truth is that suffering has become a very normal, almost expected, response to today's world. Everyone has problems, and we live in a society where we want to dump our issues on others but not share the shoulder for others to cry on. The other cold fact is that it takes energy and effort to reach out and care for each other while we carry our own individual burdens. That is just not an effort most of us want to make.

If you fall into this category, I am not judging you. I would be a hypocrite if I did. I also cannot preach to you about the importance of reaching out to those who are dealing with trials in their lives. That is a personal decision that we all must make. But from a strictly proactive safety standpoint, it is extremely important to help those in personal crisis before their downward spiral becomes a dangerous threat.

On Sunday, January 17, 2016, 24-year-old Colin Kingston murdered his former girlfriend, 21-year-old Kelsey Annese, and another man, 24-year-old Matthew Hutchinson. Kingston committed the murders with a knife, and after a brief call to his father saying that he had "brought harm" to Annese, Kingston killed himself. Kingston appears to have indicated several behavioral red flags prior to his attack on Annese and Hutchinson. The one that I want to focus on is what was reported on the evening prior to the assault. According to several sources, Kingston had been out at the nearby bar on the evening before the murders. During this time, Kingston had spoken to several people about ending his life. A few hours later, he and two innocent people were killed by his own hand.

In this day and age, when the concern of suicide is such a real and legitimate issue, there is no reason these attacks should have occurred. It's one thing if Kingston was feeling down on himself, depressed about how things were going in his life. There is little doubt that the cause of his issues likely occurred after his breakup from Annese (they were together for 3 years). Perhaps the people who he was speaking with thought that he was speaking as a man who was still heartbroken, and not a man to be taken seriously. But to state openly his desires to take his own life, and no one to do anything – it's almost unimaginable. Whether it is a person who is quite sincere about their intentions to die, or someone who is just issuing a cry for help, it is always best to err on the side of caution. Whoever heard those words that night should have kept Kingston in their sight and contacted law enforcement immediately.

This is the reason why it is so important to get involved as soon as someone begins to show these early signs of hopelessness, pain and hardship. By the time it reaches the point of thoughts of suicide, it may only be a few short hours later that they decide to follow through with their intentions, and possibly even take others with them. From a standpoint of threatening behavior toward others, many individuals who have exhibited rampage violence in some form have not been taken into custody. They have ended their own life, meaning this was their mentality prior to enacting their violence.

12. Early Indicators: Wrap-Up

Some of the first things to be watchful for in a person who may have future issues of threat-related behavior are early indicators. These are those behavioral identifiers that manifest in a person that do not necessarily require administrative action at the time. However, it should not be ignored or deemed unimportant.

Most early indicators are not seen as a threatening condition, nor should they be. The vast majority of people who exhibit these behaviors are not a threat to others or themselves, and they lead productive, positive lives. As such, we should not target a person based on these phases that they might be going through.

What makes them so important is that they lend credibility to a more serious condition when it has been identified. When a person has been assessed and, through intervention, shows a legitimate threat interest, the early indicators can be cited as additional evidence for validity.

The most important indicators to be mindful of are those in the upcoming chapters: Danger Indicators. These are those conditions that show a propensity for legitimate threat-related behavior, conditions that should be addressed as quickly as possible. Otherwise, failing to do so could result in a violent, tragic conclusion.

13. Danger Indicators: Introduction

Sometime during the day of December 6, 1989, on the campus of the École Polytechnique de Montreal, in Canada, a tragedy that is both unimaginable and largely forgotten occurred. 25-year-old Marc Lepine, a young man riddled with behavioral and clinical problems for much of his adult life, entered a second floor classroom and held the class at gunpoint. Lepine ordered all the males to exit the room, and then shot the remaining nine women. Six of these women died and three were seriously injured. Lepine then left the classroom and walked the halls and public areas, executing people at random, with a concentration on females being the target. At some point Marc Lepine turned the gun on himself, with his death putting an end to the horrific devastation. In the end, 14 women had been killed, and an additional four men and 10 women had been injured.

The École Polytechnique Massacre, and Marc Lepine in particular, is virtually a textbook scenario of threat-related behavior, and shows a life of one who provided the indicators that outlined a roadmap for an impending violent rampage of some kind. Lepine showed several examples of early indicators, those behaviors that we discussed in the previous chapters. For starters, Lepine exhibited irrational, almost violent, behavior at his place of work. His bursts of rage were so concerning that he was fired from his job (likely further unsettling him). In addition, there were many incidents where Lepine exhibited signs of suffering, going so far as to verbalize his desire to die on multiple occasions over several years to different people. Others reported that Lepine gave them observer discomfort, particularly at his place of work where he and his mother, a nurse, were employed at the local hospital.

As evident as these early indicators were with Lepine, they pale in comparison to the more serious danger indicators he also projected.

Marc Lepine showed that he was motivated by his hate toward females and his perception of the modern feminist movement; he openly communicated his intent to harm others on multiple occasions; he had an unusual, unhealthy interest in the Aryan Movement and was fascinated with the life of Adolf Hitler; he practiced multiple visits to the target prior to attacking it and purchased his weapons months in advance, thus showing pre-meditated action. In addition to this, Lepine said his final goodbyes to those he loved with cryptic messages and presents, and he left suicide notes and personal belongings with others; family and friends were seriously concerned for his safety, and his mother attempted (unsuccessfully) to get him psychiatric help. She also tried to get her son involved with social outreach programs.

The indicators don't stop there. Lepine himself cited throughout his life a desire to commit suicide. Most important, he showed the most evident of danger indicators as he experienced sudden, negative changes on a grand scale in his life. Lastly, during the post-attack investigations into his life, it was determined that Lepine exhibited psychological conditions that have been known to be associated with others who have committed rampage violence.

I certainly understand that most people aren't trained to identify these conditions. I also can imagine that it is a little unnerving to think about how to deal with someone who might show the issues like Lepine. It's okay to feel this way, and right now we should just focus on these dangerous indicators. It is important that you feel comfortable with understanding what they are; doing something about it will come later.

These danger indicators like the ones Marc Lepine presented are the catalysts that set the fire for igniting violence. With the early indicators that we reviewed in the previous chapter, it was evident that those conditions do not warrant immediate administrative action. As you saw in the definitions of each, you could understand how easy it is to overreact with early indicators. Most of those behaviors are commonplace in our society, and it is important to remain cautious without drawing undue attention to an innocent person.

The danger indicators that we will be reviewing should be of serious concern if they are identified, and attempts should be made to notify a person of authority who can assist. Although there is no template profile for how many of these indicators need to be displayed for a violent condition, it is safe to assume that the more there are then the more likely the person is to succumb to violent tendencies. Just as concerning, there have been situations where only a few have been identified and the violence was still very real. I can say though, in the many, many case studies that I have researched, I have always seen at least one of these danger indicators present in an attacker.

The Danger Indicators of Threat-Related Behavior in individuals are as follows:

- Significant and sudden changes in a person's life
- Concern of others
- Motivations of the individual
- Communications of the individual
- Interests of the individual
- Pre-meditated actions
- Consistency
- Stalking
- Suicidal tendencies
- Victimization
- Mental illness

Like the early indicators listed before, these are conditions that are case-specific. They could manifest in several different ways (like Lepine) or they may only be a one or two that are observable. They may show themselves slowly over long periods of time, or they may happen suddenly. The most important thing to take into account is that they are very serious and should not be taken for granted.

I understand the difficulty that comes with what I am asking you to do. I understand that the fear of not wanting to be seen as someone who is overreacting is a very real fear. I also understand that voicing a concern or even reporting behaviors like these are something that no one wants to be wrong about. When you report an individual for concerning behavior, it draws attention to that person. I won't lie; it will probably be humiliating to the person in question and will probably get that person upset. But you are doing the right thing; it is always the safer option to err on the side of caution rather than assume that nothing violent will ever occur.

14. Changes

From a strictly statistical study, changes in a person's life (for the worse) is the single greatest indicator of threat-related behavior. I have listed it first in the hopes that you will remember this one condition. If you forget all others, this one is the one that is most likely to trigger a violent situation.

We briefly discussed the joint study between the U.S. Secret Service and the Department of Education that was conducted after the Columbine Massacre. This study, the Safe School Initiative (SSI), was a three-year research project that was published in 2002. Its intention was providing schools in America a program for stopping future events like those that occurred in Columbine. What came of it was a report outlining "why" these incidents occurred, rather than "what" resources to use to stop future tragedies.

The SSI was thorough in its research scope; 37 incidents where an individual(s) targeted a school and committed an act of violence were reviewed. These events occurred between 1974 and 2000. Comparatively, the SSI findings are in step with those of the other prominent U.S. Secret Service study, that of the Exceptional Case Study Project (ECSP), which is the five-year research project into assassins and their targeted violence of individuals.

But back to changes…. The SSI listed an incredible statistic as it pertained to negatively perceived changes in an attackers life. Prior to the respective attack, 98% of those studied had experienced some change in their lives before committing the assault. 98%! It is the highest statistical number in this book. Virtually every single person studied, with the research transcending over 25 years, across all different kinds of gender, age, religion, criminal history, etc., had perceived a negative change in his/her life prior to the violent rampage. In some, the change was something that any one of us would have thought devastating: a failed marriage, being fired from a job, or some kind of public humiliation. I'm not saying that the violence was understandable, I just want to express that these things pushed some people over the edge.

However, not all the changes were what you and I would consider "devastating." There were times that what might have seemed insignificant to most people was a crushing blow on a personal level. Changes seem to be the ignition that starts the path to violent reactions from attackers. It might not seem like a very big deal, but it drove the attacker to commit heinous violence on a grand scale.

Various studies support the main points of change that cause people this breakdown are the following:

• Loss of a loved one – the sudden, tragic death of a person close to our hearts can be overwhelming. There is no doubt in my mind that you have experienced such loss, as have I. Sadly, it has probably occurred to you on more than one occasion. For some, this loss is more than they can psychologically bear, and they lash out to an innocent population or themselves.

• Ending a relationship – In much the same way, a breakup evokes the same kinds of feelings that come with the loss of a loved one. In a sense, something of loving value is "dying," that being the relationship. Everyone has had his/her heart broken before, but it can take its toll on people differently, even violently.

• Losing a job – This has become a major issue of threat-related behavior, particularly in the in the corporate sector. Losing a job can be extremely humiliating to a person, particularly if the job loss is based on individual performance or attitude, rather than a workforce layoff. When you combine the pressure of suddenly needing to find a new way to survive in society, with the stigma that comes with being fired, it is a huge change for the worse in a person's life. The expectation to support a family can also play a major factor in an individual's rage.

• Failure – There are those in our society who, for one reason or another, have always succeeded. It may be in academics or athletics, or they have just led a charmed life. Whatever the case, learning to lose and how to recover from it is a character building exercise that is an important lesson in life. The longer it takes for a person to learn these lessons, the less adaptable that person is to the harsh environment of our social world.

On the flipside, there seem to be people in our communities that can't seem to catch a break. Over time, too many failures begin to add up, and these people start to blame others for their defeats. Either way, the results have shown to have violent reactions in some cases.

• Public Humiliation – In this day of social media, with prevalent access to video cameras and cell phones, it is easy to publicly humiliate just about anyone. We are seeing a rise in females who are having risqué photos taken of themselves by boyfriends or strangers, only to find those photos appear on the internet for the world to see. Before, bullying used to be confined to the halls of a school or a neighborhood. Now, we are seeing adolescents being bullied online by total strangers from all over the world. Public humiliation has been expanded through technology, and it is developing a whole new generation of people who are victimized with no way to fight back.

I know that I have been through many of these changes in my life, and I know that you have as well. For me personally, I have reached such low points that I never wanted to face the world again, and the cold, dark basement of my home was a welcome retreat for escape. Sadly, the world is ideally tailored to throw these challenges into our lives.

But for me, I didn't escape from my basement by my own willpower. I left it because of my beautiful children calling for me from the top of the stairs. I slowly climbed the steps where they were waiting to hold me. Behind them my wife would watch and then join them. She would whisper, "it's going to be okay," and it was.

That is what we can do too. You will see people in your life go through these sudden, tragic changes, and it is at that time that we need to be most attentive to their suffering. Maybe you have been that person. How good did it feel that, in your seemingly darkest hour, you had others to lean on to get you through the hardship?

Some of us can't deal with the change though, and as the statistics show, it seems to be a strong stimulator for violence. Sometimes changes that you and I may consider unimportant can have major effects on other people. All that matters is that the change is important to the person dealing with it.

Changes like these can push a person to the breaking point and motivate him to commit the worst atrocities in recent memory. Even a person who led a charmed life and had a bright future can suddenly become a deranged killer.

When the legal defense team presented their arguments to the jury about their client, Jimmy (as his father called him), they painted a picture of one who was once a person of normalcy and stability. According to the defense, Jimmy was a wonderful child, brilliant and kind, gifted in athletics and academics. He was loving to his parents, and doting on his younger sister. His brilliance further showed in his aptitude for computers. Jimmy was writing computer code for his school website… in the fifth grade. He was active in extracurricular activities, including soccer, basketball and even the occasional piano lesson. On the surface, he seemed like a model child.

The exceptional child grew and became the exceptional college student. At the University of California, Riverside, Jimmy was awarded his undergraduate degree in neuroscience with highest honors. His showing of academic excellence awarded him the opportunities to become a member of several prestigious honor societies, as well as to continue his studies in neuroscience. On a side note, Jimmy was a role model for youngsters, volunteering his summers as a camp counselor to children between the ages of 7-14.

Jimmy applied (and was accepted) to the University of Colorado Denver to pursue a Ph.D. in neuroscience. However, it was during this time in 2011 and approximately a year later that the psychological wheels began to come off. Jimmy had shown some unusual behavioral traits prior to enrolling to the Ph.D. program in 2011, but these conditions went largely ignored. Within a year after being accepted in the program, Jimmy would go on to suffer a series of academic failures and would eventually drop out of school altogether. A later investigation into the life of the student would reveal a person who was manifesting darker intentions more each day.

The culmination of this manifestation came in the form of one of the most publicized tragedies of the last decade. On July 20, 2012, James Eagan Holmes (or "Jimmy") entered the Aurora Cinemark in Aurora, Colorado, during the evening of the world premiere of the film *The Dark Knight Rises*. Holmes, brandishing a small arsenal of firearms, entered the theater. Dressed as the villain of the movie, Holmes proceeded to shoot innocent movie-watchers at random. After finishing his assault, the attacker calmly left the theater through the emergency exit and was taken into custody by law enforcement without incident. Inside the building, 12 people lay dead and an additional 58 were left injured, painfully awaiting help to arrive.

If James Eagan Holmes had been a different person, our society probably would have written off his violence as an expectation. If Holmes had come from a broken home, or had been abused as a child, social experts would have argued that his rampage violence was a release of internalized rage as a victim to these incidents in his life. But Holmes was none of these; he came from a well-established family, who smothered him with love and affection.

It would have been equally easy to write off the Aurora Cinemark attacks if Holmes had shown a history of violence and criminal activity. But again, Holmes had none of these. Prior to the attack, James Eagan Holmes had not had so much as a parking ticket. His record was spotless. Holmes' actions in life clearly indicated that he understood the concept of long-term accountability. He understood that he needed to get good grades in school to have the opportunity to excel in his adult life; he understood this so well that he did better than just about any other student in his school. He also understood that he needed to be a positive, all-around member of society, thus volunteering his time to help with counseling services.

There were other, darker things that came to light about James Eagan Holmes after the Aurora Cinemark Massacre, however. From a psychological perspective, it was reported that Holmes' aunt (his father's twin sister) had dealt with bouts of psychiatric instability, suggesting that the condition may have been one that was genetically passed down. Holmes showed some unusual behavior that, although bizarre and may not suggest a violent attack, nonetheless suggested a person who was not mentally together. During one of his applications for a Ph.D. program he was pursuing, Holmes provided a thorough packet with his qualifications and a picture with himself… with a llama. Although not morbid or delusional, certainly not what one would think was appropriate for an application to such a prestigious program. Investigations also revealed that Holmes may have lead a deviant, alternative lifestyle, with reports that he had attempted (and possibly succeeded) in obtaining the services of a prostitute (or several) as recently as a week prior to the shooting. Further investigations of Holmes revealed that he had visited psychiatric services on a number of occasions of his own free will, and during an unknown time in these sessions had reported that Holmes admitted to having homicidal thoughts.

These all lend some credibility to the reasons for why James Eagan Holmes committed his violent act. But they do not address the reasoning for the "why" it occurred when it did. During Holmes' trial, the defense attempted to convince the jury (to no avail) that Holmes' was the victim of a degenerative mental health condition brought on by schizophrenia, and that this condition was what ignited the violence. Holmes' parents testified that their son slowly regressed psychologically as he matured, and they grew concerned for him.

I don't question the sincerity of the psychological team who diagnosed Holmes' condition. I don't question the sincerity of Holmes' parents and their belief. But I do not believe that James Eagan Holmes was mentally unstable, either. Evidence shows that Holmes planned out his attack over a long period of time; Holmes purchased weapons in advance, he told people on multiple occasions that he had homicidal feelings, and he booby-trapped his apartment prior to the attack.   This shows a cognizance that he knew that law enforcement would investigate his apartment for evidence, and Holmes did his best to assure that police would be met with a violent reaction. These are not the actions of mentally unstable person; they are the actions of a methodical killer, bent on sadistic harm to innocent people.

But the history of the person also suggests that James Eagan Holmes was not someone who had spent his life hungering for the taste of macabre violence, either. There is no indication in his youth of showing the symptoms that often distinguish a serial killer or predator from the rest of society. So why the sudden change? What made a seemingly normal, gifted person into a mass murderer? It focuses on the series of negative changes that happened in Holmes' life. To understand the "why," we need to go back to the beginning.

James Eagan Holmes was the child of two intellectually gifted individuals. Holmes' father was a mathematician and a scientist, with multiple degrees from UCLA, UC Berkeley and Stanford University. His mother was a registered nurse. In addition to their son, they had a daughter. Both children were close, and the Holmes' nuclear family was one that was strong and close-knit. There was no indication that James was ever abused, neglected or traumatized in his youth. There is also no indication that Holmes caused trauma to others.

Like his parents, James was very intelligent. His grades in school, his aptitude for learning, and his understanding of the intellectually challenging all came in stride for James. It is highly likely that his father and mother were much the same way in their youth, as well. I am going to bet that James, just by his own natural abilities, probably did not need to study too often in high school and even college. There are just people out there who could understand and retain complex information and regurgitate onto a test or a project when it was needed. I believe that James Eagan Holmes was one of those individuals.

As a child, I was anything but academically gifted. Even today, I am a slow-learner. My wife on the other hand comes from a family full of brilliant people. I have often admired and even envied how my wife has been able to grasp complex methodologies with ease, even as I have pored over them continuously until it would "click" in my brain.

When it comes to the intellectual aspects of learning, James Holmes and my wife are very similar. But they are also very different: even though my wife was able to quickly grasp the information given to her classes, she still went through the routine of learning how to study. She made the flash cards, she practiced rote memorization, and she read the chapter material assigned even though she probably could have contributed to it as a co-author. My wife developed the skill of learning, and she did so because she knew that one day her brilliant mind would meet its match and be challenged. When that day came, my wife wanted to be ready for it; she wanted to have the experience of understanding how to learn something in much the same way the rest of us did in our formative, early school years. So she developed her study skills, and it has benefited her to this day. I may not be as intelligent as other people, but I am confident in my ability to learn something when I need to learn it. That has come from a lifetime of study habits and practicing information retention.

I am equally confident that James Eagan Holmes did none of this. His natural intellectual abilities carried him throughout most of his academic life, and why should he have tried to learn the study habits of a well-rounded student? He was already at the top of his class in the most difficult subjects that the education system could throw at him.

The expectation Holmes put on himself for academic achievement seemed likely as well. Whether his parents put the pressure on him to meet their own academic achievements or he pressured himself is unknown. However, I do believe that Holmes certainly felt like he needed to meet their academic qualifications (or exceed them) if he was going to earn his parents respect. The various applications to doctoral programs show how important it was to him.

Something else that has not been discussed yet, but lends to the situation: when James Eagan Holmes was accepted into the Ph.D program at the University of Colorado, he was awarded money... A LOT of money. Specifically, the National Institute of Health provided Holmes with a comfortable stipend to pay for his education, something in excess of $26,000. It is not known what the specifics of the scholarship were, only that it was a grant program. Even though grants are typically understood that they do not need repayment, there is the equal understanding that they come with an expectation for academic excellence.

So now, let's put together the scenario: we have a young, brilliant mind who has been ever-confident in his intellectual superiority compared to the rest of the academic world, we have an individual who believes that he needs to succeed at this academic level to foster the relationship of his parents into his adulthood, and the federal government has now given this person their financial backing. The situation could be considered high-pressured. Holmes, though, never seemed to show signs of not being able to deal with pressure. So what happened?

I believe that James Eagan Holmes met his academic match participating in a Ph. D program in neuroscience, and it caused his life to fall apart. Holmes was likely paired up with equally gifted intellectuals like himself, but they had developed the study skills to continue to learn and adapt to their doctoral-level work. Holmes had never developed these skills, and the coursework ate him alive. What evidence suggests this? His academic performance. A student who excelled his entire academic life finished his first year in the Ph.D. program failing a critical oral exam on June 7th. It was recommended that he remove himself from the program, which he did. It was additionally reported that only a few days later Holmes would purchase a rifle.

For myself, getting a failing grade was par for the course in my early years. I certainly didn't like it, but it conditioned me to learn how to study so I wouldn't be embarrassed again. But I didn't have the pressure of a Ph.D. program on my shoulders, or the expectation of the federal government and their funding, or the thought that my genius parents would never look me in the eye again (I'm not saying that the Holmes' family would have done that, I am suggesting that was what James was thinking).

When Holmes reached this pinnacle of academia, his brilliant mind failed him. For anyone who dedicates his or her entire life to one goal, and then doesn't achieve that goal, it is a long arduous road to rebuilding one's life. This is common with young adults and their dreams in athletics. We have those who aspire (and achieve) the chance to compete in their sport at a professional level. Most however, don't have that opportunity so they have other plans. I don't believe that Holmes had another plan. When he was face-to-face with the sobering reality of his future collapsing, it destroyed him. A lifetime spent on achieving a goal for his future career was gone with a couple of failing grades, and the recommendation from the school's administration that he should pursue another venture in his life than their program. This likely caused an incredible amount of stress that fractured an already fragile psyche.

I also believe that two people were living in Holmes' mind, as well. I am not suggesting that Holmes was suffering from split-personality disorder, but rather he was a young man fractured as a person who knew it was wrong to want to kill others, and also an individual who romanticized in his mind the idea of vigilante justice, violence and revenge. I believe this because of the psychiatric visits he had while he was on campus. Holmes was not mandated by the courts to attend counseling, and he had not had any psychiatric or clinical services in his youth. Holmes began to "randomly" attend counseling. Unfortunately, the records of his sessions are closed by law so we do not know what was discussed. His psychiatrist at the University of Colorado Denver testified at Holmes' trial in 2015. During the testimony, it was made clear that Holmes had homicidal thoughts three to four times a day, but nothing specific. The psychiatrist further testified that the school officials were alerted to these disturbing admissions, and that members of the Holmes family were notified as well. Despite this, it appears that (according to testimony) there still was not valid criteria in legality of mental health to institutionalize Holmes on a 72-hour threshold.

But the important question is this: why did James Eagan Holmes seek out counseling services? If he was truly "genetically loaded" for violence, as Dr. Jeffrey Metzner, the forensic psychiatrist during the Holmes trial testified to, then why would someone with so much potential for psychological damage have the presence of mind to seek out help? Because

James Eagan Holmes knew he was falling apart, and the sudden, negative changes in his life were the catalyst that made him feel like he was losing his mind. I further believe that the mental health community failed miserably with James Eagan Holmes. He came to the professionals, of his own free will, to get help. He didn't even need this book, because Holmes identified the threat-related indicators in himself, and sought out professionals who were there to assess and act on his condition.

I do not doubt Dr. Metzner's diagnosis that was given to Holmes, that he suffered from schizoaffective disorder. But I definitely believe that the negative changes in James Eagan Holmes' life were what pushed him over the edge, and motivated him to kill 12 innocent people who were simply going to see a movie. People suffer from the same condition that Holmes suffers, but they are not homicidal psychopaths. No, something triggered that attack with Holmes, and that was the combination of his unstable mind and his intense stress.

I will make one final point on James Eagan Holmes, one that I found in an investigative article shortly after the attack. It reported that 9 minutes prior to the attack, Holmes called the switchboard at the university. No one answered, and he left no message. For a time I turned this over in my head. Why did he call the switchboard? He was sitting in the parking lot of the movie theater, fully armed with a carefully laid out plan of violence; his apartment was already booby-trapped for any law enforcement personnel who came to investigate his home after the attack. What was the point? I started to think about a person who had suffered a sudden change in his life for the worse, and that change started at the university. I also started thinking about the "two Jameses," the one who was plotting the attacks and the other who sought out counseling help by his own volition. Then it made sense. I believe that even 11 or so minutes before the attack, Holmes was still fractured and confused about what he was planning on doing. He probably saw several of his victims walking into the theater, families and couples laughing and enjoying the Friday evening in summer. Holmes tried to then call the place that could help put his life back on track, maybe give him another chance as a student. Make everything right.

Instead, James Eagen Holmes got an automated voice message. In his mind, they didn't care enough about him to even pick up the phone. At that point, Holmes' decision was made, his resolve clear.

Again, I don't question the diagnosis of James Eagan Holmes. In fact, I support it. As I mentioned earlier, and as we will discuss later, schizoaffective disorders like Holmes have been linked to other individuals who have committed rampage violence. Where I differ is the notion that the clinical explanation is the complete answer. That is absolutely not the case. If it were, then couldn't we reason that everyone who suffered from these disorders would overwhelmingly show a propensity for violence? And we know that is not true. I do believe, however, that a condition, like the one with which Holmes was diagnosed, could very well be a major ingredient in a violent mixture, if the right catalyst is applied. In the case of James Eagen Holmes, that catalyst was the sudden series of negative changes in his life.

What do you think? Do you think that what Holmes experienced was enough to push him to violence that he committed? If you don't, I respect that. Whether you agree with it or not, the important thing to understand is that you may have the ability to reach out and help a person who is dealing with sudden, significant changes in life. I would encourage you to understand how important you could be to that person, how much of a difference you could make.

People like Holmes did not use his family or friends for support, but that doesn't meant that someone who is feeling this breakdown might not turn to you. If you become that lifeline or if you even recognize this condition in someone else, know that you could be an enormous difference in preventing something terrible from occurring.

15. Concern of Others

Next time there is an attack of rampage violence in our community (and make no mistake, there WILL be one), pay close attention to the follow-up reports on the history and personal life of the assailant. News media will dig for a few days after the event and give the public as much as they can find on the attacker. The greater the tragedy, the bigger the ratings, the longer the respective news teams will report on the tragedy.

A continuing strategy that reporters will use to keep the story going is to conduct corroborative interviews with people who knew the attacker. Typically the immediate family has nothing to say, so reporters settle for a teacher that the attacker once had, or a neighbor. Classmates and adolescents are ideal, as they are excited to be on television, and are more than willing to provide a juicy quote or a sound bite.

As you may have guessed, I am no fan of the media. But even with their questionable tactics for producing a popular storyline, they do serve a purpose in helping to identify threat-related behavior. Oftentimes the individuals being interviewed for a story will admit that they recognized something different about the attacker. They may claim that he/she never fit in with the group, or that the attacker was always a menace. The person may even admit that they are not surprised it happened. Some have admitted that they attempted to notify someone of authority or tried to have an intervention, but to no avail.

Concern of Others is a fantastic opportunity for our community to recognize conditions in others that could be an indicator of future violence. Most likely, the people who are closest to the assailant are the ones who will have the greatest concern. The most popular groups that have been known to identify threats in an attacker include:

- Family members
- Close friends
- Neighbors
- Community relations (church, PTA, etc.)
- Classmates
- Co-workers

We have already discussed several mass murderers in this book. They have included Eric Harris, Dylan Klebold, Dylann Roof, Jeff Weise, Seung Hui Cho, Marc Lepine and James Eagan Holmes. During the post-investigations of all of these attackers, there were legitimate concerns of others in the attackers behaviors. In addition, all of these attackers had family members who reported a concern prior to the respective attacks. Does that mean that other members of the community don't play an important role in reporting their concerns? No. Family members are part of an inner circle in which the rest of the community is not welcome, and that allows those people the privilege of reporting. It can also act as a double-edged sword, as the "family loyalty" card is expected to be played as well. Confidentiality and airing the family laundry is largely frowned upon, even under potentially dangerous situations.

When studying individuals who carried out attacks at schools, studies suggest that in 93% of the time, attackers that engaged in rampage violence had exhibited a behavior prior to the attack that was of concern to others. Further, those individuals reported those concerns. 93%, just five percent less than the likelihood that changes in a persons life will affect a violent reaction. 93% are extremely high odds, and it works to our favor. It shows that people who are close to the attacker tend to pick up on the condition with unexplainable and instinctual behavioral radar.

Studying the data further, of those 93% of people with concerns, 88% were the concerns of at least one adult. This is important because frankly, we as a society do not take the concerns of children and adolescents as seriously as those of an adult. When a group of attackers manifest their early stages of attack-related behavior in their school years (like Klebold, Harris and Cho), and the people who would spend the most time with them are their classmates and peers, it is important that there are adults who share these young people's concerns.

Lastly, of the 93% covered, 76% were three or more people, with at least one of those individuals being an adult. As strong as the argument is for at least one adult and the concerns that they may have, having at least three lends strong credibility that there should be an intervention of some kind. As we mentioned earlier, the staff of Virginia Tech had these realistic concerns in the presence of Cho, and they made every effort to report it and have an intervening process put in motion. For whatever reason, the administrative and law enforcement entities that filtered those concerns at Virginia Tech failed to respond in an adequate manner.

Whoever you are, whatever position you may hold in your life, when multiple adults come forward with a concern of public safety because of a common individual, there is a responsibility to act. Oftentimes, the apprehension is that the individual in question will legally retaliate or that such interventions will only make the respective department look like it was overreacting. To that, I ask: if roadblocks like these are the norm (as they appear to be in today's society), then what is the point of the department? Threat Assessment Groups are designated to address these concerns, not to filter them based on strength of evidence. Every report requires the due diligence of a thorough investigation.

I continually fall back on my training as a former U.S. Secret Service agent, and I should. It is there that I was first exposed to these behavioral indicator concepts, and it is a system that is still used today by the agency to protect the most important political figures in our country and those political leaders visiting from other parts of the world. As mentioned previously, the U.S. Secret Service mandates all notifications of threats to the President of the United States must be investigated for credibility. Every single one. No matter if it is a posting on Facebook or Twitter, or a statement someone said in the heat of a political argument, or even a veiled threat ("I wish a piano would fall on that guys' head…."). If the threat has been brought to the attention of the U.S. Secret Service, you can bet that agents will respond to ensure that the threat that was made is not a realistic one.

To run down every single threat that is ever made about the President is an absolute nightmare, especially in this day in age of the internet. The popular attempts at humor through "memes" are often ways for someone to get in trouble; people would superimpose something tragic on the President, or show him in the crosshairs of a rifle. All of these are very bad things to do, and it is in your best interest to not get involved in such a situation. Too often I found that I had to explain to a person that they were in trouble for threatening the life of the most important political figure in our country, and they typically confused that with having their freedom of speech and political opinions being violated. So it is very clear: the U.S. Constitution does not give anyone the right to threaten another person. Especially the Commander-In-Chief.

But the point is this: if the U.S. Secret Service is willing to follow up on every single threat made to the principle that they are mandated to protect, then it should be equally important that law enforcement, behavioral and clinical services, and security services to do their due diligence and inquire as to any reports that the public makes. If there is a strong amount of concern from other people about an individual, there is no question that the assessing parties should move quickly and intervene.

With all of this I will say simply: trust your instincts. I am personally counting on you to do so. I hope that after you have read this section that you will come away with feeling a little more empowered about acting on your intuition. Like the section states, there is a strong probability that what you're perceiving has some legitimacy, and that you are probably not the only one sensing it.

I also understand that it is very difficult to report a person based solely on a "feeling," nor should you. But if you have an unnamed intuition about someone, don't ignore it. Pay attention and be mindful. Again, trust your instincts.

16. Motivation

Just over fours years after the assassination of President John F. Kennedy, his younger brother, Robert, made an entrance into the political arena as a candidate for the office of the president. Robert had served as United States Attorney General under his brother's direction, and had since moved from that position to holding a seat with the United States Senate from the State of New York.

1968 was a year of political and social unrest. In the United States, the popular civil rights leader and humanitarian, Dr. Martin Luther King, Jr, had been assassinated in Memphis, Tennessee. His death caused rioting in major cities across the country, and racial tensions reached a boiling point. Internationally, the United States was feeling contention from countries in the Middle East, having shown support for Israel in the region. The Vietnam War was at its peak, and the media depicted the tragedies of war as the fault of the American Serviceman. The late 1960's were a dark time for the United States of America.

The early political primaries were an indicator to how dissatisfied Americans were with their current president, Lyndon B. Johnson. Johnson, who had taken the office after the death of John F. Kennedy, had not been popular among the voter. At the conclusion of the New Hampshire Primary Election, President Johnson had been handedly defeated by challenger Senator Eugene McCarthy. President Johnson subsequently announced that he would not seek re-election, and the opportunity presented itself for Robert F. Kennedy. He saw the chance to claim the Oval Office. Robert F. Kennedy announced his candidacy for the President of the United States and almost overnight was the heavily favored choice in the eyes of America.

But not everyone shared in the fervor of another Kennedy taking a presidential election. A young and mentally troubled Jordanian, Sirhan Sirhan, was overwhelmed with anger and hostility toward Kennedy about the politician's involvement with international matters and social issues of the day. On June 5, 1968, Sirhan arrived to the Ambassador Hotel in Los Angeles, California with a .22 caliber revolver concealed on his person. The hotel was the site of where Kennedy was making his victory speech to an audience of supporters, the California Primary being his latest victory on his way to the Democratic Nomination for the Presidential election. As Kennedy left the hotel through a series of back hallways, he was met by a throng of supporters and hotel employees, with Sirhan among them. During the photographs and palm-pressing with supporters, Kennedy was exposed and Sirhan took advantage of the situation. He emptied the revolver's ammunition into Kennedy, striking him directly behind the right ear. The bullet fragments exploded in Kennedy's brain, a sick similarity to the manner in which his brother-president had died 4 ½ years before. 26 hours after the shooting, Robert F. Kennedy was pronounced dead.

Sirhan Sirhan is still alive (at the time of this writing). He has been interviewed on multiple occasions, from law enforcement investigators to court psychologists to giants in the journalism industry. Sirhan's explanations for why he assassinated Senator Kennedy has been as lengthy as the list of those who have interviewed him. After the shooting, investigations revealed that Sirhan had kept a diary journal outlining his obsession with wanting to kill Kennedy after the Senator had made a statement that he would support Israel with military intervention. One journal entry in particular read: "My determination to eliminate R.F.K. is becoming the more and more of an unshakable obsession...Kennedy must die before June 5th." Rage did not appear to be his only motivator though, as Sirhan was also quoted as saying the following:

"They can gas me, but I am famous. I have achieved in one day what it took Robert Kennedy all of his life to do."

Sirhan Sirhan's assassination of Robert F. Kennedy was fueled by his personal motivations to do so. Although there is no doubt that Sirhan had mental issues prior to and during the attack (and likely still has them today), his mental illness contributed to him developing a motivation to commit harm. That motivation was the catalyst that caused

Sirhan Sirhan to kill another human being.

Motivation however, can be just as inspiring as damning.

Dan Jansen is considered by many to be one of the greatest Olympic athletes who ever competed in the games. There have certainly been many who have done better in the games than Jansen though, especially in his own speed-skating event. Although he competed in four different winter Olympics throughout his career, he failed to deliver the results that other speed-skaters like Eric Heiden and Bonnie Blair had. Heiden and Blair each won five gold medals and Blair an additional bronze in their supremely impressive time on the Olympic ice. So what made Jansen so special? What is it that has endeared him in sports lore and Olympic history over these other athletes?

Dan Jansen had started speed skating at the behest of his older sister, Jane, to take up the sport. Jansen immediately took to racing, so much so that within a few years, he had qualified for the Sarajevo Olympics in 1984. Even though he was still only a teenager at the time, Jansen had an impressive run and gave the world a glimpse into the sport's next great athlete. Four years later the Calgary Olympics arrived, and Dan Jansen was the greatest long distance speed-skater in the world. It seemed like Olympic Gold in Calgary was going to be the first of many crowning achievements for the young champion.

But fate had other ideas. On the morning of the final race for his first of two medals, Jansen received the heartbreaking news that Jane had died of Leukemia. She was 27 years old. Jansen, stricken with grief and emotionally and mentally unstable, did not fair well in his race. While rounding his first turn on the track, Jansen crashed into the rink wall. Four days later, Jansen would repeat his abysmal performance in the second medal race with another crash. At a time that should have been a celebration of great victory, the Calgary Olympics was a horrible event that Dan Jansen was ready to move past.

As the 1992 Olympics approached, Jansen had maintained his peak performance and status in the speed-skating community. Although older, Jansen still had the presence and physical performance to defeat anyone in the world in a race on the ice. The world was tuned in to cheer for the skater, to witness redemption. No one wanted Jansen to fail, and it was time to see the events that should have happened in Calgary finally come full circle in Alberta. But like some kind of sick déjà vu, the world watched as Jansen repeated in the final events in Alberta what had happened in Calgary. Dan Jansen did not qualify for a medal in either of his races. With the next Olympics four years away, time was now against him.

But just as fate had played against Jansen for so long, it started to tip in his favor. After the Alberta games, The International Olympic Committee announced that the Summer and Winter Games would be alternated to accommodate each of the games in two year increments. Before, both games were played in the same year. Now, the world could enjoy one of the games every other year. It was decided that the Winter games that would have been played in 1996 would now be moved to 1994. Dan Jansen just got a last shot at Olympic Gold a full two years earlier than he thought he would.

It was there, in the 1994 Winter Olympics in Lillehammer, Norway, that 29-year-old Dan Jansen broke the world record in the 1000-meter speed skating race and won an Olympic Gold Medal. The icing on the cake was that the 1000-meter race was not his strongest event, and it was widely rumored that it would be the last of his career. Jansen had already raced in the 500 meter in the Lillihammer games, his preferred race and the one that he absolutely dominated during his time on the ice. But like Sarajevo, Calgary and Alberta, Jansen was bested. Dan Jansen's win in the 1000-meter race was a culmination of true perseverance and a triumph of the athletic spirit.

At a time when the Olympic headlines were tarnished by a cheating scandal focused around figure skaters Tonya Harding and Nancy Kerrigan, Dan Jansen's win reminded the world of the true meaning of the games. Just before the final race, former U.S. Olympian Mike Eruzione, the hockey player credited with scoring the winning goal against the Russians in the "Miracle on Ice" game said that Dan Jansen was, "...the true Olympian. He doesn't do it for the money or the endorsements — there aren't any for him. He works his heart out month after month, year after year, because he loves his sport…. I can't think of anyone I root for more." And the entire world shared in that sentiment.

Perseverance like what Dan Jansen displayed is the best product of motivation. Whatever his motivation first was when he took to speed-skating, there is little doubt that Dan Jansen became motivated by the promise he made to his sister that he would win an Olympic medal. The results of his motivation inspired the world, and placed him into the annals of Olympic greatness.

The behaviorally disturbed, who are committed to harm and rampage violence, are just as motivated to do harm as our Olympic speed skater was to win. Even though two types of people are polar opposites, they are both equally motivated. This is almost hard to believe, and as a sane person you should have difficulty grasping such a concept; a person who is committed to rampage violence will feel the draw, the pull of motivation to commit the heinous act(s) just as a competitor in a sport will be pulled to the challenge of Olympic competition.

Motivation can be broken down into several different criteria. Sometimes, like the case of Sirhan Sirhan, that motivation changed (probably based on his erratic mental instability). Despite that mental illness though, Sirhan maintained his motivation to kill Robert F. Kennedy, and this should be a testament to how powerful motivation can be for a killer.

Various types of motivation include:

• Notoriety/Fame – You have already seen the Sirhan Sirhan quote about his comparison to Robert F. Kennedy and fame. When it comes to attackers of schools, for example, 24% of all attackers studied, almost one in four, were motivated by the desire to be recognized and/or remembered for their actions. In 1981, less than three months after taking the Oval Office, Ronald Reagan was shot by would-be assassin John Hinckley. Hinckley, obsessed with actress Jodie Foster, determined in his mentally-disturbed mind that by assassinating President Reagan, he would endear himself to Foster through his display of power. Further, Hinckley believed that the attack would make him a household name and Foster would know about him. In this regard, John Hinckley was correct.

• Cry For Help – As we have previously discussed, suffering is an early indicator that can lead to tragic consequences, to include suicidal ideations. Prior to this occurring, those who are suffering may be motivated to get help, to stop them from harming themselves or others. Implying or stating to others that they want to commit such harm could be a strong motivator for getting help without directly asking for it. Whatever the case, it should always be taken with the utmost seriousness.

• Revenge – We have seen several examples of revenge being the motivation for threat-related violence. Many of the individuals who attacked schools and classmates cited in some reference that they were motivated to commit violence based on the feelings of ill-will that they had toward their classmates. Many of these individuals felt bullied and/or persecuted by their peers and felt that those individuals deserved retribution. In studies of attackers, a full 61% cited some kind of revenge as the motivation for their attack. This can also carry over to group violence, such as a terrorist attack. Revenge was the number one motivation for the attacks on the "Charlie Hebdo" French satirical magazine in 2015. In that incident, the Al-Qaeda terrorist group attacked the office of the publication, killed 12 people and harmed another 11. Although "terrorist affiliates" gets away from "rampage assailants," it is important to note that the revenge motivator was established quickly for recruiting in Paris. The plan was executed only a few short weeks after Charlie Hebdo released a publication mocking religious icons of the terrorist group.

• Delusions of Grandeur – Although not as much a motivator as other conditions, the idea of being "greater" than the victim has presented itself in a number of threat-motivated attacks. Returning to the Columbine assailants, Klebold and Harris confidentially mocked their community and thought themselves to be above others. Although this was not as obvious as other reasons for the massacre, it was still very much on their minds, enough so to document it in videos, online and in their own writings.

• Bringing Attention to a Cause/Concern – This is another motivator that is seen largely with terrorist affiliates rather than rampage attackers. At the beginning of the chapter we discussed Marc Lepine and his attack at École Polytechnique de Montreal. Although his thinking was troubled, Lepine set out to kill as many females as he could because he felt that they were a hindrance on his advancement in the academic curriculum. Lepine further complained about how the world favored the conditions of feminism and that he was not comfortable living a life of hindrance based on his gender. Although this is totally inaccurate and his actions completely unjustifiable, Lepine believed in his mind that his attack was bringing attention to unequal conditions in academia and business based on gender.

17. Communication

Have you ever purchased a new car? If you have, you probably didn't do it in a moment of sudden, impulsive action. Like most people, you probably did your share of research on the car and reading as much as you could online or elsewhere about it. You probably spent a great deal of time trying to figure out what color you wanted, and how you wanted the interior to be set up. You may have saved up some money for a down payment, took one for a test drive, waited until the prices came down during a holiday weekend sale-a-thon. Whatever the case, you spent your time looking in on that car, and you invested a great deal of time into the purchase.

When you got the car, then what? Did you quietly bring it home, pull it into your garage or parking space? Did you go inside and move on to the important items of the day like doing your laundry, preparing dinner or cleaning your room? Of course not! You stepped away from the car, stared at it for a moment. You stopped and admired the look of your new automobile. It was still clean and the tires were still shiny from the final detailing they received from the dealership. You took pictures with your smartphone, you forwarded those pictures to your friends and family, and probably even posted them on one (or many) of your social media accounts. Maybe your neighbors spoke with you about it, and you proudly explained the process you went through, saving up and re-searching everything, before intelligently making your choice. If you're like me, you bored your family and friends, telling them about the ame-nities of the car, like "air-conditioning" or the "hands-free phone sys-tem." Perhaps you took some friends for a ride around the area so they could experience your new car.

If you did this, don't be ashamed. Yes, it is true that it is socially con-siderate to be humble and show humility, and it is probably one of the hardest things any person can do. We are, by human nature alone, a proud group. In this day in age of social media, shouting out our great accomplishments is the norm. Online socialization is big business; it is why companies like Twitter and Facebook have done so well. We want to share in our successes, our rewards and the things that make others want what we have. Technology has never made this easier, with every person's portable phone fitted with a camera for photography and videography. It is almost a social expectation nowadays, and those who do not share the important things in their lives could be labeled introverted. Just as you and I communicate what is important to us, so do those who are planning a violent attack. This may sound ridiculous, but for someone emotionally and mentally disturbed, the planning and coordination of an attack plan is his or her life. He takes a sick pride in the hard work and effort that is being put forth into the project. For him, it is something that he is almost giddy with excitement to act out. Like you and your car, he wants to share it with the world. It is human nature to communicate those things that we value, desire, and treasure the most in our lives with others. For an attacker, the greatest desire and treasure is the future plan of attack.

So with whom would an attacker communicate his intentions? There are several possibilities, and they include:

• The Target – The most common of these incidents is when there is some kind of "stalker" situation involved and the target is an individual. The "garden variety" bomb threats are rare in this day of caller I.D. and phone tracing, and they are even more unlikely to be a legitimate threat. However, stalkers have been known to often times attempt to communicate their desires to the person of their interest. We will discuss stalking in greater detail later in Chapter 21, as it is a strong indicator of threat-related behavior.

• Law Enforcement – For many of these attackers, the idea of being in a battle of wits with law enforcement is arousing and exciting. Attackers consider it a kind of game, to keep law enforcement guessing the next move. As such, the attacker will tease investigators with hints as to future targets through letters, calls or any number of other cryptic messages. Dennis Rader, the notorious serial killer who was known to the media as the "BTK Killer," took great sadistic pleasure in taunting the police. From approximately 1974 until he was captured in 2005, Rader sent messages to law enforcement outlining his fascination with the macabre, as well as his unquenchable bloodlust.

• Family – This is a difficult situation for anyone who may have suddenly become a sounding board to a future violent crime, especially when the person who has proclaimed the intentions is the sounding board's own blood relative. As family, we often turn a blind eye to the obvious, that our loved one is planning a horrific violent rampage of some kind.

• Friends – Like family members, real friends will most likely not immediately notify authorities if someone close to them has confided in planning an attack. However, family and friends are the most likely group that will personally know the attacker who will be informed in some capacity.

• Colleagues/Co-Workers – Due to the nature of today's workplace, employers and employees are sensitive to any indication of a hostile work environment. Although this typically falls under the guise of sexual harassment or racial discrimination, any discussions of premeditated violence are usually addressed quickly. Nonetheless, there are always conditions that seem to slip through the cracks. Nidal Hasan was a U.S. Army officer who shot and killed 13 people and injured an additional 30 in an active shooter attack at the Fort Hood Army Base on November 5, 2009. Prior to his attack, Hasan had gone so far as to present a briefing to his superiors outlining a theoretical attack on the military base. The briefing was a virtual mirror of what Hasan would later commit.

• Classmates – This has happened typically in a short amount of time prior to an attack on a campus. It seems that attackers who are targeting schools will recognize certain individuals, classmates, who do not meet the criteria for being attacked. Perhaps that classmate was always kind to the attacker, or for some reason the attacker did not harbor any ill-will and did not want to see that classmate harmed on the day of the attack. Moments before the attack at Columbine High School, student Brooks Brown saw Eric Harris while Brown was having a cigarette outside. Harris approached Brown, and told him that he liked him and to leave the school premises. Brown did as he was told and a few moments later, Harris and Dylan Klebold began their killing spree.

• Teachers/Professors – Oftentimes, students with attack ideation will depict their disturbing plans through school assignments. The Columbine attackers, as well as Seung Hui Cho and Jared Lee Loughner, the assailant who shot Congresswoman Gabrielle Giffords and killed six others in the attack, all used school assignments as a publication for future attacks. Teachers and Professors should make every effort to contact an authority figure if they recognize violent work in their students.

• Social Media – A lot of times, communication of threat planning will happen in the same way that the rest of society shares in achievements, and what we have already discussed; on the internet. For many, the internet provides a safe haven for anonymity and disclosure with an unlikelihood of being pursued by law enforcement. Granted, attackers will not post their plans at length or in detail, or on a website that they have created, but they will often express their sadistic goals with others in "chat rooms." Even blogs have become a popular method of communicating violent intentions, particularly when the assailant follows an extremist group of some kind. Blogging is popular way to get a message of hate and violence to a large audience.

• Diary/Journal – Surprisingly, many attackers kept some kind of journal or diary outlining their violent intentions. Unfortunately, these writings don't come to light until after the attack, during the investigations. However, there is always the possibility that a family member, a friend or even a counselor may become exposed to the journal. If writings like this are found, it should be taken with the utmost seriousness and addressed immediately. It's one thing for a person to ramble about a desire to cause violence whether it is through the internet, to others or in public. This could be taken as a cry for help or a need for attention. But when a person is documenting violent intentions through the privacy of a personal journal, which eliminates any possibility of communicating violence for attention, typically, their violent intentions are quite real.

Some other points that are important to address about communication and threat-related behavior: when it comes to communicating their intentions, attackers more likely than not want to make sure that someone is aware of it. Studies show that in 81% of the cases researched, at least one person had information that an attacker was thinking about or planning an attack. Forgive me for sounding like a cliché commercial, but in more than 4 out of 5 instances, someone knew the attack was going to occur. Those are very favorable odds to stopping a violent situation, but only if the "right" person is made aware of it. Unfortunately, the people who have told about a plan in the past either did very little to try and stop it, or the authorities that they told did not take them seriously.

In 59% of the instances, more than one person had knowledge of the attack before it occurred. To continue on the commercial metaphor, in nearly 3 out of 5 cases, multiple people were aware of the circumstances. Even though this is a smaller amount, it lends greater credibility to a situation when it is reported. Lastly, 93 of the people who were told of an attack were a close peer such as a classmate, a friend or even a family member of the attacker. This means that it is highly probable that the person who is told will know the attacker very well, and their credibility should be taken seriously. In other words, this is not some stranger off of the street looking for a reward or notoriety.

I genuinely believe that our society takes these reports more seriously than they used to. But as we have already discussed, there still seems to be instances where inaction takes priority over caution. I will continue to hammer the point about Virginia Tech, where multiple people, academic professors and students alike, voiced their concerns about a student, and still the campus did very little to follow through with safe steps. These concerns were not made in a different era, this was less than a decade after the Columbine Massacre. If there is one thing that Virginia Tech should teach every school, every business, every community: err on the side of caution when something is reported, and don't hesitate to report something if it is communicated to you.

18. Interests: Adam Lanza and the Sandy Hook Massacre

At what point does an interest in a topic become a dangerous obsession? At what point does that obsession develop into a behavioral condition that could manifest into rampage violence? Like several of the conditions that we've already discussed, this is a tough one to identify and use as a definitive argument for threat-related behavior. If there is one thing that I am sure you have taken away by now, identifying a threatening condition in a person is not a science, but rather an art. You will not find guarantees in this book, because there are none to give. What you will find are the indicators that can curb the odds, and those things that a person is interested in can be related to some of those indicators.

We as a society tend to identify external interests with concerning behavior. Granted, sometimes a person choosing to wear alternative clothing or act in an outwardly unconventional manner may warrant some long term concern (as we discussed in the early indicator section), but what makes the difference between these interests and those external displays? The interests that we will discuss here are those things that a person has internalized, that is, what they have begun to follow and practice as a way of life. In addition, these interests have been historically associated with violent action. Such interests include the following:

• Assassins/Assassinations – This is something that seems to come up with many post-attack investigations. Attackers have documented or videotaped a confession of sorts, and during that confession they have paid homage to a previous attack that has occurred. Klebold and Harris documented in their own writing and videos their desire to start a "revolution" of sorts, and they felt that an attack of the magnitude that they planned would give them the respect they felt was deserved. Although Columbine did not ignite the violent firestorm that they predicted, it has been referenced in the ramblings and writings of other attackers since.

• Weapons – Let me preface this by stating the following: yes, owning firearms is your Constitutional Right as an American citizen, and I am not using this platform to draw undue attention to you for those rights that you responsibly practice. I seem to find myself in a constant state of defending this next section, particularly with individuals who view this as propaganda for enforcing gun control measures. That is the farthest from the truth. The vast, vast majority of individuals who own firearms in the United States do so responsibly and lawfully, and their ownership is not an indication that they plan to commit rampage violence. In fact, their ownership is testament to their desire to react and defend against it. But there is a definitive correlation that individuals who are planning an attack or have an idea to commit one also have an obsession with weapons. This includes firearms, but it is also an obsession with building homemade weapons, such as "pipe bombs" and "booby traps" through-out their residence. Instructions on how to build these devices are readily available throughout the internet and are circulated through radical groups. For example, *The Anarchist's Cookbook* has been and continues to be a popular means of reference for building homemade weapons, a "cookbook" of recipes for improvised explosive devices.

• Extremist Groups – Radicalized, anti-government organizations are well known for promoting a message of hate and anarchy in the name of revolution. Many of these organizations are militant in nature and are able to recruit impressionable individuals with a promise of unity and acceptance under a cloak of security and a guarantee of being in the forefront of a national rebellion. Aryan hate groups promote this message at length, using the backdrop of Nazi propaganda and readings like *The Turner Diaries* to gain followers. Oftentimes, these followers are youth who have been outcast from their social groups and seek a community who will welcome them. Many attackers in the past have cited a respect for Adolf Hitler prior to their attack, and some even went so far as to "dedicate" their assaults to the Nazi Movement.

• Murder/Mass Murder – It almost goes without saying; unless a student is working on a project at school (or, say, a writer is writing a book about true crime or even one on how to identify threat-related behavior in people) then they are exhibiting an unhealthy interest in a subject that could potentially influence them in a dangerous way. Multiple examples, too numerous to list in this short explanation, point back to the various kinds of violence that were influenced by the actions of previous murderers. When someone has an obsession in a topic so macabre, it could very well motivate that person to emulate it.

• Workplace Violence – Like the interest in murderers, a person who has an unhealthy interest in previous workplace violence incidents could have such an interest because he/she is studying for a possible future attack. It is important that we as a society learn from our mistakes, but this education should be done in a committee setting or a working group that has been identified to discuss and enforce safety measures in an office environment. A person who has not been placed in such a position but still has a curiosity in previous workplace violence situations may have ulterior motives.

• Stalking Incidents – We will go more in depth into stalking and their obsessive, dangerous behavior later in this section. For now, it is additionally dangerous to have an interest into the life and actions of stalking. Although I personally have not been exposed to someone who is considered a "famous" stalker, with the exception of only a noted few (As we previously discussed, John Hinckley Jr. comes to mind rather quickly and his obsessive nature toward actress Jodie Foster). In my experience, the threat-related behavior stems from a person who has an interest in the legality of stalking; what is recognized as socially and legally acceptable, and what a person can get away with. Any of these interests in any capacity should be monitored closely and addressed.

Although the interests vary in scope, the one that seems to stand out statistically is that of an individuals' interest (and exposure) to firearms and other weapons. Studies show that of the assailants who were studied, 63% had a known history of weapons use. This includes firearms, knives or other melee objects. In addition to this, 59%, nearly 6 out of 10, had some kind of experience with a firearm prior to their respective incidents. Lastly, 68% of the attackers who used a firearm in their attack obtained it from their own home or from that of a relative.

As we discussed in the previous chapter, family and friends are most likely going to be the ones with whom attackers will communicate the intents of an attack prior to the attack itself. Here, we can see that it is more than probable that, if an individual is planning an attack, then they will attempt to use means that the family provides to do so. That may mean education or even training into the use of a firearm, and it certainly seems to mean that the attacker will use the guns to which the family has access.

What does all of this mean? It means that the family is the best answer for addressing threat-related behaviors in the individual. The family is the difference maker in stopping rampage violence. The schools, the companies, the communities are excellent resources from a support standpoint, but it is the family that will keep the community safe from one of their own who could be on a path to violence. For proof of this, look no further than the story of Adam Lanza and his attack that became one of the most tragic events in the history of the United States: the massacre at Sandy Hook Elementary School.

There are any number of threat-related conditions that we could address when it comes to assessing Adam Lanza. In his very early years, Lanza showed signs of communication issues and did not like to be touched. It was reported that during these years Lanza had gone so far as to develop his own language. Lanza's "Birth-To-Three" assessment provider documented that the child "fell well below expectation in social-personal development" and that he was presented with "significantly delayed development of articulation and expressive language skills." These conditions increased as Lanza grew, and at five-years-old was reported that he was beating his head repeatedly against things and throwing tantrums. Others were powerless to calm him down.

Connecticut's Office of the Child Advocate report, "Shooting at Sandy Hook Elementary School," which documents an investigation by that office into the circumstances of Adam Lanza's life from birth until the commission of the mass murder, makes it very clear that none of the conditions of his early years could have predicted he would become a mass murderer, and I agree. However, it was more than evident that Lanza had something wrong. Further, it is important that you understand that Lanza's parents were clearly made aware of these conditions throughout their son's involvement with the schools. As the report states of Lanza's early years: "These observations underscore the importance of parental and pediatric vigilance regarding children's developmental well-being."

Lanza's socio-emotional issues became more prominent as he progressed through elementary school. It was in fifth grade that Lanza was assigned a project at school, similar to a book report but the students were required to write their own story and add illustrations. Lanza's project was called "The Big Book of Granny." The book was co-authored with another individual, who was never reported by name in any of the post-attack investigations. "The Big Book of Granny" is, to say the least, disturbing and illustrates an unhealthy interest in the macabre. It outlined in great detail a sick amount of images and text involving child murder, cannibalism and taxidermy. In a cruel twist of irony, the co-author was later diagnosed with mental illness in his adult life and was living in residential assistance at the time of the Sandy Hook Shooting. The report cited that clinical professionals noted that the school assignment far exceeded the violence that is typically found in young boys in the 5th and 6th grade. The report on Lanza goes on to detail that "The Big Book of Granny" shows conditions that suggest intense rage and even murderous intentions. Although a teacher is not certified to diagnose a condition, "The Big Book of Granny" was more than enough for a school to request that a child psychiatric intervention take place. The report makes it clear that the disturbing project from a 10-year-old boy can still not be considered valid enough to draw a direct correlation to a 20-year-old committing mass murder. But again, it showed that there was something wrong, and Adam Lanza, at ten-years-old, needed major psychiatric help.

One possible reason for this rage and hate that seemed to swell in Lanza may have been the dramatic, sudden changes in his life. His parents had separated when Lanza was in fifth grade, and like most children dealing with the new life of a fractured home, Lanza likely felt confused and upset. Taking that into consideration with the instability that Lanza had already displayed in his very early years, the changes in his life likely planted the first seeds that would grow into the eventual monster Adam Lanza would become.

After the separation, Lanza's social and mental conditions became more degenerative. Not surprisingly, his mother also showed signs of mental breakdown. Investigations revealed that Mrs. Lanza was preoccupied with a concern for her own health conditions, even though there were no medical records to support a serious ailment. As for Lanza, there was no time in these years where there is documentation to support that he saw a behavioral specialist about his increasingly noticeable downward spiral.

As Lanza progressed into his middle school years, it was obvious that he began to deteriorate socially. He became reserved and quiet, and had reached a point where he began experiencing severe bouts of anxiety, stress and obsessive compulsivity. By seventh grade, Lanza had been transferred to a Catholic school (for reasons unknown) and was cited as continuing to write long, demented stories in creative writing class. The teacher who had assigned these stories could not repeat the graphic nature of the content during investigative interviews, as they were too disturbing. She did cite that she had reported the issues to her principal. At the conclusion of seventh grade, Lanza was removed form the school and did not return to any academic institution throughout his eighth grade year.

In September 2005, during his eighth grade year, Lanza's mother took her son to the emergency room for a crisis evaluation. Mrs. Lanza voiced during this visit that she thought her son was exhibiting signs of autism, and was concerned for his long-term condition. She further noted that her son was having issues at school, issues with social groups and that issues that he was starting to show repetitive patterns that had grown worse. The discharge diagnoses included that Lanza suffered from Asperger Syndrome, as well as conditions associated with Obsessive Compulsive Disorder.

But then something unusual happened; following the initial consultation by the emergency room medical staff, Mrs. Lanza declined further long-term assistance that the medical team was more than willing to provide her son. When offered the opportunity for an extensive work up, she declined on the claims that Lanza was scheduled to see a psychiatrist in three weeks. The medical staff pressed the issue and strongly advised that staff psychiatry become more actively involved in Lanza's condition, since they had resources a their disposal that a private psychiatrist would not. Again, Mrs. Lanza refused and made it clear that she felt her son would be more comfortable under her sole, isolated care at home rather than being admitted to the hospital for treatment.

As a parent myself, I could understand that if I were approached with admitting my child into a psychiatric ward for monitoring and evaluation, I would have my reservations as well. But the difference is that I would likely do it, especially if I witnessed the actions that Lanza displayed in the first ten years of his life. Mrs. Lanza let the nurturing nature as a mother take priority over the sensible recommendations of a group of medical professionals. In addition, it was during these conversations with medical personnel that Mrs. Lanza let the penny drop; she stated that her sole reason for bringing her son to the emergency room in the first place was to get the necessary medical waiver needed so that she could keep her son home from school. Mrs. Lanza never wanted any real medical treatment from the personnel; she wanted a doctors note to get out of class. Although the medical staff offered multiple means to treat a condition that they recognized as serious, Mrs. Lanza declined any additional evaluations and referrals for her son. It was later revealed that a community psychiatrist was involved with Lanza after this visit to the emergency room. It was also determined that the psychiatrist had destroyed all records associated with Lanza, and that the professional had little memory of the child. The psychiatrist provided scant information for the investigation, only to state that Mrs. Lanza was averse to medicating her son. In addition, investigations revealed that the Lanza family was billed approximately 20 times for psychiatric sessions with the professional.

Ultimately what happened from this series of events is what usually happens; the mother got what she wanted. Despite the pleading from medical professionals and school administrators, Mrs. Lanza felt that the extreme anxiety that her son was displaying was from the environment that he was subject to live in. As such, the mother felt it best to contain her son in a closed- environment where she could home school her son and keep him from the society. The school district administrator at the time recommended against home schooling a child with such conditions, and even went so far as to suggest an unconventional method that could be entertained between the school district and the family. Mrs. Lanza refused. As for the community psychiatrist, the professional supported Mrs. Lanza's decision with a correspondence to district officials stating the following:

"(Lanza) has agreed to achieve competency in all academic subjects at home. At this point tutoring is not needed and could be viewed as counter-productive both academically and emotionally."

The Connecticut Office of the Child Advocate that filed the report on Lanza's life found that the recommendations made by the school and clinical professionals were inappropriate and non-therapeutic for Lanza. Of course, no one seemed to have an issue with it prior to Lanza killing twenty-six people.

To the credit of the school district, there were continued attempts to try and evaluate Lanza. Again, Mrs. Lanza refused, stating at the time that such evaluations were not in her son's best interests. For the next several months, Lanza was home-schooled by his parents, and all attempts by the school district to evaluate the child needed to be vetted through the family psychiatrist. Even when the school district needed standardized testing measurements, they were blocked by the family psychiatrist who sent a faxed note stating that Lanza was: "medically/emotionally unavailable to be tested (CMT)."

At this point it is important to understand that Lanza was not "home-schooled" but rather categorized as "homebound." There is an important distinction here. Home-schooling is a program that is carefully coordinated between the respective school districts and the parents or guardians of the child(ren). The programs are carefully monitored, and children are expected to perform at a high academic level (and typically do). In addition, parents are equally held to a high standard to ensure that their children maintain academic expectations and social interactions. I applaud any parent who takes on this challenge, for it truly is a labor of love.

Adam Lanza was in no way being home-schooled. "Homebound" is a status that is typically reserved for one who is too disabled to function in a school environment, even with adequate support and assistance. Through the support of their family psychiatrist, the Lanza family sought to have their son placed in homebound status. Furthermore, even though Lanza was eligible to receive ten hours of tutoring assistance from the school district, all offers for assistance were refused from the family.

What the Lanza family did was the worst thing they could have done for their son: they gave Lanza a drastic change in environment, while simultaneously refusing the assistance and repeated efforts to help from the school district and multiple medical professionals. In addition, the family psychiatrist who assisted with supporting the Lanza family and keeping the child at home went against psychiatric evaluation by peers, raising serious concerns about the medical help that Lanza was receiving. During this time period, Lanza's condition worsened and he became more and more anxious when placed in an environment that did not make him comfortable. The parents catered to the child's wishes, rather than the child's needs. The future killer was telling the warden how to run the prison, and the warden was more than willing to comply. It should be noted that Mrs. Lanza had signed an agreement with the school district authorizing officials to discuss treatment options with the family psychiatrist, and there doesn't seem to have been any plan from the school district to create a treatment plan for the child that was in their district and being homebound.

At this point, it seemed that there was a great deal of miscommunication between multiple parties. The family and family psychiatrist, the school district (with its own bureaucracy) and various medical professionals who were affiliated with Lanza on a case-by-case basis all had their own documentation and experience with the subject. But there was no way that all parties could have shared their material with one another, either legally or because they so desired. In the end, the family had the final say in how to proceed, and Mrs. Lanza felt that the best course of action for her son was to seclude him from the world. She was terribly, tragically wrong, and she would make even more mistakes still.

Adam Lanza returned to the world in the autumn of his freshman year in high school. Despite his anxiety and recommendations for homeschool education, Lanza was placed back into school after having been out for almost two years. Lanza's father had been divorced from his wife for five years at this point, and was living in another location within driving distance. During the post-attack investigation, Mr. Lanza explained that his son had been officially diagnosed with Obsessive Compulsive Disorder and Asperger's Syndrome during this time, and that he felt "relief" since he had a condition to focus on. In Mr. Lanza's mind, if the problem was discovered, then there was a solution that would fix it. By the end of his sophomore year, Mrs. Lanza felt that the anxiety and stress that her son was showing was too much for him, and she removed him from school once more. By 2006, according to his father, Lanza took an increased interest in online interactions.

Records indicate that Mr. Lanza made an honest effort to find some serious help for his son. After years of progressive social degeneration, it is likely that Mr. Lanza started to look for alternative solutions to find help for his son, those being more effective than the help Lanza was receiving from the family psychiatrist, and the methods employed by Mr.

Lanza's ex-wife. Through the Employee Assistance Program (EAP) at his work, Mr. Lanza was able to arrange an appointment with the prestigious Yale Child Study Center in October 2006. During that meeting, Lanza met with a clinical psychiatrist. The observations from the psychiatrist indicated that Lanza was difficult to interpret based on social withdrawal. However, it is evident in the psychiatrist's report that Lanza displayed enough to the specialist which indicated a strong need for further evaluation. The specialist made it clear that Lanza needed further intensive evaluation for cognitive, social and mental stability. The specialist concluded that the homebound therapy that was being instituted was having adverse effects to Lanza's well-being, and that there needed to be "tons of parental guidance."

Mrs. Lanza seemed to become confrontational with the Yale psychiatrist over the next several correspondences. She explained, via e-mail message, that the recommended medication that the psychiatrist had prescribed was unrealistic, being that her son refused to take them. Further, Mrs. Lanza went to great lengths to explain that the interview with the psychiatrist made her son too uncomfortable for her to bear, and that she was not willing to put her son through such "torture" again. Despite this, there was another independent psychiatric specialist, an Advanced Practiced Registered Nurse (APRN), who evaluated Lanza during this timeframe on four different occasions. This APRN and the Yale psychiatrist both acknowledged that they were never informed at this time that the Lanza family had been sending their son to a family psychiatrist, and were therefore never given access to any medical records. Only later was such information brought to anyone else's attention. There are subsequent reports that Lanza was finally convinced by the APRN to take some medication for instability, and according to his family, had actually made improvements. However, paranoia set in with Lanza and he began to detest his medical regimen, as well as the APRN on a personal level. With the support of his mother, Lanza quit his medical treatment, to include further visits to any psychiatric service. In March 2007, the APRN advised that the current family psychiatrist be used exclusively on the grounds that Lanza was more comfortable with the professional than any other service.

Amazingly under these circumstances, Adam Lanza and his mother focused on getting him acclimated into high school by 9th grade, and were somewhat successful in doing so. There was program set up in conjunction with the school to facilitate Lanza into the student body, and he made it clear on several occasions that he did not want to be isolated as a child with special needs. He even flourished in after-school activities, to include science club. However, Lanza was acutely aware of the special-needs classes that he was in for his anxiety and obsessive-compulsive disorder, and equated such classes as "stupid classes." In addition, the last documentation for psychiatric services (a bill) discontinued just before this time period in high school. With all of this, one group of people who went out of their way to accommodate Lanza's needs was the school staff. Teachers were frequently found to interact with each other and Mrs. Lanza in a way that would support each other through guidance and recommendations on how to work with the student. They quite simply went above and beyond, as is not surprising from those people who take on such a career.

Despite their best efforts, Lanza reverted academically and socially and returned home under the influence of tutoring coursework by his Junior year in high school. By this time, the Fall of 2008, he was co-enrolled in some college coursework in an independent study program while working toward completing his high school diploma. As it almost goes without saying, Lanza's condition continued to deteriorate. Evidence suggests that he had reached a point with his mother that their communication with one another (even together in their own home) was based on long, emotionless emails to one another that seemed to read like legal script outlining how they felt. Mr. Lanza and his son had stopped communicating by 2010. Mr. Lanza continued to make repeated efforts to interact with his son until 2012, but all attempts were for not.

During this time and the end of 2012, Adam Lanza expressed to his mother a desire to spend time with her at the shooting range, and to learn more about firearms. The Lanza family were no strangers to firearms, as they had used them regularly for recreational activity throughout their family history. Reports indicate that Mrs. Lanza was ecstatic to accommodate her son, and assisted him with learning firearm manipulation, action and reloading procedures. Despite Lanza's decades of seeming instability, Mrs. Lanza did not recognize the unhealthy interest in the use of the most dangerous weapon a private citizen could own.

On December 14, 2012, eleven days before Christmas, 20-year-old

Adam Lanza took possession of a Bushmaster XM-15 E2S rifle and a Glock 20 SF pistol from his mother's firearm locker. Sometime in the morning, Lanza killed his mother, Nancy Lanza, in the residence that they shared. Lanza proceeded to Sandy Hook Elementary School and entered the building armed. In the time span of approximately 15 minutes, Lanza killed 26 people, 20 of who were between the ages of 6 and 7 years old. The remaining six people who were killed were staff members of the elementary school, to include the school's principal. After these people were tragically killed, Adam Lanza then turned one of his weapons on himself before he could be arrested. Lanza left no suicide note, no message for reasons behind the attack. To this day, there are theories but no definitive answers as to why Adam Lanza committed one of the worst tragedies that our country has ever experienced.

First and foremost, the blame for the tragic attacks at Sandy Hook Elementary School fall squarely on the shoulders of Adam Lanza. I do not make excuses for him, and I will not let his behavioral and mental health condition throughout his life act as a defense for his horrific actions. There are many, many people in the world who have suffered in much the same way that Lanza had, and yet never committed a single crime, let alone one so unspeakable. In addition, Lanza showed a cognizance of pre-meditated action. It is this pre-meditation that shows Lanza was acting in a manner that suggests reason and understanding of what he needed to do in order to kill large groups of people. Lastly, Lanza's choice of target was likely calculated based on ease of access, attacker familiarity and minimal reaction to the deadly force he was bringing. Adam Lanza knew exactly what he was doing, and his attack was based on the evil and vile conditioning of who he had become.

But remember, the point of this whole section was to discuss "interests" of an individual, and how certain interests may be indicators for future threat-related behavior. To review, interests will most likely be exposed (and subsequently identified) by members of the family. The family has the best chance to address a person's interests before that individual acts in a violent manner. After Adam Lanza, the person most responsible for Sandy Hook Elementary, the person who had the best chance to stop the attack was Lanza's mother, Nancy Lanza.

I felt it important to go into great detail about Lanza because the tragedy at Sandy Hook is something that we as a country must never forget. Granted, we should never forget about any of the attacks, or victims of those attacks, that occur in our country. But the thought of innocent children, the oldest being 7-years-old, giddy with excitement for the up-coming Christmas holiday, and suddenly, terrifyingly having their lives ended… it's beyond comprehension. I wanted to make sure that there was no misunderstanding about the people who did what they could for Lanza… and the people who failed.

Nancy Lanza failed her son, the Sandy Hook families, the Newtown Community, and the country. Despite all of the psychiatric evaluations, the medical recommendations, the school support and the efforts by the family to get Lanza to a place of stability and normalcy, at no time should he have had access to firearms. When Lanza suddenly had an interest in guns, shooting and targeting, Nancy Lanza should have recognized this as an unusual interest from a person who had previously had no interest in interaction with anyone. I will not even bring into account her lack of willingness to work with medical staff and school officials, and their recommendations on how to better her sons condition; I will not bring into account her failure to stand up to her son, to make him take his medication; I will not bring into account that she let her son do whatever he wanted and let him run their household. But I will hold her accountable for exposing her mentally and emotionally disturbed son to firearms. The case of Adam Lanza is one that shows how serious a person's interests can be, as it could be a prelude for an attack of some kind. Lanza's mother was aware of the interest and should have stopped it at that moment. Rather than intervene though, Nancy Lanza empowered her son. The result was the Sandy Hook Massacre, her own murder and the suicide of her disturbed son.

19. Pre-Meditated Action

I doubt very seriously that you have taken a vacation without planning for it. Like most of us, you probably started by checking on the time of year that you wanted to go on vacation. You then chose the location that you wanted to go visit. You read up on the cost of travel and the most affordable way to get there, and then you started making a list of what you would need to bring with you. If you were going with family or friends, you had to account for their needs as well. These plans broke down into sub-plans; figuring out how much money you would need to save up, making sure you had adequate vacation time from work, maybe you needed to plan for someone to pick up the mail and watch the house. Maybe you had a pet that needed to be walked and fed. Perhaps your passport needed to be renewed or you needed some booster shots for where you were going.... Most of us get so excited about a vacation that we fail to remember the nightmare that went into planning for one.

A vacation is a nice, familiar way to associate to you the importance of logistical planning. One of the great successes of our military is the efficiency with which it operates. The U.S. Armed Forces can deploy anywhere in the world and establish a working base for operations in a matter of hours. From there, air and naval support can be readily available within 24 hours, as well as medical and supply needs at hand. The United States Transportation Command, also known as "USTRANSCOM" is the backbone of all of this, and there is no organization in the world that does this better.

They are the best because of the importance that is stressed on logistical planning. Like any worthwhile venture, be it a military operation or a family vacation, the success of an operation is predicated on the planning that goes into the operation in the first place. Unfortunately this works in any operation to include one that is focused on rampage violence. Attackers understand this and it is highly likely that an attack will be planned prior to the attacker commencing the attack. In those rampage violence incidents that were studied, 93% of the attackers that were investigated showed evidence of planning an attack. More alarming, virtually every single attacker had displayed behavior that was associated with planning an attack. The exact percentage was again an astonishing 93%. It is practically a guarantee that a person who is going to commit a rampage violence attack WILL plan it out, and it is even more of a guarantee that the attacker will display behavioral indicators that they are planning an attack.

So what are the indicators that the attacker will show? These are called "pre-meditated actions." These are the behaviors that an attacker will show prior to commencing his/her violence. If you are seeing an individual doing these things then you should notify authorities immediately. One last note: of those who attacked a location, 69% of those studied outlined a plan of attack at least 48 hours in advance. This means that if you are seeing someone who is displaying conditions of pre-meditated actions, you can very well make the difference in stopping it! It is more likely than not that you have caught them while they are in their planning phase, and statistically speaking, the plan of attack won't commence for at least two full days. Every second counts, but your intervention is very·important.

Pre-meditated action by an attacker includes the following:

- Attack idea/plan – As we have discussed, it is highly probable that an attack is a concept that will manifest over a long period of time. The assailant will conceptualize this over weeks, months or even years. This is the "development phase," where the attacker has already committed to the violence itself, and has now moved into a research phase. Before "field work" can be completed though, the assailant needs to determine the target, the best course of violent action and the obstacles that will stand in the way of the objective. It may sound very calculating, and it is. An attacker uses this time to outline, to develop. The good news is that if you come across an individual in this phase, the odds favor that it is the earliest form of pre-meditated action. The attacker has not moved into physically studying the location or determining the most violent attack method possible.
- The attacker approaches/visits a target – After an attacker has deter-

mined his target, he will visit it. He may only visit it once, but interviews with attackers have suggested that they visited the target on multiple occasions, and did so right up until the day of the assault. One of the biggest cases I had as a federal agent involved a search and arrest warrant of an individual. I had tracked down the suspect, as they were living "off of the grid." Rather than using their own personal social security number and address, the person had a variety of means to capture other people's personal identifiers. With those, the suspect was able to apply for credit cards and have them mailed to drop points throughout the city of Baltimore. Further, the suspect had an endless supply of identifiers from innocent people and could readily falsify driver licenses to support the credit card name. Thus, my reason for the suspect's arrest.

It took me a long time to find the suspect, and I finally caught the person through a combination of drop point locations, tailing "carriers" (people who were paid a small amount of money to pick up at drop points and carry packages and mail to a place where the suspect lived), and other means that I just should not discuss (Law enforcement has a great many methods that make their profession more difficult if they are published). To continue, I found the location of the suspect and I began preparing search and arrest warrants through the Assistant United States Attorney. Within a week, I had obtained the warrants, prepared a raid plan for my team of federal agents, and set the date for the search and arrest. I also had to watch the house. Surveillance, visiting the location and understanding the surrounding environment is an important part of preparing for an arrest, especially since you need to surprise the person you are arresting and you don't want them to surprise you by not being there on the "big day."

Attackers understand this. They are typically paranoid anyway, and that paranoia will motivate them to frequently visit the location and make sure that it has not changed in any possible way. Their concern may even make them visit the target on the day/evening of the attack.

• The attacker approaches/visits a target with a weapon – Truth be known, this may happen after they visit the target on their own, or may just do it the first time that they go to the location. This is more prevalent when the attacker is targeting a specific person rather than a location, such as in an assassination attempt. Nevertheless, violence is violence. The indicators are the same, so it is just as important to stop someone who is planning an assassination, as it is someone who is planning a rampage violence attack. The important thing to note is that when an individual brings a weapon to a target, they are willing to up the game to gain intelligence. They may be approaching a location that forbids having weapons on the premises (such as a gun-free zone). Those locations make it clear that any violation of their regulations will be met with harsh federal and state prosecutorial penalties. A person willing to violate these strict regulations to gain some insight into ease of access is a serious threat.

• The attacker will test security measures – Vulnerability testing is nothing new. Nowadays, vulnerability of a target is in the form of software, as computer hackers will saturate a server with a variety of means to expose a rift, weakness or opening where they can gain access to their target. An assailant will do the same thing, to a degree. Already unaffected by the circumstances that might result in their actions, attackers will push the threshold to see how far they can go. One of my responsibilities during my tenure with the U.S. Secret Service was ensuring the protection of multiple political figures in the United States, to include the President. The sad truth is that there are many, many people who want to harm the person who holds this office, whoever that person may be. My experience has taught me that the majority of these people are mentally unstable, and their instability is their motivation (rather than the sane person who disagrees with the politics of the person who holds the office). It is not unusual to find the mentally ill person attempting to gain access to a location where the President is present, and when they are stopped as they move through the rings of security, inevitably they will have something on them that poses a danger. Of the several occasions when I interviewed these individuals, they made it clear that it was not their first attempt at gaining access to such a location with a weapon, and each time they had managed to get a little bit closer by learning from their previous mistakes. This is certainly the case overseas, as we witness terrorist affiliates test security perimeters in the Middle East with regularity.

20. Consistency

It was Mark Twain who once wrote, "If you tell the truth, you don't have to remember anything." That, in and of itself, is a true statement. Here's a tip for you current or future parents: if you want to know what really happened with something involving your kid, have them tell you the story, then give them something to do that will take their mind off of it, then have them tell you the story again. If the story they told you the first time is true, then they should pretty much regurgitate it the second time in the same way. However, if they made it up, it will probably miss keys parts. That's because your brain accesses a memory easier than it will a story you made up on the spot. If you're really daring, you can try this technique on your supervisor or your significant other.... I don't recommend it, but the results are accurate.

It is a popular technique with law enforcement when they are interviewing a prime suspect. They will interview the person, have them leave and bring them back in for follow-up questions. If the information that the suspect told matches up on both occasions, it is likely because that person is remembering a situation. Twain was correct; we're just not wired to remember a lie like we remember the truth.

Oftentimes, those individuals who are considering an attack of some kind give off enough indicators that people become suspicious. You will probably never have to "interview" a person about their involvement with some kind of suspicious behavior, but you never know. Unfortunately, the statistics show that the most likely person you will need to confront about threat-related behavior is a family member. It's a terrifying thought, and unfortunately we have already illustrated the results of people who chose not to intervene with a relative. Family, friend or stranger, those people who are planning an attack will be paranoid and will act in such a way. They will do what they need to do and say what they need to say to deflect suspicion from them. And a lot of times, it works. We as a community will go about our lives assuming that the person's erratic behavior is their natural personality.

The irony of consistency is that the one thing that seems to persist in a person planning an attack is their unusual behavior. A person committed to violence will remain committed to its success. They show no evidence that the attack they are obsessing over, or the plans that they are making to do harm, are any more than some strange phase that they are going through in their lives. Rather, concerning behavior seems to be the norm for them. Like some of the other indicators we have discussed, this may be harder to identify, and that's understandable. Every person who is planning a violent attack does not want to be discovered, and they will do and say anything to make it harder to discover the truth about their disturbing intentions.

21. Stalking

I was once in a training course, studying the behaviors that are commonly associated with individuals who are labeled as stalkers. The instructor opened the floor to the rest the class and asked what we thought the definition of stalking might be. One of my classmates, a female, jokingly said aloud, "Stalking is situation when two people are out on a date, but only one person knows it." For such a serious subject, it did lend a light-hearted (of sorts) spin to the discussion, and it was humorous because it had a silver lining of truth. Stalkers obsess over the people that they follow, to the point that the person who they idolize is someone they internalize as an important part of their lives. The victim may not even know that they are being victimized until much later.

I have never been the victim of a stalker (at least, as far as I know). I'm grateful for this, as I have met many people who have had to go through this terrible experience. To define, a stalking situation is the unwanted or obsessive attention by an individual or group toward another person. There is a large breadth of subjectivity in this statement and it is justified. Stalking really doesn't need to have a certain number of times for it to be considered a stalking incident; if the pursuant actions of one person are making another person uncomfortable, and the recipient verbalizes their desire for it to stop and it does not, that's stalking. If you find that you are being targeted in such a way, I encourage you to take any and all action through the rights of the law to make it stop.

Just before my cousin's freshman year in college, she briefly dated a young man who lived in her hometown of Richmond, Virginia. The relationship was by no means serious, and like most people who leave for college, she moved on from her hometown life to enjoy the experiences of young adulthood without the shackles of a significant other. Although my cousin was willing to part ways with him amicably, the young man was not. The break-up ended as anything but cordial, and the young man was quite verbal in his anger toward my cousin.

The school year started, and life moved on. Within a few weeks of arriving to her school however, she was met one afternoon with a phone call to her dorm room from the front desk security. The boy from her summer had arrived to her college campus to confront her face-to-face. My cousin refused to see him, and asked the front desk receptionist to send him on his way. A week later, a fellow female student approached my cousin. The student had a single red rose in her possession. She gave it to my cousin and explained that a man had been trying unsuccessfully to gain access to my cousin's dorm room to give her the rose. The student, who was with her boyfriend at the time, asked the boy if he needed help, and he explained that he was trying to get the rose to my cousin (who he named). She told him that she knew her, and would give her the rose. This, of course, was the boy from the summer.

Fortunately, that was the last of the incidents, with the exception of one last thing that we will discuss in a moment. For now, we need to understand this situation as a whole to grasp the seriousness of it. For starters, the boy was living in Richmond, Virginia and attending Virginia Commonwealth University. My cousin was over two hours away at a college in the mountains of the Shenandoah. This boy, weeks after he was no longer seeing her, took it upon himself during the middle of the week to drive to my cousin's college. He did this on two occasions. Each round trip was approximately five hours long, and he did this during his time in school. Perhaps he had his classes scheduled in such a way as to go on a road trip like this; perhaps he was studious enough to not need the time to study or do classwork; maybe he didn't work his part-time job on that day, either. It is altogether possible that he had the financial resources to buy that kind of fuel, because anyone who has any affiliation with college students know that they are usually doing so well when it comes to money.

Most likely though, he thought in his mind that he was impressing my cousin with his show of sacrifice. That's what stalkers do, and in their minds, it looks valiant when in reality it is disturbing. The boy could have called and left a message, or even could have written a letter explaining how he felt. But he chose to drive to her school, search for her on campus, and try to physically interact with her. It was an unhealthy pursuit of an uninterested person.

One last chilling part of this story: several years later (yes, years), one of my cousin's sorority sisters from college was at a cocktail party of sorts and struck up a conversation with an older, distinguished fellow. Throughout the conversation, the young woman told the gentleman where she attended college. Throughout the conversation, my cousin's name came up in the discussion almost by accident. The gentleman stopped, and rigidly informed the woman that he knew of my cousin, and that she was the person responsible for all of the issues with his now son-in-law.... The very same boy who drove to her college to give her his rose. Even after years, this boy felt a deep resentment for her and had carried his hate of rejection into his life. As such, others had been deeply affected by it.

When it comes to the world of stalking victimization, my cousin got off lucky. There are many, many stories far worse than hers that have not ended well. Celebrities deal with these situations with regularity, and we as a society wonder why they choose to remain out of public view. With my vast experience in Executive Protection, I can't blame them. I, too, would hide from the world; you just don't know who is watching from a crowd with a stalker's mentality rather than just the passing interest of a fan. One of the most tragic cases of stalking with a celebrity was with actress Rebecca Schaeffer.

Schaeffer was considered one of the bright up-and-coming stars in Hollywood in the mid-1980's. She had stints in modeling, as well as small parts in film before she landed the main role opposite actress Pam Dawber on the sitcom *My Sister Sam*. The role was ideal for Schaeffer, as her character was the younger sister, bright, lovely and energetic with an innocence of adolescence showing each week. Although the show only lasted for two seasons, Schaeffer's appearance and performance as the girl-next-door was one that stole the hearts of suitors across the country. One boy whose attention she caught was Robert John Bardo.

Bardo's life was anything but the positive, comedic one portrayed by Schaeffer on her show. Lost in a crowd of seven children, Bardo was frequently moved due to the nature of his father's life in the military. He was also physically and mentally abused as a child by one of his siblings; he had suicidal tendencies, and had been placed in a mental health ward for emotional instability. This was all before Robert John Bardo had reached the age of 16.

Prior to the events that transpired with Schaeffer, Bardo had had multiple arrests for violence and conduct issues in public. Members of the community that knew him reported that Bardo displayed conditions of threat-related violence toward them, and erratic, unstable behavior. Bardo's emotional and mental instability limited his opportunities for work. As such, he was able to find a job at a local fast-food restaurant, but in a janitorial capacity where he was less likely to interact with the customers. The lifestyle was one that did not provide much in the way of mental, emotional and financial stimulation. Bardo found himself in a rut, and used television to escape his depressing existence. It was through the television that he discovered *My Sister Sam* and actress Rebecca Schaeffer. Bardo later described to interviewers that Schaeffer became something of a deity to him. He built a shrine to her in his apartment, and described himself as an atheist, only worshipping her. He wrote letters to Rebecca with regularity, and his obsession intensified when Schaeffer responded to one such letter by composing her own note. In it, Schaeffer told Bardo that what he wrote her was the most beautiful thing she had ever received. It is unknown if Schaeffer wrote this or had a staffer respond to her fan, but for Bardo the response only inflamed his obsession with the actress.

Rebecca Schaeffer's arrival into Bardo's life came at the right time for him. Bardo had spent his life obsessed with female pop figures of the day: Madonna, Debbie Gibson and Tiffany had all been on Bardo's radar. Just prior to the arrival of Schaeffer, Bardo obsessed over Samantha Smith. Smith had gained notoriety for composing a letter to the Soviet Union General Secretary Yuri Andropov about her fears of nuclear war between the USSR and the United States. Smith composed the letter when she was only 10-years-old, and it received a warm response from Secretary Andropov. Samantha Smith suddenly became an overnight sensation for her humanitarian efforts at such a young age. Bardo took notice of the young girl and made several efforts to contact her. He even went so far as to travel to her home state of Maine from Arizona, only to be caught by law enforcement and sent home. Sadly, Samantha Smith was tragically killed in plane crash when she was only 13-years-old. Bardo lost interest with Smith and found a new target with Rebecca Schaeffer.

Robert John Bardo's obsession with Schaeffer was a kind of lifestyle for him. For three years, Bardo's fixation grew. During her time on *My Sister Sam*, Bardo attempted to gain access to the set, only to be turned away by security. It was around the third year of stalking that Rebecca Schaeffer had begun to push out of the "good girl" typecasting, and pursued more edgy material. *My Sister Sam* had been cancelled, and Schaeffer had taken on a role in a movie called *Scenes From The Class Struggle In Beverly Hills*. In her role, Schaeffer shed her wholesome girl appearance from her sitcom days, and acted in some lovemaking scenes, as is typical in Hollywood cinema. Bardo became incensed, feeling that Schaeffer had "betrayed" him the entire time. Robert John Bardo snapped, and became determined to confront Rebecca Schaeffer.

When this feeling of betrayal finally reached a crescendo, Bardo responded to it by roaming the streets of Los Angeles, waiving a picture of Schaeffer at strangers randomly and asking them if they knew where she lived. Eventually, Bardo got lucky. He came upon a private investigator who agreed to get Schaeffer's home address for $250.00, to which Bardo agreed. For $1.00, the investigator was able to file a form with the DMV and obtain the address of Rebecca Schaeffer. Ironically, it would be the Rebecca Schaeffer/Robert John Bardo case that would close the loophole on obtaining personal information on others through the DMV.

Through this series of events, Robert John Bardo confronted Rebecca Schaeffer at her home. Unfortunately, it ended in tragedy. According to the accounts of Robert John Bardo, Schaeffer was very upset that he had come to her private residence and her animosity made him furious. For Bardo, he felt like she should be more respectful of his obsession for her, and he realized that (in his mind) she was a fraud. Bardo brought a pistol to the residence, and in that moment he drew it and fired a single shot to Rebecca Schaeffer's torso. Neighbors who heard the shooting later stated that Schaeffer screamed twice, and yelled "Why???" and then fell to the ground. Robert John Bardo fled the scene and was later picked up while aimlessly walking in Los Angeles traffic. Rebecca Schaeffer never regained consciousness and was pronounced dead approximately 30 minutes after she was shot.

Rebecca Schaeffer was 21 years old.

Stalking is a very real, very disturbing condition that can manifest into a threatening condition quickly. Like the case of Robert John Bardo, a single incident (like a role in a movie) can have tragic consequences. There is no determining what that trigger will be to set off a stalker. But it is safe to assume that there is one. Stalkers focus their lives on the lives of others, and when those innocent people do things that upset that delusional representation the stalker often has… that will likely lead to bad things.

"*She came into my life in the right moment. She was brilliant, pretty, and outrageous, her innocence impressed me. She turned into a goddess for me, an idol. Since then, I turned an atheist, I only adored her.*" – Robert John Bardo

22. Suicide

This has already come up once before, with "suffering" as an early indicator. Like that previous topic, we are not going to spend too much time on this, because it goes without saying that when a life-threatening situation is brought to your attention, you must intervene. With suffering, there is a variety of possible symptoms that could be associated with the condition. With suicide, the intentions are perfectly clear; the individual has expressed a committal to ending their own life. The threat-related behavior is there, it is just more than likely that the threat is to themselves and not others.

That is not to say that such a condition doesn't pose a threat to the outside community, however. In the U.S. Secret Service study of school attacks in the United States, it was reported that 27%, more than 1 in 4 attackers, had attributed their attack motivation to suicidal ideation. Why would a person want to kill innocent people when their desire to take their own life? It's difficult to know, as almost all individuals with a suicidal mentality who attacked a location were successful in ending their lives prior to being apprehended.

Whatever the case, whether the individuals who have made it clear that they want to take their lives are planning on killing just themselves or others as well is a moot point. Suicide prevention, due to its high volume in our society, is the most practiced form of training that our community receives for identifying and stopping threat-related behavior in a positive and proactive manner. We are trained at a young age to understand the symptoms of suicide, such as depression. We are provided multiple tools and resources to deal with these issues as they present themselves, either when we feel it ourselves or when we see it in others. There are hotlines to call for help, offices offer Employee Assistance Programs (EAP) and counselors are in abundance to get to the root of the problem that has caused the condition. When we bring it to the attention of authorities, they are mandated to follow-up in a positive and proactive manner to address the concern and make every effort to get the person help so that they can lead a productive life. When a person is provided the help that they need, these programs are very successful.

When I see the work that is being done with preventing suicide in our country (and our world) I am both thankful and frustrated. I know that the programs work, and work well. I know that we as a society have recognized that the dangers of suicide are such that we have decided to look it in the face and address it as a community. We have not brought gun debates into the equation in an attempt to curb suicides. Instead, we have recognized the conditions of behavior that manifest in a suicidal person. We have trained our community in identifying these indicators and we have resources established to notify others so that they can assess the condition. If it is determined that the situation is serious, then action is taken with a proactive objective. Family and friends are contacted to assist with developing a support base for the individual, and medication is prescribed in some cases. Over time, the person can be counseled and adjusted to a positive life.

So what do I find so frustrating? Frankly, I wonder why can't we use this same kind of formula for individuals who display conditions of threat-related behavior? It's obvious that we have had a "beta" program in place that proves that our society is more than capable of being trained to identify threatening conditions, that they can assess the level of danger in such a condition, and that action can be taken to help the individual.

The truth is that we have not had nearly enough episodes of rampage violence in our communities to concede that such measures need to be taken. If active shooters were as prevalent as suicides, then we would likely set up hotlines, train our society at a young age to identify these behaviors, and have threat-assessment teams on call at all hours to determine a next course of action. I have genuinely prayed that we would never get to the point where we would have to begin setting these programs up.

Unfortunately, we're already there. After the Virginia Tech Massacre, the Commonwealth of Virginia mandated that all public colleges and universities in the state have behavioral-assessment teams established to deal with conditions of threatening behavior. The intentions of these programs are good, but the sad reality is that they were put in place as a political answer to appease a traumatized society reeling from another school massacre. These programs are abysmal at training the community in identifying conditions of threat-related behavior, they are underfunded and they make little attempt to even notify the respective communities of their existence. Only a thorough search of the university website will reveal a phone line and a list of referenced material on threat assessments. The onus of responsibility to learn what conditions to look for in someone fall on the shoulders of the public. When an attack is still fresh in everyone's mind, programs like Virginia's Threat Assessment Team response is the answer that people look for to appease their personal feelings of security. The truth is that the positions on threat assessment teams are mostly relegated to collateral duties to individuals who wear multiple hats in their jobs. Rather than this being a dedicated group of people, it is group that meets when a situation calls for it. They could (and should) be out training the community in the conditions to watch for and report. They should be researching the latest ways to address threat-related behavior; they should be updating the community with weekly blog reports and recommendations on what to be watchful for in others' behaviors. What is further upsetting is that most of the people on these Threat Assessment Teams do not know what to train the community in in the first place.

I don't mean to make programs like Virginia's out to be something bad. It's a good start. But since there hasn't been another college or university shooting in almost 10 years in the Commonwealth, the programs have become antiquated. They need to revise the approach and become an active part of the community. Further, such programs have a great opportunity to be the standard that other programs across the country can repeat. But it seems for now the country is satisfied with the response that has been given, at least until another attack at a university or an office occurs.

23. Bullying

For a time, I categorized the effects of bullying and being bullied as a sub-category to "humiliation" that was found in "negative changes in a person's life." I have since realized through further research that the situation is far more grave, and is deserving of being addressed independently.

For starters, bullying is not something that is a sudden negative change in a person's life. A child does not go into school one day and experience harassment by other students when the harassment didn't exist the day before. Bullying is a manifestation over a longer period of time. What starts as seemingly harmless ribbing or joking becomes taunting and even physical abuse as the attacker (yes, a bully is an attacker) becomes more confident with what he/she can do to the victim. This is why it is difficult to identify in its early stages. When does social interaction between students become something more serious?

Another point that is important to make is this: bullying does not stop in school, it occurs throughout a person's life. This may include college, the military or the workforce. Even family members are notorious for bullying one another and can set the tone for the way other people will treat a victim. I have seen first hand people who are living in an assisted living residence become the victim of bullying from their co-habitants. People don't outgrow the desire to push people around if they learn it early enough in life.

Lastly, and this is most important: individuals who have been the victim of bullying have referenced their victimization as one of the reasons why they committed rampage violence or violence to themselves. Being the victim of a bully creates feelings of public humiliation, fear, anxiety, social isolation and physical pain. It creates the absolute worst, adverse conditions in children for their development. In the most extreme cases, it leads to tragic results.

Technology has not helped in addressing the situation. If anything, the creation of social interaction online has made it worse. In my day, bullying was limited to simply dealing with the person (or persons) who heckled and tormented a victim during the school day. The bullying was confined to how much exposure an attacker had to promote his angst. That exposure was usually limited to the playground, cafeteria or the gym and seen only by those there at the time. In addition, the victim was able to find some refuge, some solace when he/she retreated home. Other activities in the victims life took over, be that an extra-curricular activity or a different social life outside of the bullying arena. All of that has changed with the arrival of technology. Now, bullying is a global affair. Attackers take their torment to the internet with a barrage of verbal attacks, embarrassing videos and photographs, and invitations to total strangers to take part as well. Bullies are able to swell their ranks against a target through the internet, and the effects are devastating. The victim is in a constant state of fear and humiliation and insecurity, unsure of who may know about the experience. As such, the victim assumes everyone knows, and paranoia is frequent. The internet does not soon forget, and especially damning videos or photographs will linger online, shared for sometimes years at a time.

The irony is that victims will often seek comfort and the much-needed social interaction of adolescence in the very place that has been a stimulant to their pain: the internet. For many victims, the internet provides a virtually limitless world where a person can create an alternate persona, one that is free from verbal and physical abuse. A person can be beautiful, witty, live the life that they choose to live. If they find that the interaction is becoming uncomfortable or upsetting, the persona can be deleted and the victim can start over. Just like victims though, predators stalk the social servers as well, and they are very adept at recognizing the signs of a young person trying to escape their life. The youths are targeted, and persistence on the account of the predator can result in a threatening condition. But rather than the condition manifesting a threatening condition for the public, it creates one in the person who is already being victimized in the real world. Cyberbullying is bullying, it is bullying on a scale for which the world was ill-prepared.

By the testimony of her mother, 13-year-old Nicole Lovell had a hard life. Nicole had been the recipient of a liver transplant when she was only

10 months old, and was required to take medication twice a day just to stay alive. She was not popular in school, and her mother had confessed that Nicole had been the victim of bullying throughout her life. She had been so ostracized by her own peer group that she fled to the internet to escape her pain. It was online that she met David Eisenhauer. To Nicole, David seemed too good to be true. She was right.

Just over a year before Nicole and David would meet, WMAR-TV News in Baltimore, Maryland provided the community an expose on Eisenhauer. David, charismatic and confident, was the featured story for their "Athlete of the Week" based on his performance on the track and in the classroom. David was a successful distance runner who was finishing his Senior year at Wilde Lake High School in Columbia, Maryland, a suburb of Baltimore. He was selected over (literally) thousands upon thousands of other potential student athletes in the area for the expose, and the decision to use Eisenhauer was a sound one. Having recently been accepted to Virginia Polytechnic Institute in their coveted engineering school, Eisenhauer was no slack in the classroom. His times on the track were off the chart and he was something of a prodigy in the long-distance running. Virginia Tech was more than ready to have him on their running team. In his newscast interview, it was clear that Eisenhauer knew how good he was and was more than confident in his abilities. During the interview, Eisenhauer confidently proclaimed, "I make my personal goals achievable or just out of reach of achievable. That way I'm always constantly striving to better myself."

During his freshman year at Virginia Tech, Eisenhauer became active in online dating. It was on the popular software messenger application "Kik" that he met Nicole Lovell. Lovell was already looking for acceptance of some kind and Eisenhauer took advantage of her susceptibility. Lovell lived in the Blacksburg area, home of Virginia Tech. As such, it was easy for Eisenhauer to meet with her. Later investigations have indicated that the college student and the 13-year-old little girl began to have some kind of inappropriate relationship.

From those who knew her and what was going on (namely her peer group), Nicole Lovell had expressed that she was deeply in love, or at least infatuated, with David Eisenhauer. She had confided that she wanted to run away with him and have children. The news media reported that sexual contact had occurred between Lovell and Eisenhauer.

On the afternoon of January 30, 2016, the body of Nicole Lovell was discovered at approximately 4:00 p.m. Lovell's family had reported her missing on January 27th, and foul play had been suspected in her disappearance. Nicole's bedroom door had been barricaded from the inside of her bedroom with furniture, and there was no sign that there had been forced entry into the room. From this, it was suspected that Lovell had barricaded it herself and left the room by her own volition.

During the homicide investigation, friends of Lovell stated that she had interacted with multiple adult males online, and that she confided to friends that she had started a relationship with a student at Virginia Tech. One of these friends, Natasha Bryant, stated that Lovell had actually said that the man she was involved with was David Eisenhauer. Shortly after Lovell's death, her father had told noted television personality Dr. Phil McGraw that he was aware of his daughter's interactions with adult males online, and that it was not approved. Lovell's father further stated that his daughter had been restricted from such interaction, but she continued to do it anyway. Lastly, he never saw any indication that things had progressed to the level that they had. Within 24 hours of the discovery of Lovell's body, Eisenhauer was arrested and charged with first-degree murder.

Although the official motive for why Eisenhauer would kill Nicole Lovell was never released, it's pretty clear: David Eisenhauer became involved in an inappropriate way with a 13-year-old girl. As a young man, Eisenhauer knew this relationship was wrong but he chose to do it anyway. He likely thought that some local girl would be a simple distraction while he was away at school, someone to satisfy his deviant desires. In his mind he would be able to graduate and move on in the world, fulfilling all the ambition he showed in his WMAR-TV interview the year before. He just needed to make sure that his young girl would keep their liaison a secret.

But then something happened that Eisenhauer didn't expect; the impressionable 13-year-old girl, still learning about emotions and physical intimacy, fell in love. Like any young girl with her first love, she started talking to friends about her dreams of running away and marrying her handsome young man; she obsessed over his pictures, and nothing else seemed to matter for her but the two of them together. Lovell's lack of attention from other boys was now fulfilled with the greatest prize of all:

a handsome, successful man who was funny and kind to her, ambitious and dashing.

This was not in the game plan for Eisenhauer. He had no intention of seeing this through beyond his own physical gratification. Lovell likely told him on one or more occasion that she had mentioned him to her friends and told her friends of their involvement. No doubt this threw Eisenhauer into a spin. Suddenly, David Eisenhauer started losing sleep at night. Now he was going to be identified as a child predator rather than the successful engineer that he aspired to be. Nicole Lovell was ruining his ambitious plans for the future, and he really had no way to persuade her to stop talking. What was worse, Eisenhauer likely suspected that any attempt to break off his relationship would result in Lovell telling her parents (and eventually the authorities) of her involvement with him. When William Congreve wrote, "Heaven has no rage like love to hatred turned, nor Hell a fury like a woman scorned," he likely counted 13-year-old love struck girls among the scorned. David Eisenhauer, with his life flashing before his eyes, resolved that the only way to keep Nicole Lovell quiet was to end her life.

As if the story is not disturbing enough, it gets worse. It appears that Eisenhauer had an accomplice in his crime: Natalie Keepers. Keepers had many similarities with Eisenhauer; both were freshman at Virginia Tech; both hailed from the same area outside of Baltimore, Maryland; both were successful students in high school and had great potential to continue that success in college and further; both had never had any previous issues with law enforcement or committing crimes of any kind. But somewhere during the freshman year at Virginia Tech, it is believed that David Eisenhauer was able to convince Natalie Keepers to help him with a horrific crime: assisting with the killing of Nicole Lovell.

Keepers' involvement in the crime is best described as "strange." There is no evidence to suggest that she and Eisenhauer were ever emotionally involved, or that there was some unusual three-way involvement between the two of them and Lovell. Why would Keepers, a promising student with a bright future, suddenly risk taking part in something so macabre and disturbing? Sources have suggested that Keepers and Eisenhauer planned Lovell's murder while dining over french fries and burgers at a local fast food restaurant. Somehow, Eisenhauer was able to broach the subject with Keepers of how she could assist him with killing a little girl and hiding her body. Keepers would later confess to law enforcement that she was not present at the killing of Lovell herself, but she assisted with disposing of her body. When asked why Keepers threw away her entire future and committed such a heinous act, she explained that her involvement made her feel like she was part of a "secret club." Keepers would go on to describe Eisenhauer as a "sociopath" and she herself in a kind of apprenticeship role as a "sociopath in training."

It didn't take long for law enforcement to track down Eisenhauer and Keepers. As police approached Keepers, she was able to send a one-word text to Eisenhauer, "police," a warning to him that they had been discovered. During his interview with police, David Eisenhauer admitted that he had arranged to meet with Lovell on the night of her disappearance, and that he waited for her while she climbed out of her bedroom window after she barricaded her bedroom door. They left together to pick up Keepers, and Keepers has adamantly denied taking part in the murder itself.

On July 26, 2016, David Eisenhauer and Natalie Keepers were both indicted by grand jury in the killing of 13-year-old Nicole Lovell. Eisenhauer was indicted on charges of first-degree murder, abduction and transporting or concealing a body. Keepers was indicted on accessory to murder before the fact and transporting or concealing a body.

The sad truth is this: Nicole Lovell is gone forever. She will never have the chance to grow up, have a meaningful relationship with another person. She will never enjoy the simple pleasures of adolescence; Friday night football games with friends, prom night, graduation; Nicole Lovell will never feel the elation that comes with getting an acceptance letter to a college, or living on her own, charting the course of her life. The only exposure she ever had in anything resembling a relationship was a lie, a lie that would eventually be the motivator for a man to kill her.

It doesn't stop with Nicole. Multiple lives have been destroyed from this tragic story. The Lovells, the Eisenhauers and the Keepers will never, ever forget this horrific time in their families' legacies. Three, even four, generations from now, these families will still talk about this dark time with each other. Virginia Tech, still reeling nearly a decade after the massacre perpetrated by Seung Hui Cho, now has another tragic tale to add to their history of violence. The Blacksburg community must again try to piece together a neighborhood that has been shattered by murderous intent.

And why? Ultimately because of David Eisenhauer. There is no question that his actions caused all of this, and this is not attempt to turn blame away from the one who was responsible. But there has to be some acknowledgement of what can happen in the long-term effects of bullying, and where it can drive people. In the case of Nicole Lovell, it drove her to the means that would result in her death. The neglect and humiliation that came from her peer group forced her to find other ways to be accepted. The internet was the easiest method to do that.

The tragedy of Nicole Lovell is obviously the most extreme in the case of what could happen when enough bad conditions are put together. But online social interaction is essentially allowing our children to talk to strangers from all over the world. It is only a few smalls steps removed from having the child get into the stranger's van. With a bit of coaxing from someone convincing like David Eisenhauer, the degree of separation that comes with being online can quickly go away.

With all of this, we have gone off topic a bit. We really haven't touched on the effects that bullying has on those other individuals, those people who resolve to commit rampage violence against innocent victims. Seung Hui-Cho, Dylan Klebold, Eric Harris, Timothy McVeigh, Jeffrey Weise, Tim Kretschmer, Marc Lepine, Thomas Hamilton.... All of these individuals committed rampage violence on a grand scale, and all of them referenced, or others referenced, some kind of bullying that occurred to them in their lives. Even more disturbing is that this is only a small snapshot of attackers. The list literally offers dozens more examples, and virtually all of them make reference to a life of being bullied and harassed. The correlation is unmistakable.

Our school system is making an honest, forthright effort to address bullying in schools. Programs like the Olweus Anti-Bullying Program works with the school systems to ensure that the appropriate steps are taken at the school and family level to stop such behavior. Although the intentions are good though, the truth is that you just can't force students to like one another. The differences in culture, class status, and even athletic ability will always play in to forming peer groups. Because of that, there will always be outsiders looking in.

The best way to address bullying is to make it something so taboo that it is repulsive to the community. If a group of students were on a field trip in a local city, and they came across a stray puppy dog, and one student walked up to the puppy and kicked it as hard as he/she could, that student would be immediately ruined socially. The other students would confront him, possibly even assault him/her for what was done; they would notify their school and the student would be given some kind of counseling. Parents would be called. Even the most deviant of children would think twice before bringing that kind of issue on themselves, the act is too taboo to even consider.

That is how we need to teach bullying. It needs to be such a horrific action that the very thought of even doing it would only backfire on the bully and make them the social outcast that they look to create in their target. The fear of being considered a social reject for being a bully needs to be greater than the desire to push someone else around. Because right now, the systems that are put in place don't seem to work. Children like Nicole Lovell are still being harassed, and they are still fleeing to the internet for comfort.

Go to your child's school website and look for any information on bullying. I guarantee there is a PDF or some kind of report form to download and submit to the school. In addition, there are probably a few website links to how to prevent bullying and what to do if you know someone who is a victim…and that is probably it. There is no method to address the student's culture, which is where such actions manifest. All of the web links, studies and report forms are only an answer from an adult perspective, and they do little to stop the problem where it starts: with the kids.

24. Danger Indicators: Wrap-Up

The danger indicators that you have read in this section comprise the majority of this book, and with good reason; they are, quite simply, the most important and likely signs that an individual will show in his/her behaviors that suggest future threat-related action of some kind. Those threats may be to the community in the form of rampage violence, or they could manifest in a threat to themselves, such as suicidal tendencies. They could even promote a condition that will create long-term issues for a victim later in life, such as bullying or stalking. Studies have shown that in cases of threat-related violence stemming from these danger indicators, 54% of the attackers researched had multiple reasons for their attack. Over half of the people who committed rampage violence felt that there was more than one reason to harm other people.   In hindsight, most common criminals who are arrested for petty theft or violence are motivated by any number of reasons, but the most frequent are: they wanted money or were driven by some kind of greed, they wanted revenge for a wronging that they felt had been committed against them, or they were driven by a lustful sickness that resulted in the rape of another person. But all of these conditions were usually driven by a single intention. Granted, in many cases other issues happened that drove to further crime. After the rape of an innocent person, the attacker decided to take money from the victim's wallet, for example. Theft came from the attack, but the initial violence was with a single intent.

Attackers in rampage violence were different, at least more than half of the time. This suggests one of two possibilities: the first is that it is entirely coincidental that a potential attacker independently manifests two or more conditions that create the desire to kill innocent people at random. That seems more like a statistical anomaly than anything. The other, more realistic possibility is that these danger indicators build on one another, and that they are inter-related.

So what does this mean for us, why is this so important? For a couple of reasons. First, it stresses the importance of identifying a condition as soon as possible. By not doing so, the danger indicators become more frequent, thereby increasing the chances that something violent is going to occur. But more importantly, it presents a double-edged sword to the dangers and the answer to dealing with it. If someone is displaying danger indicators, then they are probably motivated to commit harm by more than one. But it also indicates that if they are displaying more than one indicator of danger in their day-to-day lives, then there are more people who have the opportunity to identify it and stop it.

Another point that is worthy of discussing is that studies have indicated that 31% of those who committed rampage violence never acted violently toward another person prior to their attack. Although there is strong argument to suggest that the best indicator for future violent action in an individual is previous action, it is not an absolute that we should hang our hat on. A full third of people who have committed such atrocities never had any kind of encounter, only to suddenly explode into a single violent rage. What's important about this is that you as the observer should not assume that a person won't do anything violent if they haven't done anything before. If the indicators are there, and the person is showing conditions that are in line with threat-related behavior, then it goes to say that person should be identified no matter who they are and what their previous violent actions.

One final point to consider: only 17% of attackers directly threatened a person, persons and/or the location prior to the attack. Furthermore when the person was threatened before the attack occurred, the victim was almost always a high-profile individual such as a celebrity or a political figure. In other words, if you are awaiting a bomb threat, a message or some other form of communication to move into action against a threat, you will be waiting a long time. It is 83% likely that the message will never come.

And so all of this, these indicators, these statistics, these case profiles, they all come back to you. Yes, you are the member of the community, and as I stated earlier, you are the difference-maker. It is not the clinical psychiatrist, or the law enforcement officer, or the counselor or the emergency medical technician who will identify the condition. Those people will play vital, much needed roles (as we will discuss in greater detail in the coming sections), but the initial identification of threat-related behavior is on the community itself, and those that live in it. The "community" starts with the immediate family members, then the close circle of friends, the classmates and co-workers, those people affiliated in volunteer or social groups and then strangers and people we interact with during the bustle of our day-to-day lives. The most important thing to understand is that you, the member of the community, are the best answer to identifying dangerous indicators of threat-related behavior in others.

Could you imagine what our community would be like if everyone were skilled and trained in observing behavioral threats like we are trained to identify and address a fire? Just like I said at the beginning of this book, all we are doing is learning to identify the symptoms of a potentially dangerous situation, (like a fire that is not under control) and then notifying the professionals to deal with it in a safe manner. I am confident that by teaching our society to recognize these conditions, we are paving the way to positive and proactive interventions to stop behavioral violence.

I know that this is an incredible amount of information, and I'm sure it's more than a bit overwhelming. I want to assure you that is okay, this is not something that is applied overnight. In fact, you may not have to apply it. Right now it's enough for me that you have something in your hands to explain threat-related behavior, to reference if you so choose. Because right now there is very little out there that you can read and study.

I can assure you that the best way to learn it and retain the information is to share it. I hope you share this with your community; your family, friends, your school, your children's school, your office, your social network. The more people who understand what to look for in threat-related behavior, the more people can be helped and the safer our community can be! I can only provide the information, but you are our path to safety.

Before we conclude with the "observation" phase of the book, there is one last topic that needs discussion and that is the mental health aspects of an individual: how it pertains to threat-related behavior and rampage violence. We need to tread carefully on this issue for many reasons, all of which we will address.

25. Mental Health Conditions and Threat-Related Behavior

Because of the nature of the subject, I just can't review it without making some reference to mental illness. There is no question that mental health has come to play in situations of rampage violence. For us, the sane person would not commit such atrocities, so logic suggests that the person who has attacked others so ruthlessly lacks a sense of sanity.

But we need to be very, very careful when stereotyping these mental health conditions with such violence. Most importantly (and a point I will continue to reiterate throughout this book because it is so important), the vast majority of people who suffer from mental health conditions are NOT violent. The sad truth is that the people who have attacked others have had a condition of some kind, but the majority of the people in our community who are afflicted with these illnesses do not attack innocent people. An analogy that might help explain this is that every square is a rhombus, but not every rhombus is a square; or every thumb is a finger but not every finger is a thumb.

The next point to make about mental health and threat-related behavior is that, at no time in this book or throughout, am I endorsing that it is your responsibility to identify a mental health condition in a person, to assess their mental health and/or to recommend any program for the person's betterment. This is for the mental health professional, as they are the party that is responsible for diagnosis of their patient. It is your job to identify and report behavioral concerns, it is theirs to evaluate the individual's mental stability and determine the next course of action.

The one thing that we as a society don't want to do is to lend fuel to the social stigma that comes with a person who has a mental health condition. If a person suddenly broke their arm or were bleeding profusely, there would be no question that there would be people there to help. We would call 9-1-1, others would intervene directly to stabilize the individual, and help would arrive quickly. But when it comes to mental health, a confirmed, well-documented and studied condition in science and medicine, we as a society still view it as taboo. What an antiquated type of thinking for a society that is so willing to help other incapacities. Perhaps it is because mental illness cannot be seen like other injuries or it affects a person behavior so unpredictably. Frankly, these are moot points. What matters is that we need to understand that mental illness is a medically debilitating condition like any injury, and it can be treated like any injury. People usually recognize the condition in themselves but they choose to ignore it or not get help because of the image it may cast on them. Mental health treatments are losing their stigma, but we still have far to go in our community. Whoever recognizes the condition in themselves should be praised for their willingness to get help; they should never, never be ostracized.

So if we are not going to take part in any mental health diagnosis, or likely never become involved in any aspect of mental health in an individual, then what is the point of discussing the conditions in this section? Why are we even reviewing these?

I do not know your background or how this entire program is going to be a part of your life. You may be involved in a profession that focuses on human resources, or guidance counseling; you may be a medical professional, or someone in law enforcement, or an emergency responder. You may be a stay-at-home parent (one of the most difficult jobs I have ever held, and not given the credit it is deserving from a professional aspect). What I know is that you may be given information on a person's mental health condition, and it is important to have the definitions of these conditions. The person may volunteer that they have been previously diagnosed, or you may be a parent or guardian who has been informed that child or ward under your care has a certain mental health condition. It is better to have the information and not need it, then need the information and not have it.

One last point: the information that is provided in this section (like everything in this book) has been researched and referenced at length. Resources that have been used to draw information include the Diagnostic and Statistical Manual of Mental Disorders (DSM) as well as information provided by the Mayo Clinic. The DSM is the standardized classifications of mental health disorders that are recognized by the mental health community. It is also the foundation for most (if not all) of the information provided in this section of discussion. The Mayo Clinic is widely considered the premiere center in the world for any and all aspects of medical care and research. The information provided is not based on my personal opinions; it is based on documented information from professionals. During my tenure with the United States Secret Service, my fellow agents and I were trained extensively in these conditions to assist with our own determination as to the danger levels of a person displaying threat-related behavior. Like you, we were not medical professionals who could diagnose a condition. But we used the information to help protect people like the President of the United States, and you can use the same methods to help with protecting the community.

The mental health conditions that are commonly associated with threat-related behavior and rampage violence are:

- Antisocial personality
- Bipolar disorder
- Delusion
- Narcissism
- Paranoia
- Schizotypal personality
- Paranoid schizophrenia

Antisocial Personality Disorder

The first mental health condition that we will discuss is Antisocial Personality Disorder (ASPD). With ASPD, the person typically has very little regard for the social norms of the world, and they give less regard to what is "right" and "wrong." This additionally affects the person's sense of morality, lacking a "moral compass." It is not unusual for ASPD people to violate laws and to do so with no sense of guilt or care as to the harm that they are inflicting on society. Lying and stealing are normalcy to them, and they are additionally prone to flashes of violence and impulsivity. Drugs and alcohol are known to be a staple diet. The person cares even less for the emotions of others. They are known to antagonize, treat others harshly, manipulate people and impose feelings of guilt on others.

Bipolar Disorder

This is one of those medical terms that, for one reason or another, have become popularized as a "self-diagnosing" condition. I have met many, many people in my life who have told me that they are convinced that they are bipolar. I have also had many people tell me that, from their personal observations, they are able to recognize other individuals who have bipolar symptoms. I was even once accused of being bipolar myself, although not from a medical professional or anyone trained to make such a diagnosis (and I have never been diagnosed with the condition, by the way).

We live in a society filled with people who want to look intelligent without putting the work into the study. It's easier to read a snippet or brief definition of a condition and associate it to being certified to understand it. Usually this works fine… if you are looking for directions on how to replace the brakes on your car, cook a turkey in a smoker or hang drywall. But as a means to diagnose a mental health condition? That needs to be left to the professionals.

The fundamental reason that people assume they understand bipolar disorder is because of its most obvious symptom, that being intense mood swings in the individual. Like a roller coaster climbing, banking and dropping through its cycle, a person afflicted with bipolar disorder will have intensely high feelings of joy and suddenly become (sometimes) terrifyingly angry or upset. But the confusion comes with people who are "moody," and the incorrect assumption that this is an indicator for the mood swings that a person with bipolar disorder suffers. From a medical standpoint, the DSM breaks down bipolar disorder into sub-categories for diagnosis of an individual. We don't need to delve too much into this, but it is important to understand that a person afflicted with this condition is dealing with much more than just simple mood swings that we have all had before. It is equally important to understand that (statistically) bipolar disorder is a very treatable condition with any number of combinations of medicine, therapy and even homeopathic remedies have shown great success.

There are many public figures who have bravely shared their stories of dealing with this condition. Acclaimed actors such as Richard Dreyfuss, Carrie Fisher, and Catherine Zeta-Jones have all expressed publicly that they deal with the condition every day of their lives. In literature, some of the greatest writers in history have struggled with bipolar disorder. There is wide speculation that Earnest Hemingway, Edgar Allan Poe and Lord Byron suffered from the condition, while Virginia Woolf was diagnosed with it at age 13. In media Jane Pauley, the former host of NBC's long-running "Today" morning show, has been upfront about her condition. Obviously, none of these people have been a threat to society. On the contrary, their willingness to tell us of their struggles should be considered inspirational, and would hopefully motivate others who need help to get it.

There have been a few cases of individuals who have displayed violent tendencies. But it should be made clear that although they were diagnosed with the condition, there is no correlation that bipolar disorder was what manifested their violent tendencies.

Bipolar disorder is not a strong indicator in identifying threat-related violence, but it may come up in some kind of furtherance of an assessment of a person who has shown danger indicators based on their behavior. The important thing to understand is that this is a very treatable condition and one that many people have while living successful, non-violent lives.

Delusion

Anyone who has served in a military capacity, a law enforcement unit or an emergency responder position of some kind is familiar with the responsibility that comes with manning a 24-hour "watch desk" or "duty desk." The position is a necessary one, as it is the first point of contact for an individual who is trained in the service that the unit provides. Unlike an administrative professional or an intern, the duty desk is the place where a person can speak with someone who is qualified to address the operational or field issues. It is vitally important, and also a well-hated nightmare for agents, soldiers, and police alike. During my time with the U.S. Secret Service, we shared the responsibility among all of the agents in a one-week interval, divided up about five times a year. In addition to it being the first point of contact for filtering administrative and operational needs for the office, it was also the physical location where people would come in and out of the location. In essence, the duty desk agent also acted as the first responder to any threats that might get through the building security at the front doors.

During one such rotation on the desk, I was given a first-hand account of true symptoms of delusion in another person. It was the late morning, nearing the time when people were leaving the office for lunch or going home if they were only in for half of the day. It was also a popular time for scheduled meetings, as this provided the opportunity to go out and grab something to eat while discussing plans. As such, it was not unusual to see unfamiliar faces show up at the main entrance. This was no different.

A woman came into the waiting area, well dressed and carrying a portfolio. She wore an evergreen suit with brown leather pump shoes. She was well kept; her hair was neatly trimmed and she with a close-crop haircut, similar to the popular style that many females wear that serve in the armed forces. The woman appeared to be in her mid-40's, Caucasian, and wore glasses. She smelled of a light perfume and it looked like she had spent some time on her nails, as they were painted with a conservative tan color. She had on loop earrings that I could see clearly from the nature of her hairstyle. The woman stood about 5 foot 4 inches tall and was slim. There were no indications that she had any neglect for her hygiene, as she appeared clean and her teeth were bright and complete. She looked composed, and was well spoken when she introduced herself. Judging by her appearance alone, I assumed she was an attorney or a federal agent from another law enforcement organization. I also figured that she had presented her credentials to the building security and that was how she was able to gain access to our office. She calmly waited in the adjoining room for someone to meet with her. As was customary, I met her at the entranceway to find out her reasons for being in our office.

"How can I help you?" I asked as I shook her hand.

"I am sorry for bothering you with this, I have a bit of a problem," she began. "You see, about eleven years ago I went in to the dentists office to have a filling put in one of my teeth…." The woman paused, then continued, "It was during that procedure that I given some gas that made me lose consciousness."

At this point I was certain that she was going to tell me that an assault or violation of some kind had occurred. Anyone who has had a filling would know that the procedure only requires a localized numbing anesthetic. Unless it is under extreme circumstances, there is no need for such measures as putting a person into sleep.

The woman continued, "When I awoke, I was told that the microchip implant into my brain was a success...."

I literally thought she was joking. I remember actually starting to laugh a bit because I was anticipating that she was going to do the same as an indication that she too was pulling my leg. When she continued to stare at me completely deadpan, I realized that she in fact completely serious. I quickly caught myself and went along.

"Okay..." I managed to say through my dry mouth. "Go on."

"So, my microchip has been functioning fine since the operation... no issues. I have been receiving my instructions, and I go about my day. Only now...." She paused, "I'm starting to lose some of the reception, and I think that it might be malfunctioning."

At this point, there really isn't much more to tell. She went on to explain that she went to a local police precinct, which directed her to us. Our local law enforcement counterparts knew that we dealt with individuals like this regularly, and that we were better connected to get this person the appropriate help. I asked her to take a seat and then I went back into the office to get an agent to help me with the woman. Ultimately, we interviewed her to make sure that she wasn't a danger to herself or others (which she was not by the way.... Like I said, most mentally ill people are not violent). After we spoke with her we were able to contact an organization that helped us with individuals in this mental state and they were able to further assist her.

Like I alluded to before, the truth is that individuals like this were the norm for the U.S. Secret Service. People of all kinds associate the term "Secret" in the name with clandestine and conspiracy theory work. When you combine that with the nature of the mission being the protection of high-profile political leaders, it becomes a recipe for the kind of storylines that you only see in Hollywood and fiction novels. This is also grossly inaccurate. The vast majority of work revolves around keeping up with administrative redundancy and paperwork. However, many people who have mental illnesses don't believe that. As such, the U.S. Secret Service is a lightning rod for people who are looking for answers about Area-51, Soylent Green, or just wanting to leave a love letter for their favorite politician, the same one who happens to be the father of their secret love-child.... the child who, incidentally, never existed.

But usually the interaction is phone call, a note or possibly an email or online posting. Actually having the ability to get to the front door of a field office, fooling everyone with appearance and presentation is extremely rare. It's important to understand that the woman was able to pull this off because she believed the things that were happening were real. Obviously I could not formally diagnose her as delusional, but she was acting off of something that occurred that was absolutely impossible.

Delusional disorders can be divided into varying categories, such as "erotomania" or a delusion that another person (typically someone in a public status) is in love with the afflicted. I saw this a great deal when I was an agent, as we would frequently interact with individuals obsessed with our protectees. Delusions can also be sub-categorized into whether the individual has a sense of superiority and self-importance, whether they are jealous of others, and even if they believe that they suffer from a physical or medical condition that they may/may not have.

Additionally, a person who is delusional is one who displays a repetitious nature of thinking but usually toward a non-bizarre type. They may believe that they are being stalked or followed, or being poisoned. These thoughts are not unrealistic in nature, as it occurs everyday with people all over the world. As such, it is difficult to recognize the delusion as a medical condition that needs to be treated. Most people will assume that an individual who says they are being stalked are being truthful and will try to help the victim. It can be a long time (if ever) before a person is seen as someone with a mental condition that needs some kind of treatment. Granted, there are more extreme and obvious circumstances, like the woman who I met. It was fairly easy to determine that she was not well mentally…. But not before she told me about her "symptoms." Prior to that, I may very well have invited her into the office if she had requested it. Other popular delusions with those afflicted with the condition include the belief that they have a relationship with a public figure or that they have some amazing ability or insight that no one else knows. Throughout all of this, many people who suffer from this affliction carry on in some positive capacity in life and you would likely not know about their condition unless it confronted you directly.

Delusional disorder is widely considered a challenge to treat. It is not simply handled by medication, but takes a great deal of therapy from professionals. Oftentimes, the difficulty with treatment arises when the patient refuses to accept that their belief is not a genuine one. The important thing to understand is that these people genuinely believe in the delusion, just like you and I believe that the Earth is round and the sky is blue. It is a delicate matter that should be handled discreetly by professionals, not by you and I at the moment that we are exposed to it.

Narcissism

I don't know about you, but when I think of the definition of a "narcissist" I cannot help but associate the condition to several of today's celebrities. In this age of self-importance distributed through the internet, the popularity of the "reality show," the "selfie" epidemic, Twitter accounts… the list goes on. Technology has bought humanity's narcissistic desires to a global, instantaneous level, and those who make a living off of being worshipped as an icon embrace the lifestyle the most. This seems to permeate itself into all aspects of life: entertainment, sports, music, journalism… even our own astronauts and scientists can be found promoting themselves as they watch the Super Bowl from the International Space Station, and gloat to the rest of the world how they have the best seat in the house for the game (on a side note, the only reason I bring this up is my own envy for not sitting there myself). The world today is an ideal environment for the creation, cultivation and promotion of narcissism.

To narcissists the world over I say this: to each his/her own. The desire for popularity is certainly not my thing, as I am one who enjoys the privacy of my life and keeping few quality friends in lieu of a larger group. But at the same time how dare I judge the way in which you choose to live your life? All I ask is that you please don't be offended if I haven't heard of you.

So how do you know if you are a narcissist? Well if you were offended by what you just read about me not knowing you, then you probably have the behavioral conditioning associated with true narcissism (don't take that as a diagnosis, just a joke).

The DSM seems to have a very good handle on the symptoms and conditions that are associated with narcissistic behavior. At the time of this writing, the DSM was on its fifth addition, and the category of "narcissism' had changed very little since the first series. Narcissists have an overbearing sense of self-importance. In their minds, the narcissist is "perfect," as is indicated by their inability to handle constructive criticism. They react poorly to such criticism with anger and humiliation. Additionally, because narcissists place themselves as the most important person to exist, other people are nothing more than a means to achieve what the narcissist desires. They further inflate their own value to include their personal talents, intelligence, beauty or any number of categories. The narcissist requires constant attention and positive affirmation about themselves, and demands outrageous treatment. This may be something like a certain temperature of a drink, a unique food that is impossible to find at a local restaurant, or a certain kind of clothing. The possibilities are only limited to the expectation of the person with the condition. They additionally do not take well to being in relationships, as they are self-centered and become jealous quickly.

For whatever reason, the individual has developed a condition where their sensitivities about themselves are fragile and easily shattered. The answer therefore is to compensate by building them up to be "larger-than-life," a greater person than most (if not all). Most narcissists have developed this condition through some starting point, such as physical beauty or athletic ability. It is further noted that the condition is more prone in males than females and seems to develop around the teen years and early adulthood.

It's probably not wise to give an example of a popular figure to demonstrate who might fit this profile. What I can say is that if you research the condition, many names will associate with the condition. From a threat-related behavioral standpoint though, there are several individuals throughout history who have displayed the characteristics and it is believed that the condition fueled their malevolence. One example of this is the noted serial killer Ted Bundy, who was diagnosed a narcissist prior to his execution. In a disturbing way, this diagnosis makes sense as to his rationale for violent actions. A normal person has difficulty inflicting harm on others because a normal person has a conscience. For narcissists like Bundy, all they see is fodder to forward their personal agendas.

The Mayo Clinic makes it clear that there is no medication or recommended drug therapy for the condition. Dealing with people who have narcissistic symptoms are best treated through psychotherapy, which is focused around discussions and helping the patient to understand while finding the root cause of the condition.

Paranoia

A trio of psychologists from the University of British Columbia published a report outlining similarities in psychological conditions of active shooter assailants, many of whom we have already reviewed. While researching the various writings, correspondences, and corroborative interviews of people who knew the attackers, it was determined that a common theme of each individual focused around an ever growing sense of paranoia in the individual. Reading through the journals and other documents, the psychologists determined that the internal belief of the writer (who would become the attacker) included feelings of alienation and that everyone was judging them as they went about life. The frequency of concern grew as the writing moved closer to the date of the attack, and much of the writing began to express rage at how these people perceived them.

Something I once heard a professor say in school was "even though you're paranoid, that doesn't mean that the world is not against you." This could be considered case in point for these attackers. Even though they perceived that people were mocking them, belittling or bullying them, none of this means that it was not happening. The community could very well have created an environment that drove the paranoia into these attackers. Does that justify their actions? Of course not, but it shows how important it is to not allow such behavior among one another to occur. We need to be cognizant of the long-term effects that heckling, belittling and humiliation can have on a person after the moment is over.

Paranoia (or Paranoid Personality Disorder) is described as a constant state of distrust and suspiciousness of others and the general world around an individual. The individual goes through every aspect of life believing that any action toward him/her is one of malevolence or intending some kind of harm or humiliation. Obviously, the person has a very difficult time trusting others to include close family members and/or people that they may have known for a long time. In addition, even the smallest possibility of losing that trust is one that could have long-term effects on the relationship. Something like accidently spilling a drink on the person could be perceived as a deliberate attempt to humiliate them, and that could permanently create a trust-rift in the mind of the paranoid person. Paranoia could also manifest when the person afflicted refuses to confide in others because of a fear that what they are telling them could be used to later embarrass or humiliate them, or the information could just be used against them in some fashion. Lastly, as is the point with the psychological study discussed earlier, paranoid people will hold grudges longer than most. They will feel like they have been targeted by the world, and this feeling will build up to one that could create further feelings of animosity toward others, that just won't simply go away. In the most extreme circumstances, this will eventually develop into rage with the person feeling an overwhelming desire to lash out.

In order for a person to be treated for any injury, condition or ailment, there has to be a willingness by that person to get help. For any person who has been a parent, one of the great challenges with raising a child is teaching them the importance of blowing their respective noses. A child will constantly sniffle, inhale, pick and flat-out refuse to learn how to remove the waste from their nostrils through the tried and true method. Frankly, I can't blame them. It really is a revolting condition and one that makes for many a difficult teaching session with a parent and a child. From my own personal perspective, I was able to teach both my children this by making it into a game. I simply lit a candle and challenged them to blow the candle out using only their nostrils. Obviously I monitored them carefully as to make sure that they didn't burn themselves. Each time they successfully were able to do it, I rewarded them with a small piece of candy and moved the candle back from them a little bit. This made sure that they increased the forcefulness of each "nostril blast." Eventually, this developed both an understanding of what they needed to be doing to blow their noses, and it got them used to the act so that it became second nature.

So what does this distasteful topic have to do with paranoia? It explains the challenges that come with dealing with the condition. For my children, I had many issues that I needed to overcome with them. The main point being their lack of willingness to learn how to blow their noses. I was able to overcome that through a series of games and rewards. But in order for me to make that happen, they needed to trust me. They needed to trust that I wasn't going to burn them with the candle, they needed to trust that I would reward them for their efforts, and ultimately they needed to trust that what I was doing for them was for their benefit in the long term.

Paranoia inhibits all willingness to make things better. The individuals who are assigned to help individuals suffering from paranoia must develop trust with the patient, and that trust is very difficult to establish and maintain. Oftentimes, just prescribing simple medications could be viewed as an attempt to do harm if the patient has a side effect. The side effect may be expected as part of the medication, but to the paranoid person, it was a deliberate attempt on behalf of the physician to cause harm. At that point, the trust is fractured in the mind of paranoid patient.

Paranoia has a variety of treatments, both medicinally based as well as psychotherapy. In both cases, the important thing is that the person has a willingness to get better, and that starts by trusting those who are trying to help. The best thing that you or I can do to help someone who is dealing with paranoia is to do whatever a professional recommends and to reaffirm the importance of trusting the treatment and those who are administering it.

Schizotypal Personality

The root issues of schizotypal personality disorder (STPD) focus on feelings that are associated with severe social anxiety and paranoid ideations. It is fair to say that many of the conditions that have been previously discussed can (and often do) build on one another. If you are observing one kind of symptom, it is favorable to think that other mental health issues will be there as well. Obviously, that is for a mental health professional to decide. With schizotypal personality disorder, there are definitely multiple issues with which the afflicted person is dealing.

It is believed that schizotypal personality is difficult to identify until a person reaches adulthood. This is because some of the strongest symptoms are those behaviors that are typical in children and adolescence. People with the condition will respond with introversion to many social situations, and tend to hold strong beliefs in peculiarities such as the existence of "aliens" or "unicorns." Society would write such cues off as mere youthful interests, and would further not recognize it as an issue until the person has reached the age where they should have outgrown these beliefs.

Oftentimes, people with the condition cannot form lasting, positive relationships with other people. They may consider themselves somewhat of a "loner" or introverted individuals. From my own personal perspective, I very much fit into that category; I prefer the solace of a quiet room to conduct work, I feel a pinch of anxiety when I have to "mingle" with crowds and I genuinely do not have as many friends as other people. But this is not because I am schizotypal by any means. I love my family very much and I truly enjoy their company; the people who I consider my friends are very long-term, deep relationships that I have cultivated over a long period of time. Those individuals do not cause me grief or hardship as being a part of my life. When these people, my family and friends are not near me, I miss them terribly and their presence is something I look forward to when I see them again.

People afflicted with schizotypal personality can have none of this. They cannot form those relationships with others, and they are in a constant state of distrust. As such, they develop angst toward people who should be in their circle of friends. They are further known to talk to themselves, display odd speech patterns and have odd, superstitious beliefs in the world. To make matters more difficult, when a person with the condition is motivated to get help for how they feel, it can easily be misdiagnosed as depression or anxiety. This is not meant to a criticism against those people who work in the mental health community. They oftentimes can only assess the patient based on the information that is presented at the time. STPD is long-term diagnosis, one that takes several meetings and personal analysis in the patient to articulate the justification of the condition.

Most concerning is that the condition is more frequent than most people believe. According to the American Psychiatric Association, approximately 3-4% of the population is afflicted with the condition. If you work in an office with 250 people, these statistics say that 8 to 10 of your co-workers have schizotypal personality disorder.

There have been articles written that suggest that Columbine attacker Dylan Klebold was afflicted with STPD, and shortly after the Aurora Cinemark attack James Eagan Holmes was diagnosed with the same condition.

To date at the time of this writing, the Food and Drug Administration (FDA) has not approved any medication to treat the condition of STPD. But since the condition seems to have multiple other afflictions that stimulate it, medical professionals use a variety of those drugs to treat the condition. This is where you start to read about people who are taking a "medical cocktail" of pills to deal with multiple conditions. Unfortunately, some of these drugs do not work in harmony and can cause discomforting side effects. At this point, you can understand the challenges of getting person with a condition like STPD to take their medicines regularly. Provided they are willing to take their medicines to function regularly in society, the payoff is that they have to deal with a constant state of nausea, vomiting, headaches or any number of terrible side effects that may be triggered from the volume of drugs in their system. It's a terrible Catch-22 for the person, their family and the professionals seeking to help them.

The good news is that psychotherapy has been shown to improve the conditions of many people with STPD over time. Through talk therapy, people can be "convinced" of the realities of the world; that people can be trusted and meaningful relationships can be formed. Positive encouragement seems to be a successful way of producing long-term results to fight STPD, and opportunities to succeed can only do well for the person. Developing strong bonds through social support are effective and they work. It is important that we as a community understand this, because it is the community that is going to be the key factor in providing this support base. Parents and other family members must live this life with the person everyday, and outside parties can be the difference maker in creating these strong bonds and close-knit groups.

Paranoid Schizophrenia

By all accounts, Jared Lee Loughner seemed to have had a nurturing upbringing; The only child of working parents, the Loughner family were described by neighbors as pleasant but also very private. For Jared, his early years seem to be uneventful for the most part. There were no reports or concerns of abuse or dysfunction. He had friends during his childhood, and even into high school. It was reported that he had a girlfriend during his time in high school, who later described Loughner as very sweet and incapable of violence.

As he reached young adulthood, however, Loughner became more reserved and introverted from social interaction. By his senior year in high school, Loughner had decided to drop out when he turned 18-years-old. The year was 2006. People began to take notice to significant changes in Loughner's behavioral personality; friends described him as erratic in his speaking, his thought processes became more and more irrational and he was known to randomly ask question after question that had no relevance to the conversation at the time. During this time, Loughner attended a local community college. While there he had multiple incidents with community college police. All incidents were connected with Loughner disrupting classroom activities and campus operations, to include interrupting quiet study areas. The disruptions had become so obvious and concerning that the community college had Loughner suspended from the school. He was notified that he could return if he agreed to adhere to a strict mandate of regulations that they outlined for him. Lastly, the college required that Loughner go through a series of mental health evaluations by medical professionals prior to returning to academia. Lougher did not honor the requests; he never visited a mental health professional and he never returned to the community college.

During this time period, it was reported that Jared Lee Loughner had an obsession with conspiracy theories. Later investigations revealed that he closely followed the conspiracies centered on mind control initiatives that were allegedly created by the federal government. It was also during this time that Loughner became more obsessed with finding answers to these conspiracies. To find those answers, Loughner began to follow up with political leaders. Loughner attempted to question Congresswoman Gabrielle Giffords on these issues in 2007 during a town hall meeting of sorts. A friend of Loughner's later stated that Loughner was angry at the congresswoman for how he felt she treated him during the questioning. According to corroborative sources, Loughner would become incensed at the mention of politicians, viewing them as part of the grand governmental conspiracy that he had in his mind.

On January 8, 2011, Jared Lee Loughner attended a public forum in Tucson, Arizona where Congresswoman Gabrielle Giffords was giving a speech to her constituents. Armed with a Glock 9mm pistol, Loughner began a shooting spree at 10:10 a.m. During the attack, 13 people were injured, including Congresswoman Giffords who was critically injured when she was hit in the head. Six people died in the assault. The youngest was 9-year-old Christina Taylor-Green.

Shortly after his arrest, Loughner went through a battery of psychological evaluations to determine mental stability to stand trial for his crimes and medical evaluations diagnosed Loughner with paranoid schizophrenia. It was also later determined by the courts that Loughner, despite this mental condition, was fit to stand trial. For the crimes committed on January 8, 2011, Jared Lee Loughner is serving the rest of his life plus an additional 140 years in prison.

Of all of the mental health conditions previously discussed, the vast majority of mental health professionals will concede that the one most serious to a person is that of paranoid schizophrenia. This severe brain disorder makes it very difficult for a person to interpret reality with the same sense of normalcy that most people do. The manifestations of the person could present themselves in any number of ways to include delusions, hallucinations or thinking and behavior that is extremely distorted or confused. Paranoid schizophrenia is a sub-category of the schizophrenia class. In many cases, to include Jared Lee Loughner's, the individual will not show symptoms of the condition until early adulthood. Most important, it is a condition that is chronic and never goes away. Individuals who receive treatment through therapy and/or medication may see the symptoms recede, but they will return if the treatment stops. The impact on the individual, the family, friends and medical staff is enormous for treating a person with the condition, but the effort is worthwhile. People who have the affliction and are regularly treated have been known to lead productive and positive lives. Sadly, those who go untreated can develop symptoms of depression, suicidal thoughts and desires, or may find themselves in a situation where they cannot function in society. This has often led to unemployment, homelessness and prison. In the most extreme, unusual example, someone like Jared Lee Loughner will manifest.

In addition to Loughner, schizophrenia in some fashion has presented itself in other killers: John Hinckley Jr., the individual who shot President Ronald Reagan; Mark David Chapman, the individual who shot and killed musician John Lennon; David Berkowitz, the famed "Son of Sam" serial killer from the 1970's; Ed Gein, the serial killer who was to be the inspiration for the character "Norman Bates" in Alfred Hitchcock's *Psycho*; Richard Chase, the serial killer known as the "Vampire of Sacramento" for drinking his victim's blood; and Daniel Gonzalez, who killed four people in 2009 after being inspired to do so by the "Nightmare on Elm Street" film series. All of these individuals were diagnosed schizophrenic or paranoid schizophrenic.

Conclusion

I am not a mental health professional. I have not been trained to diagnose a condition, recommend treatment, or follow up with additional sessions to monitor the patient for improvement. I cannot write prescriptions for medication, or make recommendations about what practices in the medical community are best for an individual.

But that doesn't mean that I can't read about the symptoms that are associated with mental illness. It doesn't mean that I can't determine if someone is showing signs of those symptoms. I'm not qualified to set a broken arm or surgically repair one, but I know one when I see it and I am perfectly within my expertise as a layperson to advise that the injured person should seek out medical help.

That's what we're doing here: I want to expose you to the definitions of mental health issues that are commonly associated with threat-related activity.

It is important that you do not focus heavily on the mental health portion of this book, but understand rather that this very basic information is there for you to reference should you need it. Mental Health professionals spend their entire careers analyzing, assessing, diagnosing and treating conditions in patients, and they still get it wrong. You and I are not qualified to do what they do, but we can help them by being the "eyes and ears" to recognize conditions that they can treat. In fact, mental health professionals are relying on us to do so, as they cannot be everywhere to identify conditions in others. Hopefully, this overview will lend some help to doing just that.

As I have mentioned before, and will again, the vast majority of people who are afflicted with mental health symptoms are not violent people. It is already a terribly difficult road that these people and their families are forced to walk, and I do not want to add to the burden that they carry. As unlikely as it is that they will take on a violent behavior, it is even more remote to assume that they are violent if they are receiving treatment of some kind. These individuals who recognize the conditions in themselves, and still find a way to push through the clouds to get help.... They should be commended for what they do. There are few things more difficult than for a person to look him/herself in the mirror and identify the shortcomings. When that shortcoming is something that is still considered taboo and still not socially accepted, it is a brave thing that these people do to get help. It is our responsibility to encourage others that mental health is completely appropriate and not a condition to be ashamed.

The information that we have reviewed in this first section constitutes the "Observe" portion of OA^2® and is the most voluminous of the three. As you have probably determined, it is a lot to absorb. Do I expect that you'll remember all of this after simply reading it? Of course not! I have actively studied this material for over ten years in a practical capacity in federal law enforcement as well as in the highest levels of academia. This is not the kind of material that is processed and understood overnight. It takes time to internalize it, and to make behavioral observation a way of life. In addition, it is human nature to forget most things that we review until we continually study and practice it.

And that's what you should be doing. With this book, you have the means to revisit the information in it. If you are reading this material, then chances are that you have the ability to return to it and read it again…. and you should. The more you study the material, the more familiar you will become with identifying these indicators in your day-to-day lives. Observation is already a skill that you have learned anyway, and this information will benefit you in any and all apsects of what you do.

The behavioral indicators that you have reviewed comprise a list (a very important list) of conditions that you should be watchful for in friends, family, co-workers, even strangers. You might even see some in yourself. Hopefully, you will remember the condition when you observe it and you can report it to someone who can help.

Which brings us to the next topic. When you do observe these conditions in others, what do you do? To whom do you report it? Maybe you have already seen or heard things in the past that give you reason for concern, and you attempted to notify an agency or a professional. The next section will outline a recommended approach to where to go next. Unfortunately, our national community lacks a behavioral report network to address these conditions, and as you read on, you will see that this is one of the main reasons so much violence persists. We haven't trained our community to identify the "fire," and we haven't set up the programs to get the "fire department" involved. The disconnect that exists between the everyday concerned citizen and the mental health professionals is both alarming and in huge need of adjustment.

The system that I outline is not perfect, but it is a foundation to create a streamlined way of reporting and acting on behavioral concerns if our communities adopt it. The next step in the process is to "assess" the legitimate level of danger that a person may pose, and that assessment will help to decide the next course of proactive measures to keep our communities safe.

II: ASSESS

26. Sometimes You Can't Do Anything

So I am sure that by now you have a multitude of questions, and your head is probably spinning from all the information you've read. You may feel a bit overwhelmed, being newly hyper-sensitive to the way people are acting around you. There is nothing wrong with any of this. Let's start with baby-steps, and the best way to do that is to figure out what to do next.

The first thing to understand is that there are going to be times when you can't do anything. Let me repeat that: there are going to be times that you might be exposed to something and there's not going to be anything you can do about it. Even recently I have seen concerning behavior in others and there was nothing I could do to help resolve the situation.

I recently received an online message from a "fan," or rather, my wife received it. As she was filtering through the messages of our business, this message stood out as unusual. It was approximately 17 pages in length, erratic in verbiage and referencing many of the things that we have reviewed in the previous chapters (conspiracy theories, paranoia and delusion to name a few). My wife was very concerned with the message, as it was addressed to me. In closing, the writer was seeking affirmation from me that his beliefs were legitimate. The writer had left his name, explained that he lived in California and his personal cell phone number that had an area code of the California area.

"What are we going to do?" my wife asked me.

I looked at her, a bit perplexed. "What do you mean?" I asked.

"I mean, what are we gong to do about this person who has contacted you and clearly has something wrong with him?" she responded a bid acidly.

I thought about it for a moment. I realized that the two of us had become so engrossed in discussing the topic of community interventions with concerning behavior, that the most fundamental rule had never been addressed:

Sometimes you can't do anything.

What could we have done, realistically? We didn't know this person who contacted us, so I didn't have any way to contact any relatives or friends of his; he never threatened us or said anything that implied that something harmful was going to happen, so there was no need to notify law enforcement; although his writing was erratic, showed evidence to suggest unclear thinking, this was not anything illegal. The only way to intervene in this person's life was to contact him, and that was the last thing I was going to do. I am not a counselor, and I was not going to interact with a stranger with these kinds of behavioral symptoms. Nothing good would come of that for my family or for the individual.

What I want to make clear with this story is that I believe that you have the ability to observe, assess and act on behavioral conditions in your community. In the world that you interact, be that school, work or your social life, but as you move away from that familiar ground you will have less and less resources to assist with a condition in a proactive manner.

That's why it is so important that as many people embrace proactive interventions. Where I wasn't able to do much for the person who contacted me from California, hopefully someone closer to him could do something for him.

So when can you, should you, do something? Here's a scenario: you have been asked by one of your close friends if you could pick up her 6th grade daughter from school when you go to get your own daughter, also a 6th grader. Both girls are on the same basketball travelling team, and they both have practice after school. Your friend will pick them both up from practice and drop your daughter off if you agree to take them to practice, to which you agree. If you're a parent in the 21st Century, situations like this are more common than not.

As you are driving the girls to practice, you hear them talking about a boy in their class. They start telling you about how the boy is actually a very good student, and active in some after-school activities. He's not athletic, but he is very bright and has a keen interest in science. Then the subject becomes darker and they mention that the boy told several friends who attend school that he was talking with them online about attacking a teacher. At first the other kids didn't take it seriously, but then he began mentioning plans that he has outlined and even became upset when the other kids told him that he wasn't serious.

So what would you do about this? Let's assume that you don't know this boy or his family, where would you go with this information? Would you contact the school directly, or would you go to law enforcement? Would you attempt to contact the teacher who is being threatened? Or would you act like you hadn't heard anything.

This is a huge problem with our society today. We really don't have a credible system to report these kinds of conditions. It's almost like we have taken on a mindset that reflects a "cross that bridge when I come to it" mentality. In contrast, let's return to the analogy of a fire. Do we have a means to identify a fire? Many. We have fire alarms that activate when it detects heat signatures and temperature increases. Those alarms contact multiple places; they notify whoever is near with loud sirens and flashing lights; they activate a sprinkler system; they call the fire department. There is a set series of parameters that are always the same, no matter what building you are in in the United States. In addition, if you need to act on a fire, possibly by pulling an alarm or using a fire extinguisher, all of those tools work in conjunction with the system in place. It's an absolutely fantastic, streamlined service.

But in matters of threat-related violence, we're all over the place. Granted this is not dealing with inanimate objects that have no rights and feelings... like a building on fire. But reporting concerning behavior of someone is not a violation of his or her rights or privileges. People do not have the right to say certain things and entice concern with their behavior on the grounds that it is their civil liberties and freedom to do so if they wish. As such, it is imperative that we start creating programs on a national scale that allow a concerned community to notify professionals of concerning behavior in others if it is so identified.

But what can we do now? Who can you notify if you are part of something today, in the real world? If we return to the scenario with the girls in the car, the recommendation is to notify the school's guidance counselor IMMEDIATELY. In matter of threat-related violence, the boy who is suspect has had multiple people corroborate what he has said that he plans to do. That is more than enough to begin the next phase of OA²®: Assessment. Specifically, a behavioral assessment. This is a determination into the level of danger that an individual presents to another individual or the community. In order to determine this level of danger, we need to measure the severity of the threat (or threats), the frequency of the threats (how often they occur), and the likelihood that an individual is capable of carrying out such an attack. In order to get that information, we need to be asking some questions and getting some information on the person.

Most of us will never need to conduct a behavioral assessment of an individual; you will likely do no more than identify and notify the appropriate people of a behavioral condition from here on out. The truth is, the vast majority of us will want to say something and step back while letting other people handle it. That is not a bad thing. In fact that is exactly what you should do. This includes not speaking of a report you made to other people in the community or letting your curiosity get the better of you by trying to follow-up on what the outcome was on your concerns.

But I also have to assume that if you are reading this book, then you may very well be one of those individuals who could be someone who might have to deal with something like this directly. As such, I will provide recommendations on where to go next. Also, it is always a good thing for the person reporting the concern to have a clear understanding of how the procedure works (or at least should work). For now, we're going to work a little backwards and focus on the best way to assess a report of someone's concerning behavior and how it can be determined if the individual is a danger to the community or himself/herself. We're going to assume that the information has reached the appropriate person or people to address the situation, and we're further going to assume that you are that person who is assessing the situation. You may very well be in that position at work right now: if you are a guidance counselor, a teacher, a human resources representative, a supervisor, a volunteer, an employee with a church, a law enforcement officer, a medical technician…. All of these positions are certainly capable of assessing a behavior, gathering more information and determining the best course of action. After we review this section, we're going to move into what action needs to be taken and then outline my recommendations on how to set up your respective organization to address threat-related behavior in a streamlined, efficient manner. For now, lets get into the fundamentals of assessment: the right way, the wrong way, what to look for, what to avoid, and what to ask.

One of my earliest and fondest memories growing up was of my father and his love for the great American pastime of baseball. As an only child, I didn't need to vie for the attention of my parents, so I found myself in my father's company frequently. Whether he wanted me riding coattails as much as I did is for him to disclose, but I tended to follow him at every opportunity. Sometimes it was because I was bored, sometimes I was just curious with what he was doing. Most of the time, I just wanted to be around him. I have since learned from being a father myself, parents can sometimes find difficulty with common-ground topics to discuss with their children, especially when our kids monopolize as much of a parent's time as I monopolized my dad's. There was more than one occasion that on our trips to the grocery store, the local hardware shop or just running errands that I would pepper my father with any number of questions just to stimulate a discussion. It was during this time that my dad would turn the topic of conversation to baseball. He knew it well, and it was something that we could both understand and discuss.

Although our passion for the game is equal, the excitement for the game comes from very different reasons. For me, I have always enjoyed the thrill of seeing a deep fly homerun shot out of the ballpark, a diving catch in the outfield, and the duels between great pitchers and master hitters. I have been known to record more than my share of a game or two and fast-forward to the "good parts." My father is much more methodical, an analyst and student of the game. As a child, he and his friends would spend much of their time playing baseball, watching games or playing the popular "APBA" baseball card-and-dice game, a precursor of sorts to the modern day fantasy sports. APBA instilled in him the importance of studying and buying into to those concepts that would later be known as "sabermetrics." Even today, he pours over the statistics of the hitter's percentage against a pitcher, the likelihood of on-base percentage of a newly signed player, and the ever-important probability that a prospect offers with RISP ("runners in scoring position") when he bats. He is fascinated with a pitcher's ERA ("earned run average") and even breaks these numbers down further by analyzing them during the time of the season the ballplayer is playing the game. For my father, it has always been about ensuring that his baseball team is playing the "right" players, not necessarily the "best" ones. I have every confidence that he could build a damn good baseball team just from all of the statistics that he has going through his head and how those numbers measure against different scenarios. As for me and numbers in baseball, I could care less. I just want to hear the cheering of the crowd, the crack of the bat, the homerun in the books.

None of this surprises me about my father, because analysis is his thing. A civilian employee working for the federal government for his entire career, he has been exposed to a professional lifestyle that trains its employees to embrace this methodology. Anyone who has been in a position with the government, like my father, will understand where I am going with this. A garden-variety example of this is the "matrix" model, a popular tool for helping to find an answer. The federal government loves their matrix models.

The matrix model is a scale of sorts that can give an answer to a problem based on two variables that are presented. For example, if a person wanted to measure the seriousness of a threat that was reported, the model may look something like this:

SEVERITY

		Minor (1)	Negligible (2)	Marginal (3)	Critical (4)	Catastrophic (5)
L I K E L I H O O D	Frequent (5)					
	Probable (4)					
	Occasional (3)					
	Remote (2)					
	Improbable (1)					

In the model, we see that two variables have been presented: The "severity" of the threat, and the "likelihood" of the success of the threat. If we throw some information in here, we can use this matrix. Let's say the threat went as follows, and was legitimate:

"It has been reported that there is an individual who wants to destroy a small town with a self-designed nuclear weapon. The individual who wants to do this is working alone on the project, has unfettered access to depleted uranium, and is well-trained in nuclear weapons to include their design, construction and activation."

With this information, there is no doubt that the threat is a serious one. Using the paradigm graph, we could easily assume that the likelihood of success was at the very least a "4" or "Probable." The severity of a threat could definitely meet a "5" or "Catastrophic" criteria. From these two factors, the danger level on the paradigm meets a high risk, as indicated by the hatched box area in the matrix.

From an analytical standpoint, the matrix worked to perfection. The government trains people in things like matrix models because it meets the criteria for a large group of employees to have access to a means of measuring a situation and addressing it.

But lets throw a wrench in the program. Let's say that we send our federal agents out to meet our nuclear device builder, and when they reach his location, they find that he is a quadriplegic who has no ability to move without the assistance of others. He is a gifted scientist with all the brilliance to create such a weapon, and his physical state has made him disgruntled to the world. He wants to only lash out at society.

Does this scenario still hold the same credibility on the paradigm that it once did? Is the severity of the threat still the same? Possibly. Is the likelihood of success still high? Unlikely. It has probably dropped down to about a "1" or maybe a "2," thereby throwing the concern of attack to an almost improbable or "Remote" level, making the risk low, as indicated by the diagonal lines in the matrix.

So what is my point with all of this? What am I getting at by bringing up my father, baseball and nuclear weapons, and what does any of this have to do with threat-related behavior?

It goes like this: much of the material that you have studied in this book has been analyzed at length by many people, to include federal law enforcement personnel. In many cases, people have attempted to articulate a method to measure the level of danger that a person presents to a community, another individual, or themselves based on a measurement system like the matrix model example. I am here to tell you that, when it comes to assessing threat-related behavior, there is no better measurement than a case-by-case basis of each individual situation. Throw the models, the graphs, and the charts out the window. If you are looking for a graph to tell you what to do next, you will not find it here. Sorry, Dad.

27. The Right Questions to Ask: The Behavioral Questionnaire

From here on out, we're going to assume that yours is a position that requires some follow-up review on a report of concerning be-havior. In order to prepare a quality assessment of the person, you need to get some questions answered. The more of these questions that you answer, the better your chances are of determining if the person poses a serious threat or not.

These questions look to provide into the following:

- An individual's motives/goals
- Communications that have suggested an attack
- Insight into threat-related behavior
- The likelihood of a successful attack
- Inappropriate interests that the individual may have
- Symptoms of suffering that the individual may be exhibiting
- Concern of others
- Support group information and contact

Do some of these things look familiar to you? I'm sure they do. When you look at this list, you should see the correlation between this infor-mation and the indicators that you read about in the previous section. Most important, the objective of obtaining this information is two-fold: 1) prevent the possibility of some kind of attack or rampage violence and 2) get the person who is suspect help if they need it. Notice, a portion of information that is being collected is focused on the person's individual needs for help. Identifying whether or not the person is suffering, what kind of support group that he/she has, etc…. These things are so very important for helping someone in need of it. If you so choose to use this information for prosecutorial purposes, that is your decision. But from my professional experience, the long-term goal of getting someone help is much more effective at stopping violence in the community, than simply working to have them incarcerated.

The questions themselves provide a foundation for gathering information on the individual. Hopefully, you will have a great deal of access to the person and those close to him/her to answer these questions.

What are the individual's motives or goals?

The motivation of a potential attacker is probably the single best piece of information that you can find. The individual's personal motivation is the basis for his/her concerning behavior. It may only be one thing that has suddenly happened, or it could be a condition that has gone on for a long time. Many individuals who target the politicians have done so after being incensed for years over the lawmakers' stance on topics, and their continued efforts to support that stance. In cases like these, the motivation is a single person, but the condition that motivated an attack came from a long period where rage and angst grew over time.

One other point to make about motivation: it may not be apparent during a question and answer session. You may have to draw conclusions on the motivation of the person based on what they have said in an interview without directly coming out and stating their incentive for violence.

What kinds of communication have been made or attempted from the individual that suggest an idea or intention to attack a person or a location?

In this day of online social networking and online interaction, this has become a major hub for threat-related communication. It is also very difficult to get that information to the appropriate people to address. Unless the person is communicating with someone whom they know personally and are affiliated in the same localized community (such as an office or a school), how does a communicated threat get to a person who can help? Think about it. An individual goes online anonymously in the middle of the night, makes some cryptic statements that he/she is going to attack their school in the morning, and then signs off. How can we police that, or at least report it. By law, many online services have a reporting system of some kind, but then they would need to track down the point of origin of the message, and then contact the local law enforcement affiliate with their concerns. Make no mistake, online services do the best that they can, but these kinds of communications happen more than most online organizations care to admit. And if you think that the scenario that I gave is an unrealistic one, take a look at Jeffrey Weise, the 16-year-old who attacked the Red Lake Indian Reservation and killed nine people. Hours before the attack, Weise was online verbalizing his intentions for rampage violence in the coming hours. It is unknown whether much was done about the threats, but by the time it would have taken to track down Weise, it still would have likely been too late.

This is why it is extremely important to gain as much information on a person's communications, from any and all sources. When addressing the person, ask them about their online interaction, who they communicate with; do they play social online games and interact with others? Try to discern from other people what the individual's communication preferences are. When I was an investigator, I saw a lot of agents and officers' miss key points in interviews because they pigeonholed their questions to personal communications and interactions, and failed to focus on the life of the person in cyberspace. It's a much bigger world than it has ever been and you need to make sure all the boundaries are covered.

What has the individual been involved with that could be considered "threat-related" or "attack-related" behavior?

It almost goes without saying; this is a question that could deliver a variety of answers. At this point it is the responsibility of the interviewer to "chart the course" of the interview. A person may admit to studying how to build homemade bombs, or they may think that the video games they are playing are a stimulant for threat-related behavior. Any expert in interviewing will say that the first rule of an interview is to ask open-ended questions like these, as they will provide information that would have needed to be asked otherwise. But at the same time, open-ended questions like these need to be "controlled" or kept on track so that the person being questioned does not go off on a tangent or is not misunderstood.

Does the individual have the mental stability and/or the physical ability to carry out an attack of some kind? This would include conception, planning and execution?

This is a question that is a necessary one, but also must be handled carefully. It is important that the person being questioned does not "diagnose" a condition unless that person is a medical professional. It is highly unlikely that such a professional will make such a claim, as this would be a violation of confidentiality agreements between a patient and a provider. It is okay if a person or someone affiliated as a guardian can confirm that the individual has been diagnosed with a condition. It is equally fine to document their confirmation. Additionally, it is important to document the physical conditions of the individual in question. Like a mental condition there is absolutely no justification in diagnosing an individuals physical ability or handicap that he/she displays. As I have pointed out many times already, unless you are qualified to make a diagnosis, you should not. If you meet with a person in a wheelchair, you are not in your right to suggest that they suffer from a spinal injury that has rendered their legs obsolete. However, if they volunteer the reason for their condition, you should document what they told you. Is it important to document your physical observations of a person you are questioning? Absolutely! Their physical traits and characteristics could be a strong indicator for how or why they may or may not be a threat to others.

Has the individual shown an inappropriate interest in things that may suggest concerning behavior?

Inappropriate interests are some of those things that have been covered with both early indicators and danger indicators; things such as a person's involvement with a certain organization, his/her interest in violence to an unhealthy level, and/or an obsession with conspiracy theory-type headlines. Obviously, this is another open-ended question that could result in any variety of answers that would need to be vetted on a case-by-case basis.

Are there signs/symptoms that suggest that the subject is feeling a sense of despair and/or hopelessness? Or has the subject been the victim to some kind of persecution, such as bullying or prolonged harassment by a group or individual?

Like other medically based questions this needs to be handled carefully. There is certainly nothing wrong with asking the question, as the answer could simply be "Yes." But if the individual is willing to discuss the topic, then they will probably open up at length. Additionally, this is not suggesting that if it is a third-party being asked about someone that the person being asked is diagnosing a condition, but rather they are responding to a question based on their own observations. Whatever the case, if there is any evidence suggesting that the individual in question is experiencing any of these symptoms, then it is highly recommended that the interviewer follow up with mental health providers immediately to get the individual in question some kind of help. It is equally important to recognize that there could be a possibility (and even a danger) of the individual being bullied by classmates, co-workers or other people in the community. Previous attackers noted bullying as a motivation for their attacks against others, and it is important to recognize this as soon as possible to work to avoid it manifesting into something dangerous.

Are there other people who are concerned with the person's behavior?

One major point to assessing a possible threat is corroboration. It is entirely possible that there was a misunderstanding or miscommunication as it pertains to the individual. In addition, there is also a possibility that the individual is being victimized by someone else who is holding a grudge or animosity toward him or her. As such, the individual has had an "anonymous" report sent in on him or her fabricating a bogus threatening condition. In order to better determine a person's desire to cause harm or their genuine innocence, some of the best sources for this information are corroborative interviews, or speaking with other people who can confirm or refute an issue about the person. This question helps to separate those cases into the serious/non-serious.

Is there a sense of consistency with the story that the individual is providing to articulate the behavior? In other words, does the story add up?

As we have stated earlier, it is easier to remember the truth than remember a falsehood. If you ask a person the same question on a situation that they are remembering, chances are that they are telling the truth if the story is told the same way each time they have to tell it. If you are getting different answers about threat-related behavior that they are being accused of, then there is some legitimacy that you may need to continue to monitor the individual and the situation.

What kind of support base does the person have? Family? Friends? Is it a strong support group?

This may be the case more in schools than in a workplace, but one of the most important factors in stopping rampage violence is by getting the person in question involved with a support group. That starts with family and friends. The logical person to do this would be the one who is listed as an emergency contact. Too often, I have heard cases where the business or school has put the onus of responsibility for help on the person in question, and they do so because of the fear of legal repercussion that could come from contacting an outside source. This is totally unacceptable; these people need to be contacted to help this individual.

Has the individual had a sudden, drastic change in his/her life that has taken a toll on the person?

Remember: 98% of those individuals who have committed rampage violence have had a major, negative change in their life or a series of changes in a short amount of time. There is simply no higher indicator that a person can provide to suggest that a future threatening action may occur. Next to determining a person's motivation for violence, this must be addressed. The correlation between changing conditions and sudden, seemingly impulsive violence cannot be ignored.

These questions are not meant to make you an expert in investigative techniques or train you to be an expert interviewer. Interviewing is a true talent, one that is cultivated and bettered through practice. In much the same way as professional athletes hone their athletic gifts, abilities and techniques through practice, gameplay and a modernized system of betterment, so do interviewers. Prestigious institutions like the John J. Reid School for Interviewing and Interrogation have studied and trained experts in this discipline with the most advanced and current research in effective interview processes.

But these questions can provide you with a foundation of what to look for in an individual. Do you need to sit down with the person and go through each one, checking the box as you proceed? No. If the opportunity presents itself, by all means, ask away. This is a list of the things that you are looking for, which you may be able to piece together based on facts you know or have, things people have reported, and information that has been provided from the subject in question or corroborative interviews.

Whoever is asking these questions and compiling this information is doing so from a place that has been tasked to receive it, and handle it with the strictest confidence. This location, which I call the "nexus," is where all the reports and documentation are consolidated into a single case report. These questions are part of that report.

So what is the best way to consolidate this information? I can almost guarantee that information on someone who is considering an attack will not come in all at once, or in a short time. The studies have shown that rampage violence is not based on sudden, impulsive acts, so we can assume that their condition is manifesting over a long period of time. As such, we can also assume that their behavioral indicators will be evident over an equally long period. Your nexus may only receive reporters of concern randomly.... People move on in their careers; it's important to have a place where this information can be maintained. It is also important to have a series of documents to outline the information.

28. The Right Things To Remember: The Behavioral Worksheet

One of the most common accusations against law enforcement today is that the officer or officers base their targets for arrests on "profiling" an individual rather than the crime itself. Under these circumstances, profiling refers to conditions based on a person's physical characteristics and it is these characteristics that law enforcement supposedly use to identify a target for interest for arrest. Although I will not contest that this has not happened in the past, I am very confident that the vast majority of law enforcement personnel arrest an individual based on the suspect's actions rather than their appearance.

From the perspective of this book, we will use the term "profiling" from now on in the way it was meant to be used in its original definition: we will focus on profiling from a behavioral aspect, not based on physical characteristics.

In Appendix B is a document called the "Behavioral Assessment Worksheet." The point of the worksheet is to provide a centralized record of all reports on the individual. It is also a format to draw a picture of the whole person. It is important that every person is given the benefit of the doubt in matters of behavioral assessments, and in order to do so it is necessary to understand the "complete" individual.

Obviously, this is my personal template; it can be adjusted to meet the needs of your respective business, school or organization. For example, there is a section that outlines an individual's possible military service. This would be unnecessary information for a guidance counselor at a middle school to collect.

Not every question on the template will be answered. It's important to develop as much of an assessment on a subject as possible, and the more information that can be compiled the better. But some people don't have as much in their background as others, so they will not have much information in their assessment. Because of the variety of questions that the assessment template covers, it can be adjusted to the needs of a specific party. A local law enforcement agency that has no previous behavioral assessment material, for example, may find this entire document useful. Additionally, that law enforcement unit would have more access to the information on the worksheet than a human resources manager at a private corporation.

The important thing is that the behavioral worksheet provides a group with a means to begin a documented case report on issues of concern. It also outlines a template to tailor a unique document system for each location.

Some behavioral issues that should be given special attention at any time during the assessment phase include the following:

• Maturity/immaturity - Does the individual show maturity or do they lack an understanding or willingness to accept the seriousness of the situation?
• Emotional adaptability/adjustment – Is the individual able to cope with changes that could create emotional stress, or is the person unable to emotionally deal?
• Working with others - Does the person have difficulty maintaining a professional relationship with others, to the point that peers ostracize them and are not comfortable with joint projects or assignments?
• Cultural sensitivity – Does the person assume without basis that every aspect of social interaction toward him or her is meant as a personal affront to their cultural background?
• Rigidity/stubbornness – Does the person lack an ability to compromise on any situation, even when the facts are stacked against him/her?
• Self-discipline – Does the person fail to control him or herself in any forum, be it public or private?
• Initiative/perseverance – Does the person have the willingness to see something through to completion, and if so, is his or her perseverance negatively motivated?
• Self-confidence – While there is nothing wrong with being confident

in one's actions, does this person show over-confidence suggesting a personality that believes that he/she is superior to everyone else?
• Assertion v. aggression – Does the person understand the difference between having a disagreement and becoming violent in nature?
• Conscientiousness - Is the individual meticulous with his/her planning abilities and coordination of an operation?
• Ownership and honesty – Does the person understand the concepts of integrity and accountability for his/her personal actions and/or statements?

The Ugly Truth – I don't question the sincerity of businesses and schools when it comes to their desire to keep their co-workers and students safe. But I do question the priority that these institutions place on protecting their people from rampage violence. If the seriousness of safety were as high as we were made to believe, we would have the equivalent of active shooter drills, training in proactive intervention methods, and courses to identify, protect and defend against rampage violence in something more than a one-hour automated presentation (a popular means of training in most businesses and the federal government).

The ugly truth is that the best reason a business, an organization or a school has for documenting behavioral issues in this format is due diligence. If/when an attack happens, there are going to be all kinds of legal action when the dust settles. For this reason alone, most companies will want to make every effort to show that they documented, followed through and made every attempt to get help for the attacker (if they are affiliated with the person in some way). On the flipside, if it is proven that the business had opportunities to assist a person who would later become a violent threat and chose not to help, the liability could fall heavily on the organization.

Whether it is due diligence or perhaps genuine concern for doing anything and everything possible to make a safe environment.... I don't care. In both instances, a behavioral makeup on an individual with concerning behavior works the same; through a series of questions, corroborative interviews with friends and loved-ones, and a behavioral assessment worksheet to create a case report on the "whole person."

Ultimately, the goal is to establish a means to "measure" the individual's level of danger. At the beginning of the section we discussed that there no would not be a graph, chart or matrix to measure your danger levels, but that does not mean that we can't create something to help with this. If you receive 10 reports of threats by different sources on the same person over a two year period, then this assessment system will help track that and determine the level of danger better than any other way to do it. But in order for it to work, it has to be established.

And once you have a realistic issue, what do you do then?

III: ACT

29. The Behavioral Action Team

I have never been a fan of those situations that require a group of individuals to form a committee in order to accomplish an objective. Any situation that can create an environment of "groupthink" can have serious negative impacts. I have been a part of many, many committees in my day, as I am sure that you have as well. I have been on committees that have been responsible for fundraisers at my children's school and I have been a part of committees that planned out the security measures for the G-8 Summit at Camp David in 2012. I have seen people become red-faced with anger over what the price of cookies being sold at the bake sale should be, and I have seen local politicians tossing paper airplanes back and forth to each other like children while someone was trying to provide them a safety briefing. I once had a co-worker in the U.S. Coast Guard tell me of a two-star admiral who pounded his fists on a meeting table like a five-year-old because he was not being authorized a fleet of 110-foot Coast Guard ships for his retirement ceremony. This was all during his meeting with the committee who was assigned to prepare the event.

Yes, I have had my share of committees. Despite my disdain for them though I will concede that committees, for the most part, serve a valid series of purposes. Having been on enough I can attest to their validity as being both worthwhile and important. In short, they are a necessary evil for accomplishing a task.

When it comes to assessing and acting on threat-related behavior in individuals, committees are not only important, they are vitally essential. That is the first step in the "action" phase, assuring that your organization or school has a committee to address the next steps. It further should be affiliated with the appropriate representation.

No person, no matter who they are or what position of authority they hold, should be solely responsible for acting on a decision like how to proactively respond to threat-related behavior in an individual. During my time with the U.S. Secret Service, I investigated dozens of cases involving threat-related behavior toward people that the agency was mandated to protect. I would visit with individuals who were incarcerated, with others who were relegated to the care of mental health providers, and with teenagers who sent messages on social media to strangers (wrongfully assuming that the anonymity of the internet would keep them from being found). In every single case, no matter the condition, I always worked with at least one other agent on the case in some fashion and we constantly kept our supervisor AND our headquarters division of the Protective Investigations and Assessment Division (PIAD) appraised of our status. Through all of those branches, we determined the next best course of action in every, single case. As the case agent, I was responsible for overseeing the execution of the action that was decided on.

But you don't have access to a PIAD, and you likely don't have a supervisor or an associate who is highly trained in threat-related behavior. In addition, it is almost certain that you don't have the backing and support of a major federal law enforcement agency to help you with your situation. But you still have the possibility of a threat; that hasn't changed. So what do you do?

This is the function of a Behavioral Action Team or "BAT." Having experienced a healthy background at military college, in the military and with law enforcement, I can say that I have had a great deal of experience with acronyms, as they are used frequently in all of these respective programs. They are typically easy to understand and, more importantly, easy to remember. For the sake of the reading, I will use "BAT" from here on out. I have seen similar programs or committees called "Threat Assessment Team," "Behavioral Observation and Assessment Team," and "Threat Investigation Team," all of which have their own (sometimes colorful) acronym to describe themselves. Ultimately, they all serve the same purpose: a group of individuals who oversee a program confidentially, with the goal of monitoring a condition or situation that could become dangerous if not properly addressed, and determining the best course of prompt action to stop the danger from occurring. There are many of these types of groups that are mandated by businesses and schools. We have addressed some of these earlier in the reading. As we discussed earlier, the Commonwealth of Virginia made it state law that public universities and colleges support some kind threat-assessment program to address these conditions. As such, other programs have begun to pop up in other schools and even in businesses.

But there are a few problems with these. From my personal research, I have yet to see any of these programs make a dedicated effort to train the community on a much-needed large scale. Like the one-hour PowerPoint presentation that is forwarded as "training" to public and private sector employees, these threat-assessment teams sit by idly and wait for a report to come in. This comes back to the original issue: a gross failure in notifying the public of what to identify as threat-related behavior. Am I suggesting that, even in college, high school, and perhaps as far back as middle or elementary school, we need to be training our children in identifying these conditions? Yes, I absolutely am. These are dangerous conditions, and frankly they begin to manifest early in person's growth. The sad fact is that, just as our children are our greatest priority for keeping safe, they are also probably some of the best sources to indicators of rampage violence. They must be educated in identifying threat indicators in others, just like we educate them to avoid drugs, to the issues of youth pregnancy and pre-marital sex, and to the dangers of potential child predators who stalk them.

Another major problem with today's threat assessment programs is specifically how our K-12 schools handle these situations. Colleges and businesses have the privilege of being their own entities and as such, operate groups like a BAT in their own jurisdictions, devoid of any outside micro-management. K-12 schools are not afforded this luxury, as most schools are operated with district oversight. The few school districts that have some kind of assessment program operate these from this administrative level. This is the completely wrong protocol to have when conducting an assessment. An assessment should be an attempt to determine the validity of a threat or a non-threat. Involvement of outside parties into a community may eventually become necessary, but not in an early stage of an inquiry. If there is one supremely important condition that must be met with compiling information from an interview, it is that there must be rapport between the person asking the questions and the interviewee. Any person who has credibility in conducting investigations will confirm that rapport, forthright honesty and trust between the person asking questions and the one answering them is just as important as documentation and evidence. When a school district chooses to operate an assessment, they take away an important aspect of the investigation, that the school and its staff are in a better position to handle the situation based on the established rapport and familiarity with the community. The school staff can interact with its students and families much more candidly. Someone such as the principal, the guidance counselor, or a familiar teacher will likely gain more traction on important information than an outsider. In addition, the more bureaucracy that is involved with such a sensitive subject, the less likely it is that the "personal" factor of getting an individual help will occur. In other words, the local school staff is more vested in seeing their student get help.

I am not suggesting that the school district not remain informed or "in-the-loop" on the situation. On the contrary, they are the best option for dealing with media or state government intervention if that is considered the best course of action. But like the PIAD worked with the U.S. Secret Service Field Office, the school should take the lead and keep the headquarters equivalent notified. I'm sorry to tell you, that is not how it is happening in our schools today.

So when does the information move from an "assessment" to an "action"? Simply put, there is no timetable. Individuals who are assessing reports of concern should be in a constant state of monitoring an individual's situation, compiling information to support or refute the reported behavior, and keeping a committee that decides on further action informed. Assessment and Action must work hand-in-hand.

Where should this process start? First, it has to be understood that reports of concerning behavior can and will come in at any and all times of the day, and throughout the year. Since this is the case, there must be a system to report these concerns in a way that they will reach a person with decision-making authority immediately. The Assessment and

Action Phase accomplishes three purposes: first, the urgency of safety must be addressed. That is, a protective environment for students, staff and co-workers must be maintained at all times, even when they are not present on the premises. Second, the community needs to feel like they can report a concerning condition at any time of day or night, and that it will be handled promptly. Lastly, there needs to be a set "first responder" for the information as it is reported. This "nexus" will ensure that it is not getting lost in different programs, that the proverbial left hand knows what the right hand is doing.

I have gone online and seen 24-hour hotlines set up to report issues of concern; I have seen e-mail addresses set up for specific routing messages, and I have seen PDF forms online for typing, printing and turning in. However a report goes out, it just needs to arrive with an individual in "real time" or at the moment it was sent.

So who should get the report? It depends on the organization. From a business or corporate perspective, I always recommend that the Director or Department Head of Human Resources be the recipient. From a collegiate perspective, I believe that the best point of contact is the Director or Department Head of Student Affairs. For a K-12 school, I am adamant about the point of contact being the Guidance Counselor at the school. If the information finds itself to the school district office, they typically have (or should have) a Director of Security or Head of Guidance to address the situation. It should not stay at that level, but be filtered to the Guidance Counselor at the school of the subject.

I have the utmost respect for the people who work in this industry. Human resource personnel and guidance counselors are under-valued in their respective positions, in my personal opinion. I can think of no other position that continues to work with the student through their time at a school or an employee as they move through management. As such, these people develop a great ability for rapport, interviewing people, and communication skills. "People" are their business, and they are undoubtedly the best first point of contact or nexus for assessing conditions of concerning behavior and determining the need to activate a BAT.

Obviously, businesses and academic institutions operate differently throughout our society. You and your associates know your program the best, making you the most qualified to determine how your BAT will operate. Let these recommendations help you as you map out an assessment plan for your environment.

College and University Campuses

Of all of the different kinds of organizations, the colleges and universities appear to be on the best track to establish behavioral assessment and action as a "way of life" methodology. Any person who goes online and searches for "threat assessment team" or something of the like will receive a multitude of college websites. These websites have sub-sections that outline in great detail their procedures for dealing with threat-related conditions in their staff and student body. In addition, most (if not all) have ways to contact their program, either confidentially or otherwise, to provide any and all information on concerning behavior. They are aligned with campus police, or are a division of the respective police unit, they typically have an extensive group of subject matter experts from both the college and outside to make up the program, and they are independent of any control or operation outside of the college. For any organization that needs to establish a threat assessment team, colleges and universities are doing very well with creating a blueprint to follow.

However, college threat assessment teams are not without their shortcomings, and there are still many to be addressed. First off, not every college campus has these programs. After the Virginia Tech Massacre, threat assessment teams began forming all over higher academic institutions. As it was mentioned earlier in the reading, the Commonwealth of Virginia mandated that all public institutions of higher education had at least some program in place to address these conditions as they arose. But this was a state regulation, mandated to the confines of the state lines. Other campuses chose to follow suit, but many did not. It is not as standardized across college campuses as it could be.

Additionally, the programs that are in place act in a reactionary capacity, which is the main issue with the community at large. These programs await a report to come in before they act on a situation. In the interim, these individuals who operate in these teams should be conducting training seminars for the student body, faculty and staff with regularity. Due to the nature of most of these program participants acting in a "collateral duty" capacity though, the committees make little effort to create training programs and answer questions on identification of threat-related behavior. As such, we have returned to our original problem: we expect our community (our college community) to call the fire department when they have no idea what a fire is.

The solutions for these issues are costly, but necessary for increased campus safety. The schools need to establish a group of individuals who are a dedicated cadre of people to make up the nucleus of a threat assessment team. These people would be hired for the sole purpose of being part of that team. It does not need to be many people; even the largest universities will not have many of these behavioral reports that will need response. Nevertheless, there are more responsibilities for the team members than only being called upon when there is an incident. The information is voluminous (as you can see from this book), and is in need of great study and practice. In addition, it is a full time job to train a campus community on these conditions in people and that is what these assessors need to be doing when they are not following cases. They should work in conjunction with resources that the campus can provide, such as campus security and professors or academic experts willing to donate their time.

Second, these programs need to follow the example made by the state of Virginia, and these teams need to be standardized at every single campus in the United States. They need to be as expected as campus law enforcement or school faculty. With the ever-increasing inflation of cost associated with higher education, it is travesty that these schools are not operating in such a fashion. One additional point; although Virginia has ordered all schools in the state to create these programs, the regulations are only in effect with public universities. Private schools were not mandated to comply with the law, and many have not.

Lastly, campuses need to get away from terms like "threat" in their descriptions, and get away from them quickly. If I were contacted because of concerning behavior that others had witnessed in me, and a person came to my dorm room and identified as a representative of the "threat assessment team," I would likely not be too interested in speaking with him/her. The term creates an atmosphere of danger, and the important thing is that these individuals can trust the people who approach them. The whole point of any of these programs is (or should be) to provide proactive interventions. The best form of proactive intervention is to get the person of interest help if he/she needs it, so the issue is not repeated.

I genuinely applaud colleges for the effort that they have made to keep their students safe, especially in an era post-Virginia Tech. But like a poor archer, they're missing the target. These campuses have become complacent and content with the programs that they have, when they still had more to do.

Private/Public Sector Workplace

We have been exposed to just as much rampage and active shooter violence in the workplace as we have on any academic campus, and yet the efforts we have made to address threat-related behavior in the workforce has been abysmal, at best. For all of the issues that were listed with colleges and universities, they are magnified all the more in the office environment. This is where I believe we will continue to see rampage violence increase if it is not properly addressed.

Obviously, a business, corporation or governmental office has a great number of disadvantages that a college campus does not. The business may be grand in its size, and may operate over many different areas of the country or the world. On the flipside, it may be extremely small, such as a startup business with only a few employees. Nevertheless, rampage violence does not discriminate so any kind of business or organization should assume that they could be a target.

Most organizations have a human resources division (H.R.). Due to the nature of their work including personnel, training and individual case management, they would seem to be the ideal point of contact for these kinds of conditions. Many corporations additionally have contracted agencies that specialize in providing Employee Assistance Programs (EAP's) to help the company's respective H.R. departments in sensitive situations. H.R. personnel are not qualified to provide long term mental and/or emotional health support, and most companies lack the resources to hire such a specialist. As such, EAP organizations are those that contract their services out to companies in the event that an employee is in need of assistance. It is unrealistic to not have some kind of EAP for its employees, as the stresses of life in an individual will pour over into their professional work oftentimes. Fortunately, most companies have these services and they provide a valuable service. But like other mental health professionals, they cannot assist an individual unless the condition is identified and steps are proactively made. When an indicator is recognized, it should be the H.R. division of the company or an immediate supervisor that is notified first.

Like the college campuses, businesses and corporations make little effort to train their employees in identification of behavioral indicators. Most training programs are focused on what to do in the event of an active shooter in the building, or some other form of rampage violence. I do not suggest that this information is not important, it is just as important as a fire drill. Individuals need to understand the procedure for dealing with a dangerous situation if/when it happens. However, in terms of proactively identifying conditions associated with threatening behavior, it seems the businesses make no effort to ensure that their employees are informed.

Additionally, one of the first major answers for helping people who are dealing with these issues is to help them find support. There is no greater support than that of family and close friends. With that, let me ask you: have you ever, in all of your time in school or working a job, ever not been asked to provide an emergency contact? I cannot think of one time when I have not had to provide this information, and update it regularly. The emergency point of contact is there for just this kind of reason: to involve a trusted third party in a situation where an individual is suffering. It doesn't matter if the person has a broken arm or is starting to show mental instability, that point of contact is there to be a mediator to getting loved one help! There are few things more infuriating than when I speak with businesses or schools and I bring the point-of-contact reference up as something that needs to be done. Typically I will get a look from company representatives that suggest that I might have just grown a second-head, or I am all of the sudden rambling and making no sense. Our professional societies have become so inundated with fears of violating a person's privacy and being sued that we have forgotten why we ask for information like a point of contact in the first place! Ultimately, I get to the brass tax of the discussion and it always turns to the corporate representative citing that they would need to discuss such a radical procedure with their legal department before authorizing it. I would be delighted to discuss with their legal department as well, and remind them that a failure to do anything is far more damning if something did happen.

K-12 Schools

Of these three programs, it is the K-12 schools in our country that concern me the most. To start, I want to first make it clear that I hold our schools in the highest regard, and my criticism is meant to only be constructive. If flaws are not pointed out, then they cannot be corrected and improved upon. I do not blame the individual schools and the way that they operate, because they take direction from higher authorities. I do however blame those individuals, the superintendents and school district managers who have become complacent with the safety of our children. I will discuss that in greater detail later.

The very nature of sensitivity that comes with assessing the conditions of a child cannot be overstated enough. I have the utmost respect for the importance of confidentiality in a situation that could develop in a child, and the long-term effects that could come from over-assessing the behavior or not doing enough. It is a terrible "Catch-22" of trying to determine what is best for the individual student, to taking the appropriate steps to ensure the safest school environment that we have.

Assessment of a student in the school should start with the guidance counselor. No exceptions. The guidance counselor is the person that is there to help with the emotional challenges that children face in an academic environment, to guide them to be productive adults, and to administratively work with the respective parents about special needs that a son or daughter may have. They are ideal for developing rapport with a student, and have the unique freedom to do this in a full time capacity when teachers are continuing with their responsibilities of educating the masses. As such, it is the guidance counselor of the respective school who should take the lead on all matters of cases involving concerning behavior. In virtually every instance, this is already being done in that office. We're just adding "threat-related behavior" to the responsibilities (if they are not already there).

When it is apparent that there is a serious issue that needs further action, it should be the responsibility of the guidance counselor to make that determination and bring it to the attention of the school's BAT. Like the guidance counselor, every school should operate an independent system of how to proceed with proactively addressing a concerning situation. Again, no exceptions. You see, if we look at the two previous examples of how a college assessment system and a business assessment system run (and should run), we will see that our K-12 schools have taken on the worst parts of the other two programs. Although K-12 schools are an independent location like a college, they answer to corporate oversight like a business. These institutions should be treated in much the same way that universities are responding to these issues, yet they prefer to defer the reported issue to superior authority. In addition, K-12 schools make little to no effort to train their student body in identification of threat-related behavior. Why? Do we think that our children would be too traumatized with the information? I'm not suggesting that we start teaching our kindergarten students in this subject, but middle school students most certainly need to be made aware. I'll ask again: why are we not training our children to identify and report threat-related behavior in individuals? Are we so concerned that we're going to affect their mental stability? Please, turn on the television, the internet or any news source that might come across an e-mail or a cell phone and, rest assured, your children are being exposed to far more traumatic information in the world today.

Under careful supervision, we could train our children to see these indicators and help to stop future violence. To date, I know of not one school in America that has taken on this training methodology. The sad truth is that most of these behavioral indicators will begin to manifest during the K-12 years, and the students are the most likely to be exposed to it. As such, they are the best response to identify it and address it. When I think of my own children sharing the halls with other kids who might have this hostility slowly building in them, I have a panicking urge to pull them from their school and hide them away from the world. But I also know that is just not realistic. The next best thing I can do is educate them to see these conditions in people, and instruct them on who to tell when they see it. Wouldn't it be great if we all taught our kids in the same way? How much more likely would violence in school subside if our children were educated to police their own and notify an adult of issues? I certainly believe that our children need to be protected, but I also believe that they have the right to be educated in what to watch for, to keep them safe.

But a K-12 will not have the resources that a university will have. They will not have the access to academic professors, subject matter experts, mental health professionals or personalized law enforcement at the campus. The truth is, the school doesn't need them. These individuals of expertise are fine, but the whole point of this book is to stress that you don't need to be an academic or professional expert in behavioral identification and assessments to recognize these conditions.

Here is a recommendation of some of the individuals that could/

should be on a BAT for a K-12 school:

- Guidance Counselor – Their involvement cannot be stressed enough. Rapport; personal interaction with the student body; intermediary between parents and BAT.
- Principal/Vice-Principal – Senior leadership needs to be involved as to make final determinations based on the recommendations of the BAT; maintain line of communication with the Superintendent's office and keep the school district informed.
- Law Enforcement – Any school that requests a law enforcement officer as a liaison will get it. The officer will likely be assigned as a collateral duty and will be there for BAT meetings or in the event of an investigation; excellent source for interviewing, legal action and background investigations.
- Teacher – One of several should be involved, how many depending on the size of the school. Terrific source for the "pulse" of the student body.
- School Nurse/Medical Staff – Every school has a nurse or several, and they should be affiliated with this process. Their medical expertise could be of great value during an assessment.
- Coaches – Like a teacher, coaches have a great deal of familiarity with students that other individuals might miss. Much interaction with after school activities could be beneficial.
- Clergy – Especially in private schools, clergy are well trained to discuss issues with people, and could provide great insight.
- Consultants – The need for subject matter experts may be necessary. Individuals trained in threat-related behavior, or those who are mental or behavioral health professionals should be considered at least as an "on-call" option.

This is basically a "garden-variety" setup for a BAT at a K-12 school. Obviously, it should be tailored to the specific needs of your program. Factors would include the size of the school and student body, number of employees, and size of the school district. I have interacted with school districts that have only two schools, so the superintendent's office maybe the best place to handle the situation. It really depends on the school's comfort zone to operate.

There are some additional points to consider. First, should a BAT at a K-12 school operate with a full-time staff like is recommended at a university? For the typical program, I would recommend not to do so. A university is microcosm, a place that is always operating. People live there throughout most of the year, they have a full-time police force, and individuals are independent of their families. The need for a full-time assessment team is necessary. For K-12 schools, the world is much, much smaller. The children go home, there is downtime from the institution. There should most definitely be a system to notify someone on the BAT at any hour, but the team operating in a collateral duty fashion is adequate.

This brings us to the next point to consider, though: the reason that a BAT can operate in this way is because the other group has taken on the responsibility to monitor the students during the off-hours. This is the responsibility of the parents and guardians of the children.

The most effective kind of assessment is the one that involves the community. Because of this, the parents and guardians need to be an active part of the BAT at the K-12 school level. There is not a school in the land, not an administrator in the industry that will go toe-to-toe against a parent in matters of the child, unless the child is dealing with imminent abuse then it would become a law enforcement matter. It is so important that this is a "team concept," one where the parents, guardians and the school staff are all working together in the best interest of the safety and well-being for the children. It doesn't sound like a difficult sell, does it? It's harder than most people think.

Ultimately, the purpose of any of these committees is to figure out what to do next. It's a case-by-case answer. The answer may be to reach out to a support groups, it might be to further follow a case and see if the situation is getting worse or better, it may be to call a mental health specialist or a behavioral clinician…. or it may require that law enforcement get involved. What I know right now is that these responsibilities are typically falling on the shoulders of one or a few individuals, with little documentation or due diligence into responding with providing helpful alternatives. Additionally, there is a significant lack of educating the community what to look for in concerning behavioral conditions, how to address them and how to report them to a trusting cadre of people who can and will help. It's a glaring need in administrative policy that must be corrected.

The most frustrating part is that the financial commitment to creating such programs is negligible to any organization. Other than a mental health provider specifically contracted to address a case, or a consultant is brought in to provide training for staff, then the cost seems to be very minimal. Online notifications such as e-mail or texting, additional 24-hour phone lines and "on-call" cell phones seem to be a small price for the need of the service. There may be situations where a few employees would be needed to be hired, such as in the instance of university and colleges, but schools and most businesses are more than capable of handling these responsibilities with some training and research.

The true issue with why our businesses and academic institutions are not doing more is that they are playing the odds. In the grand scheme of things, the odds of there being an incident of rampage violence in a school are virtually impossible. Of the 129,000+ public and private K-12 schools in America today, there have been 84 school shootings between 2013 and 2015. Statistically, there is about a .00065 percent chance that a school you and your family are affiliated with at this grade level will have some firearm altercation. It's almost an insignificant concern.

Of course, that is how the situation looks right now, in 2016. In the 1950's, the statistics were even lower when studying this form of violence, and yet 60 years later we have seen huge increase in the threat. Hopefully we will see a steady decline in the condition over the next 60 years. Hopefully.

30. Filling the Gaps

Those individuals first hired with the United States Secret Service are exposed to a battery of courses during time in training to become Special Agents. As previously noted in Chapter 5, these courses encompass two separate training facilities in Georgia and Maryland, with each lasting approximately four months. During that time, cadets are indoctrinated into aspects of the work that include federal law, firearms proficiency, defensive tactics, driver training, cyber security, and physical fitness. In addition to these, there are a myriad of specialized programs that are specific to the federal agency with which the cadet is employed. For example, cadets who are hired to work for the Bureau of Alcohol, Tobacco and Firearms have a much different jurisdiction than those who have been hired to enforce tax laws with the IRS and therefore train in areas specific to their jurisdiction.

Like most people that attended these training courses, I was grateful when it was finished. Despite the rigors of the training, it was a worthwhile education. There has been so much that I have been able to apply in my real life that I learned while at FLETC and RTC. As an additional credit to my instructors, even after more than ten years of having completed the training, the lessons are still fresh in my mind and useful.

With everything that I learned there, one lesson was relentlessly preached throughout the entire training and continued to be something practiced in the field long after training was over. The retention of information in most training courses is minimal, but this one particular lesson was always stressed to trainees, and applied in one's career.

It was the lesson of "filling the gaps."

I'm going to tell you something that the U.S. Secret Service would rather I not share: it is very, very likely that the agents that you see with the President have never actually been to that location prior to the moment that they arrive. From a security standpoint, do you think it makes much sense to have bodyguards not know their way around where they are when they are escorting someone? And yet what I am telling you is accurate: every time you see the President pull up in his motorcade to a grade school or an office building, ready to give a speech on a White House agenda, the agents that are with him and who are responsible for keeping him alive have most likely never been to the building that they are walking into prior to that initial arrival. They have limited knowledge of the layout of the building; where the hallways lead and where they dead-end; they are just as familiar with a new building and its floor plan as you and I would be if we went there ourselves. You would think that the protective detail of the President of the United States has that information committed to memory and that each movement has been carefully rehearsed. I'm sorry to tell you that it's not the case.

So how do they do it? How does the United States Secret Service keep the most important political figure (and others) safe? I'm afraid that I can't go into those details. I will only add that, rest assured, the President and others who are protected by the U.S. Secret Service are in very safe, capable hands. I will just say that it takes a cast of thousands of performers to pull off the production.

But again, how do agents effectively protect a person in a room or other area with which they are unfamiliar?

They fill the gaps. It is a well-learned concept and has been proven to be most effective.

What does this mean? What is "filling the gaps" supposed to signify? It's the concept that there are always, always exposed points in a security area. No one is completely, 100% protected from dangers, not even a person under the protection of the U.S. Secret Service. When agents enter an unfamiliar place, such as a meeting room, they don't stand right next to the protectee. Have you ever seen a video of the President or Vice-President speaking to the media with his agents standing right next to him like a shadow? No, because the agents have already moved to somewhere else to fill the gaps. They are fanning out, making observations of security concerns and addressing them as quickly and efficiently as they can in the time they have. This may be something simple like standing against a door, or placing themselves in front of a window, or blocking a person who they don't want near the protectee. Agents watch each other and see what the other agents have already addressed and then move on to a weak spot that is still exposed.

It's a great way to protect a person, especially when it is totally unrealistic to know every single location in the travels of someone as important as the President of the United States. Filling the gaps is also a terrific way to maximize the usefulness of the protection detail. I challenge you to find a security detail that has been trained by the Secret Service that is idly standing around when they have arrived to a location with the person they are escorting. Granted, you may see this other agents standing in a hallway or a stairwell, but not the protection detail that is surrounding the President. As for the people in the hallways, that is their job; they are post-standers assigned to a very specific location. And while they are in that location, they are responsible for filling their own gaps in their coverage zone.

So what does all this talk about "filling the gaps" mean to you? Why am I telling you this? Because it's not a concept that is reserved solely for the U.S. Secret Service. Like everything else in this book, it can be applied to make your community a safer place, and it is fairly easy to do. I certainly used it more than once in my career, and not in a security capacity. I often found that during an arrest warrant or assisting with searches, there were always things that needed to be done that hadn't been assigned, were overlooked or were unexpected. Times like that necessitated individuals who would see these holes and could fill them effectively.

"Filling the gaps" is crucial for maintaining safety in any environment. And it's what you are going to do to ensure that your community is prepared for threats when they arise.

Just like I was unable to know every hallway, every room, every stairwell that I would enter when I was protecting a person during my time as a Secret Service Agent, I also can't know what you want to do. I can assume you want to protect something, as that is most likely why you're reading this book.

From the perspective of a parent, my concern has been and always will be the level of safety that my children's school provides for the students. Since my children started attending the school, my wife and I have become very active in the PTA, in the after-school activities and with the students and faculty themselves. I have even made it a point to substitute teach a time or two myself, something that I found surprisingly enjoyable and personally rewarding.

I must admit that my involvement was more than just idle interest in helping out with my children's school. In a way, it was a sort of surveillance of the program. I wanted to know how the school operated, what they had planned for in the event of emergencies, and how they addressed issues of concern when they arose. You may think that this was a bit of going a bit too far, but I disagree. This is the place that I entrust with the lives of my children. If you are thinking that maybe I was doing too much, maybe you should consider that you're not doing enough to watch out for your own children.

I am pleased to say that my children's school did a fine job with safety measures; they practiced emergency lockdown procedures regularly with the students and staff; they maintained an outstanding nursing staff to assist with any and all medical conditions, and they communicated well with local emergency responders to ensure that all parties were on the same security page.

But although their plan was good, it was not absolute. Like most things, there is always room for improvement. I was trained in many aspects of safety, and I was able to easily recognize some of these as shortcomings in their program. To the credit of my children's school, when I approached them with these minor concerns, they were more than enthusiastic to modify what they were doing to provide a safer environment. The school's leaders understood that the goal was the safety and well being of the students and the staff, and they welcomed the input from someone with my background.

The results carried themselves over to the church that shares the campus grounds with the school. I was approached by the parish and asked to oversee improving their security measures. Like the school I was able to review what the church had already done, and make recommendations for improvements based on what was missing. In both cases with the school and the church, the results have been improved safety and security measures for an ultimately safer environment.

Unfortunately, I can almost certainly guarantee that my results were more atypical than the norm. Most school districts are in the habit of turning away parents when the administration is questioned about things like academics, budget issues and safety procedures. Inquiries are usually directed to the school district website, where a link outlining contact phone numbers or PDF templates for reporting issues can be found. On occasion, the school district will attach documentation that summarizes some safety and security procedures on a high-end level, but the specifics of safety and security are not provided in detail.

I understand the reasoning for this: a security detail that is readily available to a large group of people offers itself the opportunity to be used for nefarious means. If there were security measures published for Columbine High School or Virginia Tech, how much worse would those attacks have been? Frankly, that information should remain with those who need it when the time comes.

But we aren't focusing on reactionary security and safety; we're talking about proactive measures, and that comes back to identifying and assessing threat-related behavior. There is nothing wrong with you expecting for your children's school (or your employer, or your community) to outline to you how they go about addressing behavioral concerns when they are reported. And they should, you are absolutely entitled to know.

But here's the truth of the matter: your children's school doesn't have a realistic way to identify and address concerning behavior in the student body. If they say that they do, I encourage you to challenge it. Challenge it by requesting the specific steps of how they go about compiling reports, documenting cases, and following up. Again, as a parent you are absolutely entitled to this information, and it is something that they should be doing, but they do not.

This is how you start filling in the gaps. You find out where the gaps are, and to do that, you need to know what they have. If they lack any of these things, then you know that is something that needs to be addressed. These are the gaps that should be filled:

- Notification
- Training
- Liaisons
- Awareness

Notification

There should be a clear notification system that you can use to alert administrative staff about a possible behavioral concern. This should not just be a form that can be printed and simply filled out and sent in when it is convenient. It needs to be (at the very least), a notification system that will arrive to a person with decision-making authority when the report is made. Oftentimes schools, business and neighborhood watch groups use a secured e-mail or even a phone number for these notifications. Unfortunately, concerning behavior is not typically recognized as something that requires immediate action. As such, these reports are not considered worthy of justifying the added costs to implement a real-time notification system.

And frankly, I have never understood why. We have already reviewed (and cited with studied references) that there are high probabilities that attackers will have communicated their intentions to at least one person prior to an attack, that at least one person was involved in the attack planning in some capacity, that in cases where three or more people had been made communicated some ill-intent, at least one person would be a responsible adult. So my question again begs: if it has been shown to be statistically realistic that an attacker of any kind is likely going to communicate their vile intentions prior to an attack, doesn't it make sense to have a notification system that responds quickly?

The answer is that many people believe that we have that system in place already, and that system is 9-1-1. Yes, emergency responders do excellent work with the community, but what most people really don't understand is that the 9-1-1 systems in our community are already working on life-threatening issues at that very moment: people trapped in fires, life-threatening medical conditions, car accidents are a few examples. For the average 9-1-1 caller the danger is already happening. Identifying concerning behavior in others is a pending, possible issue. A person simply communicating ill intent is not enough justification to take a first responder away from a situation where life hangs on a thread. Nevertheless, concerning behavior is important enough that it should be reported, and done so in an expeditious way. Downloading an online form is not enough. Forms can be filed away in a folder, forms can be misplaced, and forms can be forgotten.

With schools in particular, they should have a much better system in place to make notifications of concerning behavior in others. Systems need to be set up and then shared with the community. It needs to be explained how to use the system, who it notifies, what information is needed and what happens when a report is made. This shouldn't be on a pamphlet that is sent home once a year; it should be reminded on a regular basis, posted throughout the campus and user-friendly. It should be clearly stated what the notification system is intended for, and that should cover situations such as bullying to cyber threats to things students are saying to one another in and outside of schools. Additionally a similar system should be set up in businesses for employees if they feel that there is something that needs to be reported as it pertains to the workplace.

It may be very possible that your children's school or your office has these procedures in place... but I'm going to say that I doubt it. You should check for yourself, ask questions about how the administration and supervisors go about dealing with these concerns when they arise. Is it really so much to ask to have something like this in place? A real-time notification system for the community that will alert administrative staff to a possible threat? Can you imagine if every school, every business had this? If our national community had these systems in place, would it really make things worse, or better? It would certainly make things safer, and it is all based on proactive, positive interventions.
This is what it means to "fill the gaps."

Training

Do you think that your children's school staff are being trained in preventive safety and security measures, or are you just assuming that they are? Do you know what they are trained in, or are you just assuming that they being trained in "something" that will keep the students and staff safe?

Have you ever thought to ask these questions, or are you comfortable with your schools program? Perhaps you felt like you were asking about something that you shouldn't, or that you were prying somewhere that was none of your business. I can assure you that you have absolutely every right to know what procedures are being taken to keep your children safe when you are not there.

Maybe at your office, you are trained to deal with threat-related violence. I will guess that the amount of exposure you have received in something like this boils down to an online slide presentation that you have to review every year or so. The slides probably focus more on how to deal with a situation when it becomes a crisis rather than recognizing behaviors to prevent a person's condition from escalating. You probably view it more as a nuisance and a waste of your work time than anything else. I'm inclined to agree with you; I too have seen my fair share of these slides, as they are a thorn in the side of every government employee. We all know what they are meant to do as well: they legally protect a business from being held liable for not training their employees in safety and security measures should something happen. In reality, these "training videos" don't do much.

Yet, we are perfectly content to allow this limited amount of training as enough for those people who watch our children while we are away—our teachers and school staff. Honestly, why would you think that their training into safety and security would be any different from what you receive?

I don't blame the teachers for what they are given; it's not their fault. The many, many teachers that I have spoken with on this very topic are as frustrated as you are with having to sit through this terrible "training," and that they are not given more to help them with their day-to-day interaction with students. Teachers recognize that training programs like online reviews of safety measures and distributed pamphlets provide very little value to dealing with real life dangerous situations. They of all people understand the importance of maintaining the interest and enthusiasm of a student, and they know that one of the least effective methods is a slide presentation on a computer. If it actually worked so well, then every teacher in America would use it on every student, and we know that's not happening (thankfully). There are some kinds of training that should be applied like this, such as the annual training on how to use the intranet of the company or the school. But when it comes to providing for the safety of our children, our teachers deserve better.

Start asking your schools what they are doing to improve their training methods in identifying and assessing threat-related behavior for their employees. Our teachers are some of the best people to be trained in this kind a proactive approach. Very early in their respective careers, educators of all kinds develop a keen insight into youth that few others have. Even parents only understand their own children, but teachers understand all based largely on the exposure to the broad range of children each and every year that comes with their careers. They see how children interact in their subcultures, they overhear students' conversations, and they observe kids socialization among one another. In a very short time teachers can already assess when a student is having a bad day or something has happened. Teachers are the ideal candidates for identifying unusual conditions of behavior, particularly with children and adolescents, in our society.

Equally so, they are the best to deal with it. It is most likely that an individual who commits an atrocity such as an active shooter attack will have started to develop their condition at an early age. We have already seen this with attackers like Seung Hui Cho, Adam Lanza and Jeffrey Weise. Doesn't it then make sense to train those individuals who would have the most exposure to adolescents the best in indicators of threat-related behavior?

And why stop there? Why should the schools, or companies, or the community in general, not get some kind of overview training in this as well? How effective would a community be when our youth is being monitored for changes in their behavior at home and in school, by parents and teachers on the same page to identify the same conditions? It would be very effective. We just need to convince the right people that it is a worthwhile effort.

There should be a clear understanding of what kinds of training the staff at a school and a business receive as it pertains to behavioral concerns of others. These training programs should be outlined in clear detail so that the community knows exactly what the staff is capable of doing (and what they are expected to do) in the event of a situation. In today's financially strapped education system, the majority of our teachers are subjected to limited training that they are required to do online, typically consisting of only a few hours (at the very max). Additionally, this training is not meant to train them in identifying indicators of potential issues, but rather reacting to a situation once it occurs. This is a terrible way to go about this. The same can be said for the training in the corporate world and the public sector. Most employees are given slide-based presentations online that describe how to appropriately react to a concerning situation. There is little in the way of personal training programs to teach people how to address issues before they manifest into something dangerous. It is important that you hold your schools and business accountable for ensuring that the staff and the community are provided a better way to train people.

Liaisons

I hope that your children's school, or your office, or your neighborhood have a close, working relationship with your emergency responders. I don't mean that you have a group of people who are standing by and ready to assist you if you call for help. We all have that. Your school should have several people who are assigned as liaisons to their campus. You certainly want an officer or someone in a law enforcement capacity to be in this position. Am I suggesting that an officer is assigned exclusively in this position? No, peace officers have a huge responsibility to protect and serve the community as a whole, so it is unrealistic to take a person away from that to walk around a school all day. There are some schools throughout the country , however, that are assigned an officer exclusively. These are typically known as School Resource Officers (SRO). SROs are sworn officers of the law, and are more than qualified as a liaison to law enforcement and other emergency responder organizations. Additionally, SROs are usually filling a slot that is recognized as a need at that school for a certain reason. This may be that the school is located in a high-crime area, or there have been major issues of violence that transcend that of a typical school.

But the majority of schools in our country don't have SROs. And if you are in a corporate office, you definitely won't have something like this. The extent of corporate protection revolves around the use of contracted office security, and they are almost always responsible for the main entrance of a building and not the specific offices throughout the complex.

If your school, office or neighborhood doesn't have one or several emergency responder representatives assigned as a liaison, then there is a major gap in your process that needs to be filled.

Law enforcement is not only encouraged to maintain these relationships with the community, they are expected to do so. But what most people fail to understand is that law enforcement (and their EMS/first responder counterparts) will come if/when they are invited to. Police will not force themselves on a community if the community does not want them present. Most neighborhoods, schools and businesses assume that they are wasting a precinct's time by requesting a few visits a year.

This couldn't be further from the truth. The police recognize that the most functional, safest communities are those that work in conjunction with law enforcement to ensure a protective environment. They want to take part in the community and form bonds with the citizenry. It's our responsibility to invite them in. Especially in the schools.

There is absolutely nothing wrong with a school requesting that a law enforcement officer be assigned to their school in this capacity. This officer would act in such a way as to lend a police perspective to a possible threat-issue that has been reported and to consult on how law enforcement can intervene. Additionally, officers have a multitude of invaluable resources that are exclusive to their jobs and can be used in a legal capacity to assist the school in helping a troubled student and his/her family in a positive way. Lastly, a familiar officer interacting with the students, staff and parents is a great presence of positivity and safety, even if they are present only a few times in the school year. Other emergency responders, such as members of the fire department, EMS and local or state emergency management members are also excellent options to act as a school or community liaison.

Awareness

You can set up the best notification system in the world; you can have the best training that money can buy; you can convince an entire police division to work with your program in a liaison capacity.
None of it matters if no one buys into it.

The true success of proactive identification and intervention revolves around the community itself. If everyone continues to move through the routine of school, work and home with the idea that someone else will recognize the issues and take care of them, then all the preparation means nothing. The greatest machine in the world is useless if there is no one to operate it.

The community has to buy into the belief that they make a difference. They must trust that the methodology works and that it is keeping everyone else safe. They have to understand the greater picture and why such measures are being done.

Oftentimes, that is not a message people easily embrace.

The biggest issue when attempting to fill the gaps is that it will, inevitably, cause something that is already in place to be adjusted or possibly removed. People, by nature, don't like change. Change means re-learning, and re-learning something is an uncomfortable process that alters a person's life. It's easier to resist the change than to embrace it. Trust me, I have spoken with enough schools and businesses to know that they would rather take their chances with the statistical probability that they will not be threatened instead of creating safeguards against a violent attack of some kind.

The best way to involve the community is to increase awareness. Slogans, school involvement, participation, evening meetings, all of it. It's so important that proactive interventions are not swept away as an after thought, and that the parents, teachers, students, employees, neighbors, everyone are ever vigilant. It needs to become as common and accepted as a 9-1-1 service or a suicide prevention hotline. In many ways, that's what a behavioral notification system is: a hotline to notify professionals of concerning behavior and possible threatening actions by others in the community.

Conclusion

Is this the end all/be all of filling the gaps? Most likely, no. But it is the garden variety for most places. There may be other nuances of a building or a school that are unique to its system, and those gaps will need to be filled as necessary. You will just have to maintain an open-mind and think about what things need to be addressed. But what you have here is good start.

There will be the naysayers who will adamantly oppose recommendations like these. Some will call it "radical," or suggest that it is the kind of system that starts to breed paranoia in a community. It will be implied that teaching the public about threat-related behavior and then giving them a means for reporting is inviting disaster. The claim is that programs like these create an opportunity for people who are angry at others, or scorned, or delusional, to file false reports against one another. There will even be those in the community who will feel that they are not qualified to address these issues in any manner whatsoever.

I know these kinds of people are out there because I meet them regularly. I have given presentations to groups and I rarely remember a time where there wasn't at least one person who felt compelled to express their strong disagreements.

I will tell you what I have always, always told them—I respect their opinion. I also make it a point to advise that it is the community's responsibility to help in any and all ways to ensure a safe neighborhood, a safe workplace… a safe school for ourselves and those with whom we share it.

I don't subscribe to the naysayer mentality, because at the conclusion of the meetings where I am publicly questioned, I am cornered by many more who privately want to help, who want to make a difference, and are tired of seeing innocent people fall victim to active shooter and mass violence. I meet with people who are frustrated, and have grown more and more concerned with the way the world is, and cannot accept that there is no way to prevent it.

Our path to safety is a proactive one, and it starts with identifying the underlying behaviors that manifest threats, continues with assessing the level of danger that these behaviors could be, and finishes with acting on the assessment, ensuring that all the gaps in the process are filled.
I don't just expect that you (the parent, the citizen, the teacher, the spouse) are capable of doing these things; I'm counting on it. You are the only chance to stop senseless violence from continuing in our country. And I know that you can do it.

CONCLUSION

I was a Special Agent with the United States Secret Service on the day of the Sandy Hook Massacre.

The agency was in a chaotic state. The official election had just ended, and agents were returning from their poststanding assignments across the country, back to their respective field offices to the welcoming embrace of backdated criminal casework and overdue vouchers. Additionally, the agency was dealing with a series of terribly embarrassing public relation issues, stemming from a variety of poor decisions on behalf of several employees. For myself, I had recently been diagnosed with a condition that prohibited me from continuing in the position. Literally, the job would have killed me if I continued at it. I was in a place where I was transitioning to an analytical role at the Washington, D.C. Headquarters. While my transfer was finalized I sat in my field office answering phones as the duty desk agent, keeping a close eye on the news for any sudden threats to our country.

On one such morning, December 14, 2012, the news began to report a shooting at Sandy Hook Elementary School.

Remembering back, it was a surreal moment. I just stared at the television in numb silence; I could not believe that something so horrific had occurred. The initial reports had mentioned that a few people in a school had been shot. It was only later that the full gravity of the attack was reported. I felt ill, and I became almost panic-stricken thinking of my own children as they were in their own schools, their own day cares. I called my wife at her office, and she was in total shock as I explained what was being reported. The video images of people at the scene in tears, a woman sobbing uncontrollably with no chance of comfort…. I am still haunted by their grief, by their loss.

During this time in my life, I was completing my graduate degree in Strategic Security. I only had a few more classes left, and I had already planned on pursuing a doctorate in the same discipline. I also knew that if I wanted any chance of being accepted into the program then I would need to complete a graduate thesis to show my ability to thrive in doctoral studies. My thesis was a focus on how we as a society could prevent rampage violence proactively in our K-12 schools. Needless to say, you can imagine the sick irony I felt with the Sandy Hook Massacre happening at the same time I was completing my research on such a similar topic.

At the same time, the thesis, my career path and my job status at the time gave me an ideal place in my life to know a great deal about active shooter violence. It afforded me the chance to research the issues that caused the violence, and the best studies for how to deal with the conditions as they manifested. I also knew that my own agency, the United States Secret Service, employed these programs regularly to keep those under their purview of protection safe. Lastly, I knew that they had conducted studies and published recommendations on how to protect schools from what had just happened at Sandy Hook. All they needed to do now was enlist the help of their agent and officer cadre to offer programs to train the community in what they already knew.

So that was what I set out to do initially: I compiled information on how my agency could provide this service to the public. I approached my supervisors about pitching a program like this to senior management at Headquarters, and offered my expertise to assist. This offer was met with nothing short of disgust and contempt. The agency was not interested in keeping people safe who were not under their personal umbrella of protection. My requests were unequivocally denied.

I knew at that point that my career with the U.S. Secret Service was over. I could not in good conscience continue with an agency that had all the resources and research in the world to help with protecting our schools and still made absolutely zero effort to do so. I needed to pursue this with organizations that cared about keeping their children safe. A year and four months after the Sandy Hook Massacre, I resigned my position. I wanted to offer programs to K-12 schools to train teachers, students and administrators in identifying and positively and proactively address threat-related behavior before it manifested into conditions of violence. If any group cared about the safety and security of children, it would be the school districts.

I could not have been more wrong.

After planning the program for over a year, I started to compile contact information on school districts across the United States. I simultaneously completed my graduate degree and was accepted into the doctoral program to continue my studies, so between that and my experience as U.S. Secret Service Agent, I felt very, very comfortable with the information. I also felt comfortable with the idea that anyone could be trained in identifying these behavioral indicators in others. Most people already knew the indicators they observed, all I was doing was applying definition to their observations. If nothing else, it created a sense of empowerment: the people who would regularly second-guess what they were seeing in others would now believe that their observations were legitimate, and would then do something about it.

Over the 2015 year, I reached out to 207 school districts across Virginia, Maryland and nearby east coast affiliates. The training was offered free of charge to any school district, and I was willing to travel to the location of their choice. I offered training programs of one-hour, eight-hour and even more in-depth training if requested. I received direct responses from two school districts telling me to never contact them again. The other 205 simply let me know that they were not interested.

207 school districts. Administrators and superintendents who claimed that their top priority was the safety and security of their students decided to turn away a free one-hour training session on identifying threat-related behavior and potentially stopping active-shooter violence in their schools. If you are disturbed by that thought, you can imagine how I felt at the end of 2015.

One school, however, gave me a chance. It wasn't one school district, it was one school. Resurrection-St. Paul School in Ellicott City, Maryland contacted me and offered me the opportunity to speak with the staff. In addition, they gave me the chance to train the staff for an entire eight-hour class. RSPS recognized the innovative approach that I was proposing, and were open-minded to the possibilities that the methodology had for keeping children safe in their own school. The course response exceeded my expectations, and I left that day with a glimmer of hope that there were people who understood this idea.

From there, I took a different approach. The rejection from the school districts taught me a valuable lesson, one that I should have already known as a father and that I am embarrassed to say that I forgot: no one cares more for the safety of a child than his or her parents.

Parents, guardians, family, close friends were the audience that I sought. My research showed me that they were also the best defense against threat-related violence. The research further supported that identifying behavioral indicators of violence didn't stop with children either; it permeated itself into every facet of life. Troubled co-workers, adults, anyone could experience these conditions at any time in their life. It wasn't just a school problem, students weren't just the target. It was a social issue that was starting to morph into a national epidemic. By reaching out to families, they could then take what they learned to their offices, their businesses, friends at other schools. The opportunities for increasing the safety of our national community were endless.

But how could I reach out to individual parents when I couldn't even get a school district to talk to me? Obviously, no school was going to provide the contact information of its parents, and I would never think to ask for it. I considered Parent-Teacher Associations, but another difficult pursuit, as each operates differently at each school.

Frankly, it was damn frustrating. What truly upset me was the positive response I received from members of the community on the program. I had teachers tell me that they loved the idea of the approach, guidance counselors expressed that it was exactly the kind of system that needed to be established to help with issues that they saw every school year. Most importantly, I interacted with parents who wanted a program like this implemented in the school. Oftentimes, these discussions would move into the person's own observations. Like a previous chapter stated, "everyone has a story." I implored these people to contact their schools and have them contact me. The response they received was similar to my own: not interested, don't bring this up again.

Only after speaking with my close friends and family did I realize that the problem wasn't the methodology, the problem was my approach to teaching others about it. I was basing my training on the decision of a bureaucratic system. Another hard lesson learned. If you want a bureaucratic system to listen to your arguments, all you need to do is convince their boss to make it happen. That is why this book exists: if I can't persuade the schools, the universities, the companies to change the way they do things, then I will go over their heads and tell you, the reader, instead. You are the client, the parent, the co-worker, the employee.

I will make sure that you, the individual most affected by bureaucratic regulations, understand that the organizations that you trust with your safety and the safety of your children seem to have more pressing issues on their agenda.

I genuinely hope that after reading this book you will recognize that OA$^{2®}$ (or a system similar to it) is needed in our schools, our universities and our corporations. We need to train our community through these organizations to work together to recognize these conditions and address them before they become another Sandy Hook Elementary. I have done all that I can, honestly. I have outlined everything about the training into one compilation, I have published it on a grand scale, and I have made it easily accessible to anyone who chooses to use it. I have provided documentation to help start a program, and I have outlined the best way to set it up. I have even left a way to contact me for advice.

OA$^{2®}$ is the exact right course for stopping rampage violence in our society. You are the best answer to a question that has plagued our community for too long. I now place the responsibility on you, the reader, to forward the program in your child's school, your office, your neighborhood.

I cannot promise that this methodology will stop rampage violence or active shooters in our community… but if we use this system, we will stand a much better chance of preventing this kind of violence in the first place. That I can promise.

For that reason alone, isn't it worth it to make the effort? If anything mentioned in this book can help pave our path to safety, shouldn't we do everything we can to make it happen for ourselves and our loved ones?

You know the answer. We should.

REFERENCES

INTRODUCTION

Page 4: *"On the morning of September 16, 2013..."* Johnson, K. and Ledger, D. "Moment By Moment: How The Navy Yard Shooting Unfolded." USA Today. 18 September, 2013. Retrieved from http://www.usatoday.com/story/news/nation/2013/09/17/navy-yard-gunman-killed-for-more-than-30-minutes/2828585/ on 1 July 2016.

6: *"After several minutes of firing..."* Johnson, K. and Ledger, D. "Moment By Moment: How The Navy Yard Shooting Unfolded." USA Today. 18 September, 2013. Retrieved from http://www.usatoday.com/story/news/nation/2013/09/17/navy-yard-gunman-killed-for-more-than-30-minutes/2828585/ on 1 July 2016.

7: *"Sometime during the first alarm..."* Weiner, Rachel. "Navy Yard victim Arthur Daniels helped save boss's life." The Washington Post. 25 September, 2013. Retrieved from https://www.washingtonpost.com/local/crime/navy-yard-victim-arthur-daniels-helped-save-bosss-life/2013/09/25/7fd15a22-260e-11e3-b75d-5b7f66349852_story.html on 1 July 2016.

8: *"But they likely did hear something..."* "Rampage at the Navy Yard: What Happened Inside Building 197?" The Washington Post. 25 September, 2013. Retrieved from http://www.washingtonpost.com/wp-srv/special/local/navy-yard-shooting/scene-at-building-197/ on 1 July 2016.

9: *"For those who knew Aaron Alexis..."* Johnson, K. Jervis, R. and Wolf, R. "Aaron Alexis, Navy Yard Shooting Suspect: Who Is He?" USA Today. 16 September, 2013. Retrieved from http://www.usatoday.com/story/news/nation/2013/09/16/aaron-alexis-navy-yard-shooter/2822731/ on 1 July 2016.

— Brown, P. and Payne, E. and Pearson, M. "Navy Yard Shooting Survivor: 'I Got Lucky.'" CNN. 18 September, 2013. Retrieved from http://www.cnn.com/2013/09/18/us/navy-yard-shooting-main/ on 1 July 2016.

10: *"Nearly 10 years later..."* McLaughlin, E. "Flags in Navy Yard Shooter's Past Apparently Not Red Enough." CNN. 19 September, 2013. Retrieved from http://www.cnn.com/2013/09/18/us/navy-yard-alexis-red-flags/ on 1 July 2016.

10: *"Later in 2008..."* McLaughlin, E. "Flags in Navy Yard Shooter's Past Apparently Not Red Enough." CNN. 19 September, 2013. Retrieved from http://www.cnn.com/2013/09/18/us/navy-yard-alexis-red-flags/ on 1 July 2016.

11: *"As if these issues were not enough..."* Botelho, G. and Sterling, J. "FBI: Navy Yard Shooter 'Delusional', said 'Low Frequency Attacks' Drove Him To Kill." CNN.. 26 September, 2013. Retrieved from http://www.cnn.com/2013/09/25/us/washington-navy-yard-investigation/ on 1 July 2016.

12: *"This last statement to ELF..."* Botelho, G. and Sterling, J. "FBI: Navy Yard Shooter 'Delusional', said 'Low Frequency Attacks' Drove Him To Kill." CNN. 26 September, 2013. Retrieved from http://www.cnn.com/2013/09/25/us/washington-navy-yard-investigation/ on 1 July 2016.

21: *"In early 2016..."* Associated Press. "First Graders Suspended After Plotting To Kill Classmate." Fox News. 31 March, 2016. Retrieved from http://www.foxnews.com/us/2016/03/31/first-graders-suspended-after-plotting-to-kill-classmate.html on 1 July 2016.

23: *"For the defenseless school..."* State of Colorado, Office of the Governor. Columbine Review Commission Report. By William Erickson, et al. May 2001.

24: *"The project was completed..."* Vossekuil, B., R.A. Fein, M. Reddy, R.Borum, and W. Modzeleski. The Final Report and Findings of the Safe School Initiative: Implications for the Prevention of School Attacks in the United States, Washington, DC: U.S. Secret Service and U.S. Department of Education, July 2004.

26: *"While planning attacks of this nature..."* Payne, E. and Sanchez, R. "Charleston Church Shooting: Who Is Dylann Roof?" CNN. 23 June, 2015. Retrieved from http://www.cnn.com/2015/06/19/us/charleston-church-shooting-suspect/ on 5 July 2016.

26: *"Attackers usually communicate..."* Vossekuil, B., R.A. Fein, M. Reddy, R.Borum, and W. Modzeleski. The Final Report and Findings of the Safe School Initiative: Implications for the Prevention of School Attacks in the United States, Washington, DC: U.S. Secret Service and U.S. Department of Education, July 2004.

27: *"In many cases..."* State of Colorado, Office of the Governor. Columbine Review Commission Report. By William Erickson, et al. May 2001.

28: *"There is no one profile..."* Vossekuil, B., R.A. Fein, M. Reddy, R.Borum, and W. Modzeleski. The Final Report and Findings of the Safe School Initiative: Implications for the Prevention of School Attacks in the United States, Washington, DC: U.S. Secret Service and U.S. Department of Education, July 2004.

29: *"Most attackers are known..."* Vossekuil, B., R.A. Fein, M. Reddy, R.Borum, and W. Modzeleski. The Final Report and Findings of the Safe School Initiative: Implications for the Prevention of School Attacks in the United States, Washington, DC: U.S. Secret Service and U.S. Department of Education, July 2004.

31: *"Most of the time, attackers displayed..."* Vossekuil, B., R.A. Fein, M. Reddy, R.Borum, and W. Modzeleski. The Final Report and Findings of the Safe School Initiative: Implications for the Prevention of School Attacks in the United States, Washington, DC: U.S. Secret Service and U.S. Department of Education, July 2004.

I. OBSERVE
42: *"The media never really provided..."* Borum, R. (2000). Assessing Violence Risk Among Youth. Journal of Clinical Psychology, 56 (10), 1263 – 1288.

51: *"I am not diagnosing the condition..."* Volkmar, F. (ed.). (2013). Encyclopedia of Autism Spectrum Disorders. New York: Springer.

52: *"It is important that a community..."* Associated Press. "Shooter Obsessed With Violence." Fox News. 23 March, 2005. Retrieved from: http://www.foxnews.com/story/2005/03/23/shooter-obsessed-with-violence.html on 19 August 2016.

57: *"Now let's take another scenario..."* Bendavid, N. "Soccer Violence Escalates in Europe." The Wall Street Journal. 29 April, 2015. Retrieved from: http://www.wsj.com/articles/soccer-violence-escalates-in-europe-1430308902 on19 August 2016.

61: *"On April 16, 2007..."* Commonwealth of Virginia. "Report of the Virginia Tech Review Panel", 2012.

— *"On April 16, 2007..."* Mozingo, J. et al. "An act of terror and an act of hate: The Aftermath of America's Worst Mass Shooting." The Los Angeles Times. 13 June, 2016. Retreived from: http://www.latimes.com/nation/nationnow/la-na-orlando-nightclub-shooting-20160612-snap-story.html on 19 August 2016.

62: *"For several months prior..."* Bowers, M. "Virginia Tech Professor Nikki Giovanni Reflects on Tragedy." The Virginian-Pilot. 5 April, 2008. Retrieved from: http://pilotonline.com/news/virginia-tech-professor-nikki-giovanni-reflects-on-tragedy/article_3eb71e85-57b0-5b62-971a-be3245b5eef7.html on 19 August 2016.

63: *"If there was any silver lining..."* Virginia Code 23-9.2:10.

70: *"On Sunday, January 17, 2016..."* Adams, C. "'Distraught' Former Student Allegedly Ex-Girlfriend and Another Student in Murder-Suicide at SUNY Geneseo Just One Week After Break Up." People. 19 January 2016. Retrieved from: http://www.people.com/article/suny-geneseo-murder-suicide-colin-kingston-stab-ex-girlfriend-break-up on 19 August 2016.

75: *"Sometime during the day..."* Bindel, J. "The Montreal Massacre: Canada's Feminists Remember." The Guardian. 3 December 2012. Retrieved from https://www.theguardian.com/world/2012/dec/03/montreal-massacre-canadas-feminists-remember on 19 August 2016.

75: *"The École Polytechnique Massacre..."* Weston, G & Aubrey, J. "The making of a massacre: the Marc Lepine story, Part I-II". The Ottawa Citizen. 7-8 February 1990.

76: *"The indicators don't stop there..."* Montreal Coroner's Report, Marc Lepine, 10 May 1991, Sourour, T. Investigating Coroner – Attachment C.

79: *"The SSI was thorough..."* Vossekuil, B., R.A. Fein, M. Reddy, R.Borum, and W. Modzeleski. The Final Report and Findings of the Safe School Initiative: Implications for the Prevention of School Attacks in the United States, Washington, DC: U.S. Secret Service and U.S. Department of Education, July 2004.

82: *"When the legal defense team..."* O'Neill, A. "James Holmes Life Story Didn't Sway Jury". CNN. 11 August 2015. Retrieved from http://www.cnn.com/2015/08/02/us/13th-juror-james-holmes-aurora-shooting/ on 19 August 2016.

82: *"The exceptional child grew..."* Whitaker, B. "Colo. Suspect James Holmes "smart" but "quiet" teachers and neighbors say". CBS News. 20 July 2012 Retrieved from http://www.cbsnews.com/news/colo-suspect-james-holmes-smart-but-quiet-teachers-and-neighbors-say/ on 19 August 2016.

— *"The exceptional child grew..."* Dedman, B. "Photos of James Holmes, Camp Counselor for Underprivileged Kids." NBC News 21 July 2012 Retrieved from http://www.nbcnews.com/news/investigations/photos-james-holmes-camp-counselor-underprivileged-kids-v12878372 on 19 August 2016.

82: *"Jimmy applied..."* Auge, K. & Brown, J. "James Holmes was one of the elite in neuroscience before Aurora theater massacre." The Denver Post 4 August 2012 Retrieved from http://www.denverpost.com/2012/08/04/james-holmes-was-among-elite-in-neuroscience-before-aurora-theater-massacre/ on 19 August 2016.

82: *"The culmination of this manifestation..."* KABC-TV "Aurora Colo. Theater Shooting Timeline, Facts." ABC 7. 26 July 2012 Retrieved from http://abc7.com/archive/8743134/ on 19 August 2016.

83: *"There were other, darker things..."* Reference: O'Neill, A. "James Holmes Life Story Didn't Sway Jury". CNN. 11 August 2015. Retrieved from http://www.cnn.com/2015/08/02/us/13th-juror-james-holmes-aurora-shooting/ on19 August 2016.

— *"There were other, darker things..."* Allan, N. "Batman Colorado Shooting: James Holmes was nicknamed 'the llama' ". The Telegraph 12 August 2012. Retrieved from http://www.telegraph.co.uk/news/worldnews/northamerica/usa/9470911/Batman-Colorado-shooting-James-Holmes-was-nicknamed-the-llama.html on 19 August 2016.

— *"There were other, darker things..."* Chapman, B. & Lysiak, M. "Dark Knight Suspect James Holmes was too freaked out to perform with prostitute one week before Aurora shootings, sex worker says." New York Daily News. 30 July, 2012. Retrieved from http://www.nydailynews.com/news/national/joker-lame-excuse-lady-knight-article-1.1124657 on 19 August 2016.

— *"There were other, darker things..."* O'Neill A., "Will Mental Illness Save Holmes' Life?" CNN 3 August 2015 Retrieved from http://www.cnn.com/2015/07/16/us/holmes-aurora-theater-shooting-jury-choice/ on 19 August 2016.

84: *"These all lend some credibility..."* O'Neill A., "Will Mental Illness Save Holmes' Life?" CNN 3 August 2015 Retrieved from http://www.cnn.com/2015/07/16/us/holmes-aurora-theater-shooting-jury-choice/ on 19 August 2016.

84: *"I don't question the sincerity..."* Healy, J. "Colorado Killer James Holmes Notes': Detailed Plans vs. 'A Whole Lot of Crazy'" The New York Times 28 May 2015. Retrieved from http://www.nytimes.com/2015/05/29/us/james-holmess-notebook-and-insanity-debate-at-aurora-shooting-trial.html on 19 August 2016.

— *"I don't question the sincerity..."* Bolton, A. "Inside Colorado Threater shooter James Holmes Booby-Trapped Apartment." USA Today 10 September 2015 Retrieved from http://www.usatoday.com/story/news/nation-now/2015/09/10/james-holmes-aurora-theater-shooting-booby-trapped-apartment/71996544/ on 19 August 2016.

84: *"James Eagan Holmes was the child..."* Miles, K. "James Holmes San Diego upbringing examined as he faces trial in shooting of 71". Huffington Post 23 July 2012 Retrieved from http://www.huffingtonpost.com/2012/07/23/james-holmes-san-diego-background_n_1696081.html on 19 August 2016.

85: *"The expectation Holmes put on himself..."* Associated Press, "Holmes Rejected From University of Iowa: Do NOT Offer Admission." CBS News 19 September 2012 Retrieved from http://www.cbsnews.com/news/holmes-rejected-from-u-of-iowa-do-not-offer-admission/ on 19 August 2016.

86: *"Something else that has not been discussed..."* CBS D.C. "James

Holmes Received $26K Grant from Bethesda-Based National Institutes of Health." CBS DC 24 July, 2012. Retrieved from http://washington.cbslocal.com/2012/07/24/james-holmes-received-26k-grant-from-bethesda-based-national-institutes-of-health/ on 19 August 2016.

86: *"I believe that James Eagan Holmes..."* Rogers, A. "Colorado Shooting Suspect Failed an important exam only hours before buying a gun." Business Insider. 25 July, 2012. Retrieved from http://www.businessinsider.com/colorado-shooting-suspect-failed-exam-2012-7 on 19 August 2016.

— *"I believe that James Eagan Holmes..."* Goode, E. & Kovaleski, S. & Healy, J. & Frosch, D. "Before Gunfire, Hints of 'Bad News'" The New York Times. 26 August 2012 Retrieved from http://www.nytimes.com/2012/08/27/us/before-gunfire-in-colorado-theater-hints-of-bad-news-about-james-holmes.html on 19 August 2016.

87: *"When Holmes reached this pinnacle..."* Goode, E. & Kovaleski, S. & Healy, J. & Frosch, D. "Before Gunfire, Hints of 'Bad News'" The New York Times. 26 August 2012 Retrieved from http://www.nytimes.com/2012/08/27/us/before-gunfire-in-colorado-theater-hints-of-bad-news-about-james-holmes.html on 19 August 2016.

87: *"I also believe that two people..."* Frosch, D. "James Holmes' Psychiatrist Testifies in Colorado Theater Shooting Trial." The Wall Street Journal. 16 June 2015 Retrieved from http://www.wsj.com/articles/james-holmess-psychiatrist-testifies-in-colorado-theater-shooting-trial-1434484324 on 19 August 2016.

87: *"But the important question is this..."* Steffen, J. "Aurora Theater Shooting Trial, The Latest from Day 57". The Denver Post 27 July 2015 Retrieved from http://www.denverpost.com/2015/07/27/aurora-theater-shooting-trial-the-latest-from-day-57/ on 19 August 2016.

88: *"I do not doubt Dr. Metzner's diagnosis..."* Associated Press, "Doctor who found James Holmes sane says mental illness caused him to attack Colorado theater." Fox News. 27 July, 2015 Retrieved from http://www.foxnews.com/us/2015/07/27/doctor-who-found-james-holmes-sane-says-mental-illness-caused-him-to-attack.html on 19 August 2016.

88: *"I will make one final point..."* Rowlands, T and Spellman, J. "James Holmes Called University 9 minutes before shooting, attorney says." CNN.

31 August 2012. Retrieved from http://www.cnn.com/2012/08/30/justice/colorado-shooting/ on 19 August 2016.

— *"I will make one final point..."* Bolton, A. "Inside Colorado Threater shooter James Holmes Booby-Trapped Apartment." USA Today 10 September 2015 Retrieved from http://www.usatoday.com/story/news/nation-now/2015/09/10/james-holmes-aurora-theater-shooting-booby-trapped-apartment/71996544/ on 19 August 2016.

92: *"When studying individuals who carried..."* Vossekuil, B., R.A. Fein, M. Reddy, R.Borum, and W. Modzeleski. The Final Report and Findings of the Safe School Initiative: Implications for the Prevention of School Attacks in the United States, Washington, DC: U.S. Secret Service and U.S. Department of Education, July 2004.

92: *"Studying the data further..."* Vossekuil, B., R.A. Fein, M. Reddy, R.Borum, and W. Modzeleski. The Final Report and Findings of the Safe School Initiative: Implications for the Prevention of School Attacks in the United States, Washington, DC: U.S. Secret Service and U.S. Department of Education, July 2004.

92: *"Lastly, of the 93% covered..."* Vossekuil, B., R.A. Fein, M. Reddy, R.Borum, and W. Modzeleski. The Final Report and Findings of the Safe School Initiative: Implications for the Prevention of School Attacks in the United States, Washington, DC: U.S. Secret Service and U.S. Department of Education, July 2004.

95: *"But not everyone shared in the fervor..."* Associated Press, "Sirhan felt betrayed by Kennedy" The New York Times. 20 February 1989 Retrieved from http://www.nytimes.com/1989/02/20/us/sirhan-felt-betrayed-by-kennedy.html on 19 August 2016.

96: *"Sirhan Sirhan is still alive..."* Federal Bureau of Investigation, "Federal Bureau of Investigation: Robert F. Kennedy Assassination Summary. 56-156-3217 Federal Bureau of Investigation 4 May 1977 Retrieved From https://vault.fbi.gov/Robert%20F%20Kennedy%20%28Assassination%29%20/Robert%20F%20Kennedy%20%28Assassination%29%20Part%201%20of%203/view on 19 August 2016.

96: *"They can gas me, but I am famous..."* Ayton, M. "Inside the minds of America's Presidential Assassins." The Los Angeles Times. 17 April 2014

Retrieved from http://www.latimes.com/opinion/op-ed/la-oe-adv-ayton-assassinations-20140418-story.html on 19 August 2016.

98: *"At a time when the Olympic headlines..."* Hilton, L. "Jansen Persevered Despite Olympic Disappointments." ESPN Classic. Retrieved from http://www.espn.com/classic/biography/s/Jansen_Dan.html on 20 August 2016.

— *"At a time when the Olympic headlines..."* Korneheiser, T. "Finally, Jansen Stands as Lord of the Rings" The Washington Post 19 February 1994. Retrieved from http://www.washingtonpost.com/wp-srv/sports/longterm/olympics1998/history/1994/articles/94-tkjansen.htm on 20 August 2016.

99: *"You have already seen the Sirhan Sirhan quote..."* Vossekuil, B., R.A. Fein, M. Reddy, R.Borum, and W. Modzeleski. The Final Report and Findings of the Safe School Initiative: Implications for the Prevention of School Attacks in the United States, Washington, DC: U.S. Secret Service and U.S. Department of Education, July 2004.

---: *"You have already seen the Sirhan Sirhan quote..."* Stanglin, D. "Would-be Reagan assassin John Hinckley Jr. to be freed." USA Today 27 July 2016 Retrieved from http://www.usatoday.com/story/news/2016/07/27/would--reagan-assassin-john-hinckley-jr-freed/87607638/ on 20 August 2016.

99: *"We have seen several examples of revenge..."* Vossekuil, B., R.A. Fein, M. Reddy, R.Borum, and W. Modzeleski. The Final Report and Findings of the Safe School Initiative: Implications for the Prevention of School Attacks in the United States, Washington, DC: U.S. Secret Service and U.S. Department of Education, July 2004.

— *"We have seen several examples of revenge..."* Vinograd, C. et al. "Charlie Hebdo Shooting: 12 Killed at Muhammed Cartoons Magazine in Paris." NBC News 7 January 2015 Retrieved from http://www.nbcnews.com/storyline/paris-magazine-attack/charlie-hebdo-shooting-12-killed-muhammad-cartoons-magazine-paris-n281266 on 20 August 2016.

100: *"Although not as much a motivator..."* Cullen, D. (2009) Columbine, Hachette Book Group, New York, New York.

102: *"For many of these attackers..."* Rosen, R. "The Floppy Did Me In." The Atlantic 16 January 2014 Retrieved from http://www.theatlantic.com/technology/archive/2014/01/the-floppy-did-me-in/283132/ on 20 August 2016.

103: *"Due to the nature of today's workplace..."* Priest, D. "Fort Hood Suspect warned of threats within the ranks" The Washington Post. 10 November, 2009. Retrieved from http://www.washingtonpost.com/wp-dyn/content/article/2009/11/09/AR2009110903618.html on 20 August 2016.

103: *"This has happened typically in a short amount of time..."* Lederman, J. "Friend of Columbine Killers Still Seeking Answers" Monroe Patch 28 November 2012 Retrieved from http://patch.com/connecticut/monroe/bp--friend-of-columbine-killers-still-seeking-answers on 20 August 2016.

103: *"Oftentimes, students with attack ideation..."* Reid, T., "Newly Released Columbine Writings Reveal Killers Mind-Set" The Washington Post 7 July 2006 Retrieved from http://www.washingtonpost.com/wp-dyn/content/article/2006/07/06/AR2006070601438.html on 20 August 2016.

— *"Oftentimes, students with attack ideation..."* Kleinfield, N, "Before Deadly Rage, A Life Consumed By Troubling Silence." The New York Times. 22 April, 2007. Retrieved from http://www.nytimes.com/2007/04/22/us/22vatech.html?_r=0 on 20 August 2016.

— *"Oftentimes, students with attack ideation..."* Carcamo, C. and Mello, M. "Reports detail Jared Loughner's behavior before the shooting." The Los Angeles Times 27 March 2013. Retrieved from http://articles.latimes.com/2013/mar/27/nation/la-na-ff-jared-loughner-20130328 on 20 August 2016.

104: *"Some other points that are important..."* Vossekuil, B., R.A. Fein, M. Reddy, R.Borum, and W. Modzeleski. The Final Report and Findings of the Safe School Initiative: Implications for the Prevention of School Attacks in the United States, Washington, DC: U.S. Secret Service and U.S. Department of Education, July 2004.

105: *"In 59% of the instances..."* Vossekuil, B., R.A. Fein, M. Reddy, R.Borum, and W. Modzeleski. The Final Report and Findings of the Safe School Initiative: Implications for the Prevention of School Attacks in the United States, Washington, DC: U.S. Secret Service and U.S. Department of Education, July 2004.

— *"In 59% of the instances..."* Vossekuil, B., R.A. Fein, M. Reddy, R.Borum, and W. Modzeleski. The Final Report and Findings of the Safe School Initiative: Implications for the Prevention of School Attacks in the United States, Washington, DC: U.S. Secret Service and U.S. Department of Education, July 2004.

107: *"This is something that seems to come up..."* Siemaszko, C. "Columbine Killers Craved Fame – Tape" The New York Daily News 13 December 1999 Retrieved from http://www.nydailynews.com/archives/news/columbine-killers-craved-fame-tape-article-1.846829 on 20 August 2016.

109: *"Although the interests vary in scope..."* Vossekuil, B., R.A. Fein, M. Reddy, R.Borum, and W. Modzeleski. The Final Report and Findings of the Safe School Initiative: Implications for the Prevention of School Attacks in the United States, Washington, DC: U.S. Secret Service and U.S. Department of Education, July 2004.

— *"Although the interests vary in scope..."* Vossekuil, B., R.A. Fein, M. Reddy, R.Borum, and W. Modzeleski. The Final Report and Findings of the Safe School Initiative: Implications for the Prevention of School Attacks in the United States, Washington, DC: U.S. Secret Service and U.S. Department of Education, July 2004.

— *"Although the interests vary in scope..."* Vossekuil, B., R.A. Fein, M. Reddy, R.Borum, and W. Modzeleski. The Final Report and Findings of the Safe School Initiative: Implications for the Prevention of School Attacks in the United States, Washington, DC: U.S. Secret Service and U.S. Department of Education, July 2004.

110: *"There are any number of threat-related conditions..."* Office of the Child Advocate, Shooting at Sandy Hook Elementary School: Office of the Child Advocate. State of Connecticut. 21 November, 2014.

110: *"Connecticut's Office of the Child..."* Office of the Child Advocate, Shooting at Sandy Hook Elementary School: Office of the Child Advocate. State of Connecticut. 21 November, 2014.

110: *"Lanza's socio-emotional issues..."* Office of the Child Advocate, Shooting at Sandy Hook Elementary School: Office of the Child Advocate. State of Connecticut. 21 November, 2014.

— *"Lanza's socio-emotional issues..."* Office of the Child Advocate, Shooting at Sandy Hook Elementary School: Office of the Child Advocate. State of

Connecticut. 21 November, 2014.

— *"Lanza's socio-emotional issues..."* Office of the Child Advocate, Shooting at Sandy Hook Elementary School: Office of the Child Advocate. State of Connecticut. 21 November, 2014.

111: *"One possible reason for this rage..."* Office of the Child Advocate, Shooting at Sandy Hook Elementary School: Office of the Child Advocate. State of Connecticut. 21 November, 2014.

111: *"After the separation, Lanza's social and mental conditions..."* Office of the Child Advocate, Shooting at Sandy Hook Elementary School: Office of the Child Advocate. State of Connecticut. 21 November, 2014.

112: *"As Lanza progressed into his middle school years..."* Office of the Child Advocate, Shooting at Sandy Hook Elementary School: Office of the Child Advocate. State of Connecticut. 21 November, 2014.

112: *"But then something unusual happened..."* Office of the Child Advocate, Shooting at Sandy Hook Elementary School: Office of the Child Advocate. State of Connecticut. 21 November, 2014.

112: *"As a parent myself, I could understand..."* Office of the Child Advocate, Shooting at Sandy Hook Elementary School: Office of the Child Advocate. State of Connecticut. 21 November, 2014.

— *"As a parent myself, I could understand..."* Office of the Child Advocate, Shooting at Sandy Hook Elementary School: Office of the Child Advocate. State of Connecticut. 21 November, 2014.

113: *"(Lanza) has agreed to achieve competency..."* Office of the Child Advocate, Shooting at Sandy Hook Elementary School: Office of the Child Advocate. State of Connecticut. 21 November, 2014.

114: *"To the credit of the school district..."* Office of the Child Advocate, Shooting at Sandy Hook Elementary School: Office of the Child Advocate. State of Connecticut. 21 November, 2014.

114: *"Adam Lanza was in no way being homeschooled..."* Office of the Child Advocate, Shooting at Sandy Hook Elementary School: Office of the Child Advocate. State of Connecticut. 21 November, 2014.

114: *"What the Lanza family did was the worst thing..."* Office of the Child Advocate, Shooting at Sandy Hook Elementary School: Office of the Child Advocate. State of Connecticut. 21 November, 2014.

115: *"Adam Lanza returned to the world in the autumn..."* Office of the Child Advocate, Shooting at Sandy Hook Elementary School: Office of the Child Advocate. State of Connecticut. 21 November, 2014.

115: *"Records indicate that Mr. Lanza made an honest effort..."* Office of the Child Advocate, Shooting at Sandy Hook Elementary School: Office of the Child Advocate. State of Connecticut. 21 November, 2014.

116: *"Mrs. Lanza seemed to become confrontational..."* Office of the Child Advocate, Shooting at Sandy Hook Elementary School: Office of the Child Advocate. State of Connecticut. 21 November, 2014.

116: *"Amazingly under these circumstances..."* Office of the Child Advocate, Shooting at Sandy Hook Elementary School: Office of the Child Advocate. State of Connecticut. 21 November, 2014.

117: *"Despite their best efforts, Lanza reverted..."* Office of the Child Advocate, Shooting at Sandy Hook Elementary School: Office of the Child Advocate. State of Connecticut. 21 November, 2014.

117: *"During this time and the end of 2012..."* Office of the Child Advocate, Shooting at Sandy Hook Elementary School: Office of the Child Advocate. State of Connecticut. 21 November, 2014.

117: *"On December 14, 2012..."* Office of the Child Advocate, Shooting at Sandy Hook Elementary School: Office of the Child Advocate. State of Connecticut. 21 November, 2014.

121: *"They are the best because of the importance..."* Vossekuil, B., R.A. Fein, M. Reddy, R.Borum, and W. Modzeleski. The Final Report and Findings of the Safe School Initiative: Implications for the Prevention of School Attacks in the United States, Washington, DC: U.S. Secret Service and U.S. Department of Education, July 2004.

122: *"So what are the indicators that the attacker will show..."* Vossekuil, B., R.A. Fein, M. Reddy, R.Borum, and W. Modzeleski. The Final Report and

Findings of the Safe School Initiative: Implications for the Prevention of School Attacks in the United States, Washington, DC: U.S. Secret Service and U.S. Department of Education, July 2004.

129: *"Schaeffer was considered one of the bright..."* Dawsey, D. and Malnic, E. "Actress Rebecca Schaeffer Fatally Shot at Apartment" The Los Angeles Times 19 July, 1989 Retrieved from http://articles.latimes.com/1989-07-19/news/mn-3788_1_rebecca-schaeffer on 20 August 2016.

129: *"Bardo's life was anything but the positive..."* Braun, S. and Jones, C. "Murder suspect seemed as determined as victim". Eugene Register-Guard. 24 July, 1989.

129: *"Prior to the events that transpired with Schaeffer..."* Nicol, B. (2006) Stalking. Reaktion Books. London.

130: *"Rebecca Schaeffer's arrival into Bardo's life..."* Associated Press, "Man Accused of Killing Actress said to have gone to Samantha Smith's Hometown." Associated Press News 24 July, 1989.

130: *"Robert John Bardo's obsession with Schaeffer..."* Nicol, B. (2006) Stalking. Reaktion Books. London.

131: *"When this feeling of betrayal..."* Welkos, R. "Public Records Led Suspect to Actress-Victim". The Los Angeles Times 22 July, 1989 Retrieved from http://articles.latimes.com/1989-07-22/news/mn-3291_1_public-record on 20 August 2016.

131: *"Through this series of events..."* Ford, A. "Suspect on Tape Tells of Actresses Last Words". The Los Angeles Times 22 October 1991 Retrieved from http://articles.latimes.com/1991-10-22/local/me-114_1_bardo on 20 August 2016.

— *"Through this series of events..."* Axthelm, P. "An Innocent Life, A Heartbreaking Death". People. 31 July 1989. Retrieved from http://www.people.com/people/archive/article/0,,20120867,00.html on 20 August 2016.

132: *"She came into my life in the right moment..."* Nicol, B. (2006) Stalking. Reaktion Books. London.

133: *"That is not to say that such a condition..."* Vossekuil, B., R.A. Fein, M.

Reddy, R.Borum, and W. Modzeleski. The Final Report and Findings of the Safe School Initiative: Implications for the Prevention of School Attacks in the United States, Washington, DC: U.S. Secret Service and U.S. Department of Education, July 2004.

138: *"By the testimony of her mother..."* Helling, S. "Slain 13-year-old Virginia Girl Nicole Madison Lovell Struggled With Bullying and Shared Pain Online, Says Mother." People. 2 February 2016 Retrieved from http://www.people.com/article/nicole-lovell-internet-activity-virginia-tech on 20 August 2016.

139: *"Just over a year before Nicole and David would meet..."* WMAR-Baltimore "Student Athlete of the Week: David Eisenhauer" ABC 2 News. 19 Mar 2015 Retrieved from http://www.abc2news.com/sports/local-sports/student-athlete/student-athlete-of-the-week-david-eisenhauer on 20 August 2016.

139: *"During his freshman year at Virginia Tech..."* Jouvenal, J. "Former Va. Tech Students indicted in killing of Blacksburg middle schooler" The Washington Post 26 July 2016 Retrieved from https://www.washingtonpost.com/local/public-safety/former-va-tech-students-indicted-in-killing-of-blacksburg-middle-schooler/2016/07/26/1b1e48c2-5344-11e6-b7de-dfe509430c39_story.html on 20 August 2016.

139: *"From those who knew her and what was going on..."* Associated Press and Daily Mail Reporter "Murdered Virginia Girl 'always talked of running away' with student accused of stabbing her to death: Friend says 13-year-old wanted to get married and start a family with college freshman, 18" The Daily Mail 9 February 2016 Retrieved from http://www.dailymail.co.uk/news/article-3438835/Friend-says-slain-teen-talked-running-away-defendant.html on 20 August 2016.

140: *"On the afternoon of January 30, 2016..."* Keneally, M. "Timeline of Alleged Abduction and Slaying of 13-Year-Old Virginia Girl." ABC News 3 February 2016 Retrieved from http://abcnews.go.com/US/timeline-alleged-abduction-slaying-13-year-virginia-girl/story?id=36686517 on 20 August 2016.

140: *"During the homicide investigation..."* Associated Press and Daily Mail Reporter "Murdered Virginia Girl 'always talked of running away' with student accused of stabbing her to death: Friend says 13-year-old wanted to get married and start a family with college freshman, 18" The Daily Mail

9 February 2016 Retrieved from http://www.dailymail.co.uk/news/article-3438835/Friend-says-slain-teen-talked-running-away-defendant.html on 20 August 2016.

— *"During the homicide investigation..."* Duncan, I. "Former Columbia and high school track star charged with abduction and murder of Virginia teen" The Baltimore Sun. 30 January 2016 Retrieved from http://www.baltimoresun.com/news/maryland/crime/bs-md-abduction-arrest-20160130-story.html on 26 August 2016.

141: *"As if the story is not disturbing enough..."* Helling, S. "Va. Tech Suspect in the death of 13-year-old girl allegedly told police she was a 'sociopath in training.'" People. 23 May 2016 Retrieved from http://www.people.com/article/nicole-lovell-killers-david-eisenhauer-natalie-keepers-sociopath-in-training on 20 August 2016.

141: *"Keepers' involvement in the crime..."* Associated Press. "Former Virginia Tech Students Indicted in Slaying of Teen." The Denver Post. 27 July 2016. Retrieved from http://www.denverpost.com/2016/07/27/grand-jury-to-meet-on-students-charged-in-virginia-slaying/ on 25 August 2016.

142: *"It didn't take long for law enforcement..."* McLaughlin, E. "Natalie Keepers: Once-promising student now face prospect of prison" CNN. 8 February 2016. Retrieved from http://www.cnn.com/2016/02/08/us/blacksburg-virginia-natalie-keepers-profile-nicole-lovell/ on 26 August 2016.

142: *"On July 26, 2016..."* Associated Press. "Former Virginia Tech Students Indicted in Slaying of Teen." The Denver Post. 27 July 2016. Retrieved from http://www.denverpost.com/2016/07/27/grand-jury-to-meet-on-students-charged-in-virginia-slaying/ on 25 August 2016.

145: *"Studies have shown that in cases..."* Vossekuil, B., R.A. Fein, M. Reddy, R.Borum, and W. Modzeleski. The Final Report and Findings of the Safe School Initiative: Implications for the Prevention of School Attacks in the United States, Washington, DC: U.S. Secret Service and U.S. Department of Education, July 2004.

146: *"Another point that is worthy of discussing..."* Vossekuil, B., R.A. Fein, M. Reddy, R.Borum, and W. Modzeleski. The Final Report and Findings of the Safe School Initiative: Implications for the Prevention of School Attacks in the United States, Washington, DC: U.S. Secret Service and U.S. Department of Education, July 2004.

146: *"One final point to consider..."* Vossekuil, B., R.A. Fein, M. Reddy, R.Borum, and W. Modzeleski. The Final Report and Findings of the Safe School Initiative: Implications for the Prevention of School Attacks in the United States, Washington, DC: U.S. Secret Service and U.S. Department of Education, July 2004.

151: *"The first mental health condition..."* Mayo Clinic Staff, "Antisocial Personality Disorder" mayoclinic.org. Retrieved from http://www.mayoclinic.org/diseases-conditions/antisocial-personality-disorder/home/ovc-20198975 on 20 August 2016.

152: *"The fundamental reason that people..."* Mayo Clinic Staff, "Bipolar Disorder" www.mayoclinic.org. Retrieved from http://www.mayoclinic.org/diseases-conditions/bipolar-disorder/basics/definition/con-20027544 on 20 August 2016.

— *"The fundamental reason that people..."* National Institute of Mental Health "Bipolar Disorder" www.nimh.nih.gov Retrieved from https://www.nimh.nih.gov/health/topics/bipolar-disorder/index.shtml on 20 August 2016.

152: *"There are many public figures..."* Chi, P. "Richard Dreyfuss Opens Up About His Battle with Bipolar Disorder" People 11 November 2013 Retrieved from http://www.people.com/people/article/0,,20754443,00.html on 21 August 2016.

— *"There are many public figures..."* Kennedy, L. "20 Questions for Carrie Fisher" WebMD 3 November 2010 Retrieved from http://www.webmd.com/mental-health/addiction/features/questions-for-carrie-fisher on 21 August 2016.

— *"There are many public figures..."* Huffington Post "Catherine Zeta-Jones Leaves Treatment for Bipolar Disorder" Huffington Post 21 May 2013 Retrieved from http://www.huffingtonpost.com/2013/05/21/catherine-zeta-jones-bipolar-treatment_n_3312701.html on 21 August 2016.

— *"There are many public figures..."* Dalsimer, K. "Images in Psychiatry: Virginia Woolf" American Journal of Psychiatry 161(5). May 2004.

— *"There are many public figures..."* Pauley, J. (2004). Skywriting: A life out of the blue. New York: Random House.

156: *"Additionally, a person who is delusional..."* Bressert, S. (2014). Delusional Disorder Symptoms. Psych Central. Retrieved from http://psychcentral.com/disorders/delusional-disorder-symptoms/ on 16 August 2016.

156: *"Delusional disorder is widely considered..."* Bressert, S. (2013). Delusional Disorder Treatment. Psych Central. Retrieved from http://psychcentral.com/disorders/delusional-disorder-treatment/ on 16 August 2016.

157: *"The DSM seems to have a very good handle..."* Mayo Clinic Staff, "Narcissistic Personality Disorder" Mayo Clinic. Retrieved from http://www.mayoclinic.org/diseases-conditions/narcissistic-personality-disorder/basics/definition/con-20025568 on 21 August 2016.

158: *"For whatever reason, the individual..."* Mayo Clinic Staff, "Narcissistic Personality Disorder" Mayo Clinic. Retrieved from http://www.mayoclinic.org/diseases-conditions/narcissistic-personality-disorder/basics/definition/con-20025568 on 21 August 2016.

158: *"It's probably not wise to give an example..."* Samuel, D. & Widiger, T. "Describing Ted Bundy's Personality and Working Towards DSM-V" Independent Practitioner (2007), 27 (1), pp. 20-22.

158: *"A trio of psychologists..."* Nye, J. "Inside The Mind Of A Mass Killer: Intense Paranoia Drives Killers Not A Detached Sense Of Reality, Study Finds" The Daily Mail 29 July 2013 Retrieved from http://www.dailymail.co.uk/news/article-2380994/Inside-mind-mass-killer-Academics-deny-loner-theory-say-killers-detached-driven-paranoia-revenge.html on 21 August 2016.

159: *"Paranoia (or Paranoid Personality Disorder)..."* Bressert, S. (2014). Paranoid Personality Disorder Symptoms. Psych Central. Retrieved from http://psychcentral.com/disorders/paranoid-personality-disorder-symptoms/ on 21 August 2016.

161: *"The root issues of schizotypal personality disorder..."* Mayo Clinic Staff, "Schizotypal Personality Disorder" Mayo Clinic. 1 April 2016. Retrieved from http://www.mayoclinic.org/diseases-conditions/schizotypal-personality-disorder/home/ovc-20198939 on 21 August 2016.

161: *"Oftentimes, people with the condition..."* Bressert, S. (2014). Schizotypal Personality Disorder Symptoms. Psych Central. Retrieved from http://psychcentral.com/disorders/schizotypal-personality-disorder-symptoms/ on 16 August 2016.

162: *"Most concerning is that the condition..."* American Psychiatric Association. Diagnostic and Statistical Manual of Mental Disorders. 4. Washington: American Psychiatric Association; 2000.

162: *"There have been articles written..."* Greenspan, S. "Murder Most Foolish: Are Some School Shooters Gullible?" Psychology Today 7 February 2011 Retrieved from https://www.psychologytoday.com/blog/incompetence/201102/murder-most-foolish on 21 August 2016.

— *"There have been articles written..."* Steffen, J. & Ingold, J. "Psychiatrist: Theater Gunman Suffers From Personality Disorder" The Denver Post 4 June 2015 Retrieved from http://www.denverpost.com/2015/06/04/psychiatrist-theater-gunman-suffers-from-personality-disorder/ on 21 August 2016.

163 *"By all accounts, Jared Lee Loughner..."* Cloud, J. "The Troubled Life of Jared Loughner" Time. 24 January 2011 Retrieved from http://content.time.com/time/magazine/article/0,9171,2042358,00.html on 21 August 2016.

— *"By all accounts, Jared Lee Loughner..."* Hennessey-Fiske, M. "Jared Lee Loughner's High School Girlfriend: 'He was completely different back then than he is now'" The Los Angeles Times 12 January 2011 Retrieved from http://articles.latimes.com/2011/jan/12/nation/la-na-arizona-shooting-girlfriend-20110113 on 21 August 2016.

163: *"As he reached young adulthood, however..."* Cloud, J. "The Troubled Life of Jared Loughner" Time. 24 January 2011 Retrieved from http://content.time.com/time/magazine/article/0,9171,2042358,00.html on 21 August 2016.

— *"As he reached young adulthood however..."* Anglen, R. "Jared Lee Loughner, Suspect in Gabrielle Giffords shooting, had college run-ins" The Arizona Republic 9 January 2011 Retrieved from http://archive.azcentral.com/news/articles/20110109jared-lee-loughner-gabrielle-giffords-arizona-shooting.html on 21 August 2016.

164: *"During this time period..."* Montopoli, B. "What Does Jared Lee

Loughner Believe?" CBS News 10 January 2011 Retrieved from http://www. cbsnews.com/news/what-does-jared-lee-loughner-believe/ on 21 August 2016.

164: *"On January 8, 2011..."* Lacey, M. & Herszenhorn, D. "In Attacks Wake, Political Repercussions." The New York Times 9 January 2011 Retrieved from http://www.nytimes.com/2011/01/09/us/politics/09giffords.html?_r=0 on 21 August 2016.

— *"On January 8, 2011..."* CBS News "Victims of the Tucson Shooting Rampage" CBS News 8 January 2011 Retrieved from http://www.cbsnews.com/news/victims-of-the-tucson-shooting-rampage/ on 21 August 2016.

164: *"Shortly after his arrest, Loughner..."* Lacey, M. "Suspect in Shooting of Giffords Ruled Unfit for Trial" The New York Times 25 May 2011 Retrieved from http://www.nytimes.com/2011/05/26/us/26loughner.html on 21 August 2016.

— *"Shortly after his arrest, Loughner..."* Duke, A. "Loughner Sentenced To Life For Arizona Shooting." CNN 8 November 2012 Retrieved from http://www.cnn.com/2012/11/08/justice/arizona-loughner-sentencing/ on 21 August 2016.

164: *"Of all of the mental health conditions previously discussed..."* Bengston, M. (2016). Paranoid Schizophrenia. Psych Central. Retrieved from http://psychcentral.com/lib/paranoid-schizophrenia/ on 19 August 2016.

— *"Of all of the mental health conditions previously discussed..."* Mayo Clinic Staff, "Schizophrenia" Mayo Clinic. 24 January 2014. Retrieved from http://www.mayoclinic.org/diseases-conditions/schizophrenia/basics/definition/con-20021077 on 19 August 2016.

165: *"In addition to Loughner, schizophrenia..."* Taylor, S. "Shootings By Hinckley Laid to Schizophrenia" The New York Times. 15 May 1982. Retrieved from http://www.nytimes.com/1982/05/15/us/shootings-by-hinckley-laid-to-schizophrenia.html on 19 August 2016

— *"In addition to Loughner, schizophrenia..."* CNN Library "Mark David Chapman Fast Facts" CNN. 3 May 2016. Retrieved from http://www.cnn.com/2013/03/23/us/mark-david-chapman-fast-facts/ on 19 August 2016.

— *"In addition to Loughner, schizophrenia..."* American Psychological Association, "David Berkowitz" American Psychological Association 17 February 2012. Retrieved from https://www.apa.org/ed/precollege/undergrad/ptacc/csi-student-paper.pdf on 19 August 2016.

— *"In addition to Loughner, schizophrenia..."* Thomas, K. "Somber look at serial killer Ed Gein" The Los Angeles Times. 4 May 2001. Retrieved from http://articles.latimes.com/2001/may/04/entertainment/ca-59065 on 19 August 2016.

— *"In addition to Loughner, schizophrenia..."* Markman, R & Bosco, D (1989). Alone with the devil. NY: Doubleday.

— *"In addition to Loughner, schizophrenia..."* Wright, S. "Schizophrenic serial killer who murdered four people in attack inspired by horror film" The Daily Mail. 2 March 2009. Retrieved from http://www.dailymail.co.uk/news/article-1158908/Schizophrenic-serial-killer-murdered-people-attack-inspired-horror-film-failed-NHS.html on 19 August 2016.

II. ASSESS
178: *"What are the individual's motives or goals?..."* Fein, R.A., & Vossekuil, B. (1998). Protective intelligence & threat assessment investigations: A guide for state and local law enforcement officials (NIJ/OJP/DOJ Publication No. 170612). Washington, D.C.: U.S. Department of Justice.

178: *"What kinds of communication have been made..."* Fein, R.A., & Vossekuil, B. (1998). Protective intelligence & threat assessment investigations: A guide for state and local law enforcement officials (NIJ/OJP/DOJ Publication No. 170612). Washington, D.C.: U.S. Department of Justice.

179: *"What has the individual been involved with..."* Fein, R.A., & Vossekuil, B. (1998). Protective intelligence & threat assessment investigations: A guide for state and local law enforcement officials (NIJ/OJP/DOJ Publication No. 170612). Washington, D.C.: U.S. Department of Justice.

179: *"Does the individual have the mental stability..."* Fein, R.A., & Vossekuil, B. (1998). Protective intelligence & threat assessment investigations: A guide for state and local law enforcement officials (NIJ/OJP/DOJ Publication No. 170612). Washington, D.C.: U.S. Department of Justice.

180: *"Has the individual shown an inappropriate interest..."* Fein, R.A., &

Vossekuil, B. (1998). Protective intelligence & threat assessment investigations: A guide for state and local law enforcement officials (NIJ/OJP/DOJ Publication No. 170612). Washington, D.C.: U.S. Department of Justice.

180: *"Are there signs/symptoms that suggest..."* Fein, R.A., & Vossekuil, B. (1998). Protective intelligence & threat assessment investigations: A guide for state and local law enforcement officials (NIJ/OJP/DOJ Publication No. 170612). Washington, D.C.: U.S. Department of Justice.

181: *"Are there other people who are concerned..."* Fein, R.A., & Vossekuil, B. (1998). Protective intelligence & threat assessment investigations: A guide for state and local law enforcement officials (NIJ/OJP/DOJ Publication No. 170612). Washington, D.C.: U.S. Department of Justice.

181: *"Is there a sense of consistency..."* Fein, R.A., & Vossekuil, B. (1998). Protective intelligence & threat assessment investigations: A guide for state and local law enforcement officials (NIJ/OJP/DOJ Publication No. 170612). Washington, D.C.: U.S. Department of Justice.

182: *"What kind of support base..."* Fein, R.A., & Vossekuil, B. (1998). Protective intelligence & threat assessment investigations: A guide for state and local law enforcement officials (NIJ/OJP/DOJ Publication No. 170612). Washington, D.C.: U.S. Department of Justice.

182: *"Has the individual had a sudden, drastic change..."* Fein, R.A., & Vossekuil, B. (1998). Protective intelligence & threat assessment investigations: A guide for state and local law enforcement officials (NIJ/OJP/DOJ Publication No. 170612). Washington, D.C.: U.S. Department of Justice.

III. ACT

202: *"The true issue with why our businesses..."* National Center for Educational Statistics "Fast Facts" U.S. Department of Education. Retrieved from http://nces.ed.gov/fastfacts/display.asp?id=84 on 29 August 2016.

— *"The true issue with why our businesses..."* Everytown For Gun Safety "Analysis of School Shootings" Retrieved from http://everytownresearch.org/reports/analysis-of-school-shootings/ on 29 August 2016.

Appendix A:

Charging Documents

Newport Police Department   Page: 1
Incident Report   09/17/2013

Incident #: 13-17827-OF
Call #: 13-17827

Date/Time Reported: 08/07/2013 0620
Report Date/Time: 08/07/2013 0714
Status: No Crime Involved

Reporting Officer: OFFICER SETH MOSELEY
Assisting Officer: OFFICER ERIC CORMIER
Approving Officer: SERGEANT FRANK ROSA

Signature: _____

Signature: _____

#	EVENTS(S)

LOCATION TYPE: Hotel/Motel/Temp. Lodgings   Zone: BEAT 1/124
MARRIOTT HOTEL
25 AMERICAS CUP AVE Apt. #405
NEWPORT RI 02840

1 INFORMATION RECEIVED

#	PERSON(S)	PERSON TYPE	SEX	RACE	AGE	SSN	PHONE

Moseley #364

On August 7, 2013 I was assigned to car 1. At about 0623 hours Officer Cormier and I were dispatched to the Marriott Hotel, room 405 for a harrassment report. I responded from city yard.

On arrival we met with ▓▓▓▓▓. ▓▓▓ stated that he is a naval contractor and that he travels often. ▓▓▓ went on to explain that while getting onto his flight from Virginia to Rhode Island he got into a verbal altercation with an unknown party in the airport. ▓▓▓ believes that the individual that he got into an argument with has sent 3 people to follow him and keep him awake by talking to him and sending vibrations into his body. ▓▓▓ stated that he has not witnessed any of these individuals, but believes they are two black males and a black female. ▓▓▓ stated that he first heard them talking to him through a wall while at the Residence Inn in Middletown. ▓▓▓ then packed up and went to a hotel on the Navy base where he heard the same voices talking to him through the walls, floor and ceiling. ▓▓▓ stated that he moved to his third hotel and is currently at the Marriott. ▓▓▓ first said that the 3 individuals were speaking to him through the floor. Then ▓▓▓ stated that the voices were coming through the ceiling. ▓▓▓ stated that the individuals are using " some sort of microwave machine " to send vibrations through the ceiling, penetrating his body so he cannot fall asleep. When I asked ▓▓▓ what the individuals were saying to him he would not elaborate. ▓▓▓ stated that he has never felt anything like this and is worried that these individuals are going to harm him. ▓▓▓ stated that he does not have a history of mental illness in his family and that he has never had any sort of mental episode. I advised ▓▓▓ to stay away from the individuals that are following him and to notify NPD if they attempt to make contact with him. ▓▓▓
▓▓▓▓▓▓▓▓▓

Suspicious Persons
August 7,2013
Sgt. Frank C. Rosa, Jr.

    While assigned to OIC on August 7, 2013, I reviewed this report for approval. Based on the Naval Base implications and the claim that the involved subject, one ███████ was "hearing voices" I made contact with on duty Naval Station Police ████████████. I advised ██ of the report and the claims by ██████. I then faxed ██ a copy of the report. ██ advised me that ██ would follow up on this subject and determine if he is in fact, a naval base contractor. No further action at this time.

                      ** Portions of this report have been redacted **

Appendix B:

Behavioral Assessment Worksheet

BEHAVIORAL ASSESSMENT WORKSHEET
Copyright © 2016 by DTAC Publishing

Date/Time:			Location:		

Interviewer:			2nd Interviewer/Witness:		

Subject: (last, middle, first)			Case Name/Number:		

Subject Address:			Subject Telephone:		

Date of Birth:	SSN:	Race:	Gender:	Height:
___/___/___ M D Y		___: Black ___: White Other:_____	___: M ___: F	___ft. ___wt.

Weight:	Eyes:	Hair:	Complexion:	Build:
___ lbs.	___:Brown ___:Black ___:Blue ___:Hazel ___:Green Other:_____	___: Brown ___: Black ___: Blonde ___: Red ___: Gray Other:_____	___: Acne ___: Pale ___: Dark ___: Freckles ___: Tan Other:_____	___:Thin ___:Medium ___:Heavy ___:Obese ___:Sickly Other:_____

Appearance:	Eyesight:	Hearing Issues:	Head Trauma:	Vision Issues:
___:Disheveled ___:Neat ___:Casual ___:Bizarre ___:Body Odor Other:_____	___:Normal ___:Glasses ___:Contacts ___:Artificial ___:Blind Other:_____	___:Yes ___:No If Yes, Explain:	___:Yes ___:No If Yes, Explain:	___:Yes ___:No If Yes, Explain:

| 2 | BEHAVIORAL ASSESSMENT WORKSHEET |

Physical Deformity: *(explain)*

Physical Complaints: *(explain)*

Substance Abuse:	**Type(s) of substance(s):**	**Frequency & amount of abuse:**
___:N/A ___:Alcohol ___:Drugs Other:_____		

Driver's License:	**Citizenship:**	**Scars/Marks/Tattoos:**
#:_____ State:_____ Exp: Date: ___/___/_____ M D Y		

Criminal History:
_____
_____
_____

Was the subject deceptive or chose not to reveal any aspects of criminal history? ___: Y ___: N
Explain:
_____
_____

Does the subject have a history of violent crimes? ___: Y ___: N
Details:
_____
_____

Does the subject have a history of destructive, assaultive or aggressive behavior? ___: Y ___: N
Details:
_____
_____

Evidence of targeted violence? ___: Y ___: N

___: Menacing Behavior   ___: Violence at home   ___: Harassing Behavior   ___: Violence at work/school

___: Stalking Behavior   ___: Violation of restraining order   ___: Violence directed toward public figure

___: Other (describe) _____

3 BEHAVIORAL ASSESSMENT WORKSHEET

MENTAL HISTORY

Mental Status:

General Status: Cooperative   Uncooperative   Passive   Evasive   Manipulative

    Frank/Candid   Defensive   Hyper-sensitive   Hostile   Threatening

    Suspicious   Other:_____

Level of Orientation: Full   Partial   Disoriented

Thought Process: Clear   Confused   Illogical   Erratic   Racing

Hallucinations: Visual   Auditory   Commands   Other:_____

Has any action been taken in response to a hallucination? ___:N ___:Y(explain)
_____
_____

Thought Content: Appropriate   Bizarre   Paranoia   Homicidal/Suicidal Thoughts

*Details:*_____

Delusions: Persecution   Grandiosity   Obsessive   Deviance/Erotomania

*Other:*_____

Mood: Depressed   Elated   Anxious   Guilty   Guarded

    Embarrassed   Flat   Scared   Angry   Irritable

    Other:_____

Suicidal Thoughts/Attempts: Never   Single Event   Multiple Times   Distant Past   Recently

*Explain:*_____

4 BEHAVIORAL ASSESSMENT WORKSHEET

Psychiatric Medications: ___:Y ___:N

Doses:_____

Current Prescription: ___: Y ___:N

Mental Hospitalizations: ___:Y ___:N

Type of Commitment: Voluntary Involuntary Suicide Attempt Unknown

Organizational Interests/Affiliations: ___:Y ___:N Type:_____

Is the subject interested in organizations that advocate or is associated with violence? ___:N ___:Y(explain)
_____
_____

Does the subject support views/ideals of extremist groups in a non-member status? ___:N ___:Y(explain)
_____
_____

Weapons Ownership: ___:Y ___:N

Type:_____ Reason for Ownership:_____

Recent acquisition: ___:Y ___:N Purpose for acquisition:_____

Weapons access: ___: Restricted ___: Unrestricted Location:_____

Fascination with weapons: ___:N ___:Y(specify)_____

Specialized Training:

___: Basic Firearms Training ___: Advanced Firearms Training ___: Sniper Training

___: Firearms use, but no training ___: Explosives Training ___: Pilot Training

___: Chemical/Biological Training ___: No Specialized Training

___: Other(describe)_____
_____

5 BEHAVIORAL ASSESSMENT WORKSHEET

SOCIAL/ENVIRONMENTAL FUNCTIONING

Living Arrangements:

___: Alone   ___: Spouse   ___: Children   ___: Parents

___: Relatives   ___: Friend   ___: Roommate   Other:_____

Recent Change: ___:Y ___:N _____ (*date*) _____

Association with Family/Relatives/Friends:

Nature/Quality of relationship with parents/siblings/other relatives:

___: Close   ___: Supportive   ___: Distant   ___: Strained   ___: Estranged   ___: Violent

Relative(s):_____

Frequency of personal/interactive contact with parents/siblings:

___: Frequent   ___: Occasional   ___: Infrequent   ___: None

Explain:_____

Nature/Quality of relationship with friends/associates:

___: Close   ___: Supportive   ___: Distant   ___: Strained   ___: Estranged   ___: Violent

Individual(s):_____

Frequency of personal/interactive contact with friends/associates:

___: Frequent   ___: Occasional   ___: Infrequent   ___: None

Explain:_____

Indication that any family/friends/associates are afraid of subject or what subject might do? ___:N ___:Y

*(explain):*_____

_____

| 6 | BEHAVIORAL ASSESSMENT WORKSHEET |

Is there evidence of substance abuse or mental illness in the subject's family? ___:N ___:Y

*(explain):*_____

Current Life Situation:

___: Employment   ___: Relationship   ___: Living Arrangements   ___: Social Support/Networks

___: Family   ___: Other *(explain)* _____

Has the subject experienced a traumatic event during the last year?

___: Major Illness or accident   ___: Loss of an important person in a relationship

___: Change in daily structure   ___: Significant Failure

___: Loss of status   ___: Experience of rejection

___: Other crisis/situational life stressor(s) *(explain)* _____

To what extent are the subject's actions consistent with his/her statements? (explain) _____

_____

Grievances/Resentments:

___: Economic   ___: Political   ___: Employment   ___: Family

___: Marital   ___: Military   ___: Government   Other: _____

___: Recent change _____

Interest in assassins/assassinations:

___: Gathered information/reading   ___: Talked with friends/family

___: Written to past attackers   ___: Observed media presentations on assassinations

___: Visited assassination sites   ___: Modeled self/identifies with assassins

___: Collected articles/photos of public figures   ___: Memorialized ideas in journal/diary

___: Internet/Social Networking activity   ___: Other _____

7 BEHAVIORAL ASSESSMENT WORKSHEET

ANALYSIS

Attack-Related Behavior: (*including but not limited to the following planning strategies*)

___: Inappropriate interest in assassins or assassinations, weapons: militant/radical/extremist ideas or groups; murder/mass murder(ers)/workplace and/or school violence/stalking incidents

___: Inappropriate communications

___: Efforts made to learn workplace/school security measures

___: Test security measures at workplace/school

___: Observation of workplace/school schedule and activities

___: Multiple approaches to workplace/school with unclear motives

___: Engaged in menacing, harassing and/or stalking-type behavior

___: Follow, visit or approach with a weapon

___: Dressed to fit into workplace/school environment

___: Deceptive behavior to gain access to restricted areas

___: Other attack-related behavior involving rational planning or analysis: (*explain*) _____

_____

To what extent has the subject's behavior changed over time moving in a direction toward or away from attack?

(*explain*): _____

_____

Organizational Ability:

How capable is the subject in planning and/or carrying out an attack?

___: Disorganized ___: Minimal ___: Average ___: Well-organized ___: Sophisticated ___: Other

How much concern among those who know the subject well that he/she might take action based on inappropriate

ideas? (explain): _____

---

8 BEHAVIORAL ASSESSMENT WORKSHEET

Motivation:

___: Notoriety/Fame   ___: Cry for help   ___: Bring attention to cause   ___: Revenge

___: Suicide by police   ___: Change government policies   ___: Be stopped from carrying out attack

___: Get someone in trouble   ___: Other (*explain*): _____

Does the subject appear to be seeking opportunity for attack with multiple targets based upon motive? ___:N ___:Y

(*explain*): _____

CURRENT EVALUATION

To what extent is the idea of attack-related behavior viewed as an acceptable or necessary action?

What indications are there that the subject considers target violence as a desirable way to achieve objectives to improve a situation, or to resolve any problems?

Based on life circumstances, to what degree is there an urgency of any risk posed by a subject to a workplace/school/individuals/self?

Likelihood in foreseeable future of a major change in the subject's life circumstances that would cause subject to pose a risk to workplace/school/individuals/self?

Other considerations not mentioned?

9 BEHAVIORAL ASSESSMENT WORKSHEET

Additional Comments/Concerns:

_____: Interviewer _____: Signature

_____: 2ⁿᵈ Interviewer _____: Signature

_____: Date _____: Time

10 BEHAVIORAL ASSESSMENT WORKSHEET

MILITARY SERVICE RECORD

Military Branch: ___: n/a   Military Service Number: _____

___: U.S. Army   ___: USMC   ___: National Guard

___: U.S. Navy   ___: USCG   ___: Foreign Service

___: USAF   ___: Reserves   VA Claim Number: _____

Dates of Service:

EOD - ____/____/_____   DOD - ____/____/_____   Military Rank Upon Discharge: _____
(*Enter*   *mm   dd   year*   *mm   dd   year*
on Duty)

Combat Duty: ___: N ___: Y	**Disciplinary Action:** ___: N ___: Y	**Discharge:**
Dates of tours: _____ _____ _____	___: Non-judicial punishment	___: Honorable ___: Dishonorable
	___: Court martial proceedings	___: Other than honorable
Number of tours:	Explain: _____	___: General ___: Medical
Location(s): _____ _____ _____	_____ _____ _____	___: Convenience of Government
		___: Bad Conduct
		___: Other

Additional Comments/Information on Military Service:

11 BEHAVIORAL ASSESSMENT WORKSHEET ⟍

EMPLOYMENT HISTORY

Occupation: _____	*Employment Status:*	Unemployed due to:
_____	___: Full Time ___: Part time	___: Mental Illness
_____	___: Retired ___: Other	___: Layoff/Firing
_____		___: Transient Status
Currently Employed: ___: N ___: Y	*(explain):* _____	___: Physical Disability
		___: Confinement
		___: Other _____

Is the subject a student? ___: N ___: Y

Level of Education: ___: 1-6 years ___: 6-11 years ___: High School Graduate ___: GED

___: College ___: Bachelor's Degree ___: Graduate School ___: JD

___: Doctorate ___: Technical School ___: Business ___: Certificate

Name of educational institutions: _____
_____
_____

Current employer/point of contact: _____ Employment dates: _____ to _____

Duties performed: _____

Employment address: _____ Telephone: _____

Supervisor's name: _____ Position: _____

Previous employer/point of contact: _____ Employment dates: _____ to _____

Duties performed: _____

Employment address: _____ Telephone: _____

Supervisor's name: _____ Position: _____

12. BEHAVIORAL ASSESSMENT WORKSHEET

Subject's behavior in work environment/functioning with co-workers: _____
_____
_____

Reaction to stress in workplace: _____
_____
_____

Job Perception:

___: Satisfied ___: Dissatisfied ___: Disgruntled ___: Harbors grudges

___: Other *(explain)*: _____

Sources of Income:

___: Job ___: Retirement ___: Unemployment ___: Disability

___: SSI ___: Welfare ___: Alimony ___: Other

___: Recent change _____ Date: _____

Marital and Family History/Status:

___: Single ___: Married ___: Separated ___: Divorced

___: Widowed ___: Remarried ___: Recent Change _____ Date _____

Name of Spouse/Ex-spouse or partner: _____ *Relationship* _____

Current Address: _____ *Contact Information* _____

Nature/Quality of relationship with spouse:

___: Close ___: Supportive ___: Distant ___: Strained ___: Estranged

___: Recent Change _____ Date _____

Number of Children: _____

Name: _____ *Date of Birth* _____ *Quality of Relationship* _____

Name: _____ *Date of Birth* _____ *Quality of Relationship* _____

Name: _____ *Date of Birth* _____ *Quality of Relationship* _____

13 BEHAVIORAL ASSESSMENT WORKSHEET

Made in the USA
Middletown, DE
06 December 2016